Revealing America

Revealing America

Image and Imagination in the Exploration of North America

James P. Ronda

University of Tulsa

D. C. Heath and Company

Lexington, Massachusetts   Toronto

Address editorial correspondence to:
D. C. Heath and Company
125 Spring Street
Lexington, MA 02173

Acquisitions: James Miller
Development: Sylvia Mallory
Production: Carolyn Ingalls
Editorial Design: Cornelia Boynton
Photo Research: Rose Corbett Gordon
Production Coordination: Michael O'Dea
Permissions: Margaret Roll

Published simultaneously in Canada.

Printed in the United States of America.

International Standard Book Number: 0-669-35175-X

Library of Congress Catalog Number: 95-77978

10 9 8 7 6 5 4 3 2 1

For
John L. Allen,
Friend and Trail Guide

PREFACE

For many years textbooks and classroom lectures prominently featured the story of the exploration of North America. Every American history survey course, whether on the secondary or college level, included sections on the explorers. Willingly or not, students were enlisted in the ranks of the Coronado, Champlain, and Lewis and Clark expeditions. The tales those recruits heard were all about courage and adventure in distant and unknown places. And the stories always ended in triumph as the forces of civilization tamed the savage wilderness. More overtly than most other aspects of American history, exploration history celebrated the invasion of America and lent legitimacy to the conquest of the continent. Explorers were actors in a morality play that passed for history. The audience never doubted either the rightness of the explorers' missions or the outcome of the journeys.

Over the past three decades, this vision of exploration came to represent much of what was wrong with traditional conceptions of the American past. Books about exploration focused on the lives of a few European and American men to the exclusion of anyone else. Other actors on the exploration stage either waited in the wings or had bit parts. As the practice of American history expanded beyond the narrow confines of presidential elections and party politics, the old explorer stories sounded increasingly irrelevant. Retracing familiar expedition routes promised little for instructors and students interested in the lives of African-American ironworkers, Iroquois clan mothers, and New England mill women. Explorers seemed a relic from long bygone eras, not worth much space in print or time in class.

Revealing America aims at putting exploration back into the mainstream of American history. Building on work done by historians, geographers, and anthropologists, this book features an expanded understanding of exploration and its consequences. More than thirty years ago, the distinguished historian and documentary editor Donald Jackson wrote that it was "no longer useful to think of the Lewis and Clark Expedition as the personal story of two men." In his *Letters of the Lewis and Clark Expedition*, Jackson printed documents that touched on art, science, and Native American cultures as well as diplomacy, politics, and cartography. *Revealing America* continues this approach and extends it to include explorations by all sorts of travelers and adventurers.

Meriwether Lewis and William Clark sometimes called their exploring party "the Corps of Discovery." *Revealing America* offers readers both a larger Corps of Discovery and a more spacious continental stage. The documents printed here also propose a broader definition of exploration, one that encompasses journeys and discoveries of many kinds. While *Revealing America* is organized chronologically, it does not move in just one geographic direction. Older histories of exploration swept readers along in a triumphant march from east to west. Reflecting the complex travels made by many explorers, *Revealing America*'s stories move in many directions. Journeys have always been at the heart of the American experience, whether the travelers were Kiowas coming into the country through a hollow log or tourists on the transcontinental railroad. Exploration stories connect us to the larger histories of the continent. Every generation explores America anew. Each journey reveals another America.

Zebulon Montgomery Pike once called the members of his Mississippi River expedition "a Dam'd set of Rascels." In writing *Revealing America,* I have relied on a whole company of rascals and adventurers. Like so much of my work on the exploration of the American West, this book was inspired by John L. Allen. John took me up the trail to the place where history and geography meet. I could not have had a better guide. His work remains the measure of all others. Charles E. Rankin has more than once opened the pages of *Montana: The Magazine of Western History* for me and allowed me to test ideas on a wider audience. At the University of Tulsa I have enjoyed steady support from Kimberly S. Hanger, Gordon Taylor, Norman Grabo, Sidney F. Huttner, and Lori N. Curtis. The Gilcrease Museum has become a second home, and I am deeply grateful to Sarah Erwin, Anne Morand, Dan Swan, Shane Culpepper, and the museum's director, Joan Carpenter Troccoli, for making me a part of so distinguished an institution. *Revealing America* benefited from careful readings and thoughtful comments by John L. Allen, University of Connecticut; Mark A. Eiffler, University of Nebraska, Kearney; John R. Finger, University of Tennessee, Knoxville; Barry Gough, Wilfrid Laurier University; Mark Harvey, North Dakota State University; David R. Lewis, Utah State University; Darlis A. Miller, New Mexico State University; B. Gene Ramsey, Southeast Missouri State University; Donald B. Smith, University of Calgary; Alan Taylor, Boston University; and Michael Welsh, University of Northern Colorado. I have also learned much from James L. Axtell, Dayton Duncan, Gary E. Moulton, John R. Wunder, William L. Lang, and William Goetzmann. The staff at D. C. Heath has assisted and supported me in many ways; I thank history editor James Miller, production editor Carolyn Ingalls, permissions editor Margaret Roll, and designer Cia Boynton. And as always, anyone who writes about the exploration of North America recognizes the debt owed to Bernard DeVoto, Donald Jackson, and David B. Quinn.

Revealing America has made its own journey from idea to publication. I have had two constant companions along the trail—my wife Jeanne and my editor Sylvia Mallory. Both gave encouragement, advice, and direction in measures far greater than I deserved. For what is good in this book the rascals deserve much of the credit; for what has strayed off the trail the blame is mine.

J. P. R.

CONTENTS

3   Edging into America, 1590s–1680s   67

4 The Clash of Empires 106

5 In Search of the Passage to India 135

6   # The Western Fur Trade and the Santa Fe Trail   174

CHRONOLOGY

986–1010	Norse voyages to Greenland and Vinland.
1492	First Columbus landfall.
1524	First survey of North America's Atlantic coast, undertaken by the Florentine mariner Giovanni da Verrazzano.
1528–1536	Journey of Alvar Núñez Cabeza de Vaca.
1534–1536	Jacques Cartier's two voyages to the Gulf of St. Lawrence and as far up the St. Lawrence River as present-day Montreal.
1539	Fray Marcos de Niza searches for golden cities and fabricates Cíbola.
1539–1543	Hernando de Soto expedition into the present-day Southeast.
1540–1542	Francisco Vásquez de Coronado launches his quest for Cíbola.
1584–1590	English voyages to Roanoke (present-day North Carolina) organized by Sir Walter Ralegh.
1598–1605	Juan de Oñate explores the Southwest, including present-day Arizona, New Mexico, Texas, Kansas, and Oklahoma.
1607	Jamestown founded.
1608	Samuel de Champlain establishes Quebec at the site of what had been Stadacona.
1609–1616	Champlain's expeditions as far inland as the eastern shore of Lake Huron.
1634–1670	French missionary and trading expeditions into the Great Lakes.
1642	Establishment of Montreal.
1670	Hudson's Bay Company chartered.
1673	Louis Jolliet and Father Jacques Marquette explore the Mississippi River down as far as the mouth of the Arkansas River.
1678–1687	René-Robert, Cavalier de La Salle leads explorations in the Great Lakes, down the Mississippi, and along the Gulf Coast.

long before the traveler saw it. Reflecting on his reading, Thoreau asked, "Was not Asia mapped in my brain before it was in any geography?" The artist George Catlin shared a similar view. Looking at the northern Great Plains along the Missouri River, he proclaimed the plains "a place where the mind could think volumes." Catlin might have added that he had thought volumes about Indians and the West even before he saw the plains. The power to "think volumes" prepared explorers to expect some things and ignore others. Imagination (and sometimes fantasy) shifted their reports, maps, and other records toward one set of conclusions at the expense of others. The distinguished historical geographer J. Wreford Watson once wrote that "it is not what people actually see so much as what they want to see, or think they see." For most who went on a far journey, nothing was more important than paths made in the mind.

The conjectures and calculations of imagination pushed aside notions of unknown territories and empty spaces. No explorer or traveler was ever fully persuaded that the lands beyond home were truly unknown, really a howling wilderness. Cherished ideas about human societies, plants, animals, and the land itself rushed in to fill the unknown countries even before Europeans paid their first uninvited visits. Ideas permeate the documents in this collection. Indeed, the history of exploration and travel is as much intellectual history as it is the story of trails, passes, and camping places. As Thoreau confided to his journal, "In the spaces of thought are the reaches of land and water over which men go and come. The deepest and most original thinker is the farthest traveled."

The ideas found in this collection cover the full range of North American history. In these journeys we see the lure of personal wealth and capitalist values, the power of religious conviction, the force of national empires, and the changing definitions of nature and the human community. Ideas nurtured and shaped every journey, no matter who made it. Ideas about landscape were always close at hand, whether travelers pondered the road ahead or the shape of the final destination. Willa Cather once noted that to European immigrants the Great Plains seemed "not a country at all, but the material out of which countries are made." As those immigrant travelers assembled their own version of home on the plains, they were guided by ideas about the landscape rooted deep in the past and now carried to a new place. This collection echoes with long, acrimonious, and sometimes fatal arguments about the North American landscape. The Northwest Passage and the dream of the wealth of Asia in the pockets of Europe was as alive for nineteenth-century railroad travelers like William Frazer Rae and Samuel Bowles as it had been for such early adventurers as Jacques Cartier and Peter

Pond. Countries of wealth and power lured those who traveled with Francisco Vásquez de Coronado as well as those who struggled to reach California along with George and Tamsen Donner. Images of gardens and deserts were everywhere as Europeans tried to define American spaces. Rejecting Native American definitions, every outsider sought to put his or her name and mark on the land. As contemporary nature writer Barry Lopez explains, "Desire causes imagination to misconstrue what it finds." Pedro de Castañeda, Mary Richardson Walker, and Robert Louis Stevenson all made journeys of desire and imagination. Ideas about life and land directed those journeys and in turn suggested what desire imagined would be found. Beauty and meaning were more than in the eye of the beholder. They were in the minds of every journey maker.

The second theme of this collection is the journey itself. Thoreau packed his bags and made his journeys without ever going far from home. Such homebound ventures would not have satisfied the explorers and travelers whose lives and ideas fill these pages. They expected that journeys of the mind would prompt travels in the physical world. Their journeys were of many kinds, shapes, and varieties.

Modern readers, conditioned by rapid travel from one look-alike airport to another, need to appreciate these differences. Not every passage by land or water was the same. Troubled and broken passages could reveal more than ventures that ended on time and home safe. Some travels were driven by the passion to find a single place when the location of the place and the nature of the route to it were not well known to Europeans. Coronado, on horseback in pursuit of the elusive Quivira, saw the Great Plains quite differently than did railroad-traveling, Denver-bound Walt Whitman. Other journeys took land-company explorer Christopher Gist and fur trader Gabriel Franchère to places already located and charted. Gist and Franchère were not tourists. Their travels were more about business strategies and the politics of empire than a search for memorable personal experiences. The noteworthy official explorations of North America in the nineteenth century were scientific survey journeys. And governments in the United States and Canada launched large-scale exploring parties with many missions. William Clark, Henry Youle Hind, and other explorers played roles as scientists, diplomats, and agents of expanding empires. Finally, there were journeys that modern readers might too easily and too quickly dismiss as mere tourism. The distinctions among explorer, traveler, and tourist are more artificial than real, more bound to the world of dictionaries than to the terrain of journeys and revelations. For Native Americans, many Europeans appeared like tourists—tourists determined to make the commonplaces of native life into things strange and exotic. Thoreau grasped the nuances in words like *explorer*, *traveler*, and *tourist*. "Go where we will on the *surface* of things," he explained, "men have been there before us and our boundaries have literally been run to the South Seas, on the old patents. The frontiers are not east or west, north or south; but wherever a man finds a fact." Finding the fact and revealing its meaning could come at any time.

The third theme in this collection is the central role of native people in the history of North America. From the earliest conjectures that philosophers and geographers made about a larger world, there was the assumption that other beings—perhaps human, perhaps not—inhabited the lands beyond. Few Europeans who thought about countries other than their own conjured up an empty world. Voyagers in the age of Columbus expected to find an Eastern world filled with the peoples of Japan, China, and India. Once the Americas began to take shape in the European imagination, there was no doubt that these were inhabited lands as well.

There are many ways to see native people as principal actors in the American historical drama. We might read Native American literature, look at objects fashioned and used by native people, listen to traditional songs and stories, or visit places made special in native history. Reading the accounts of encounters between native people and newly arrived strangers is one more way to appreciate the complexity of exploration across the cultural divide. Narratives of mutual discovery let us travel to places at once very old and strangely new.

The Americas at the end of the fifteenth century saw nothing less than the collision of two old worlds. Out of that collision came new places, new peoples, and new ways of being. This was a genuinely "New World," a world that called for mutual exploration as individuals struggled to make sense of each other. When read with an eye toward cultural diversity and a common humanity, exploration records give modern readers an opportunity to be present at moments of encounter. At the same time, the real limitations of such records must be acknowledged. They are not objective, literal transcripts of encounter events. The narratives themselves were built on European expectations about native people and the physical landscape. Few explorers escaped believing that native people were either gentle children of nature or savage brutes. Few travelers saw strange landscapes in terms other than what was already familiar. Such preconceptions did not preclude accurate reporting, but they posed an ever-present barrier to fuller cultural understanding. Thus modern readers might best think about exploration and travel narratives as a kind of constructed reality, an engineered landscape of the past meant to flatter Europeans. But native voices are within our hearing if we have ears to hear.

This book offers voices and views from the past that are revelations. To appreciate exploration and travel as revelation, consider what happened in the Americas after 1492. The European intellectual tradition was driven by a passion to count, name, qualify, and classify. The act of defining peoples, places, and things and then mastering them infused European life and learning. Revelation was part of the process of definition, whether one was revealing and defining a mountain or the life of a community. Once revealed and named, the mountain or an entire people might become subject to the will of European outsiders. Revelation, in short, was all too often the beginning of conquest. Exploration was at the sharp edge of the invasion wedge. As historical geographer Brian Harley explains, European speculations about seemingly empty places sought more than adding to the sum of geographic and scientific knowledge. Talk of "opening the West" meant incorporating it into a larger imperial system. Opening a place and revealing it were steps in the process of closing and dominating it.

In *Heart of Darkness*, a novel with much to say about exploration and revelation, Joseph Conrad offers this powerful observation. "The conquest of the earth, which mostly means taking it away from those who have a different complexion or slightly flattened noses than ourselves, is not a pretty thing when you look into it too much." The readings in *Revealing America* stimulate just that sort of deep look. The revelation may not always please or reassure. Arrogance, greed, and violence often lurk down the trail or around the next river bend. Exploration accounts, once read as tales of romance and adventure, tell other and sometimes more troubling stories. The cultural landscapes of North America were and remain rich and complex. Invasion and conquest loom large in the landscape of the past. Yet we discover other terrain features as well. Courage, compassion, and understanding were also a part of that revealed territory.

What historian James Axtell has called the American encounter created a new world of vast and often terrifying dimensions. The records of exploration and travel take us to that new, sometimes unsettling, country. By listening to the voices of travelers like Fray Marcos de Niza, Marie de l'Incarnation, Thomas James, and Virginia E. B. Reed, we can trace that country's boundaries and probe its interior. Thoreau knew the relationship between such listening and a quickening of the mind and spirit. "To travel and 'descry new lands' is to think new thoughts and have new imaginings."

SUGGESTIONS FOR FURTHER READING

Carter, Paul. *The Road to Botany Bay: An Exploration of Landscape and History.* New York: Alfred A. Knopf, 1988.

Christie, John A. *Thoreau as World Traveler.* New York: Columbia University Press, 1965.

Elliott, J. H. *The Old World and the New, 1492–1650.* Cambridge, England: Cambridge University Press, 1970.

Lopez, Barry. *Arctic Dreams: Imagination and Desire in a Northern Landscape.* New York: Charles Scribner's Sons, 1986.

Meinig, D. W. *The Shaping of America: Volume One, Atlantic America, 1492–1800.* New Haven, Connecticut: Yale University Press, 1986.

———. *The Shaping of America: Volume Two, Continental America, 1800–1867.* New Haven, Connecticut: Yale University Press, 1993.

Schuma, Simon. *Landscape and Memory.* New York: Alfred A. Knopf, 1995.

Slotkin, Richard. *Regeneration Through Violence: The Mythology of the American Frontier, 1600–1860.* Middletown, Connecticut: Wesleyan University Press, 1973.

Wright, John K. *Human Nature in Geography.* Cambridge, Massachusetts: Harvard University Press, 1966.

A NOTE ON TEXTS

The selections offered in this book are not meant as a substitute for the longer and fuller versions available in many scholarly editions. In the service of accessibility, I have edited and modernized the texts, silently adding punctuation and correcting spelling when necessary.

"The excursions of the imagination are so boundless . . ."
—Henry David Thoreau

Revealing America

North America

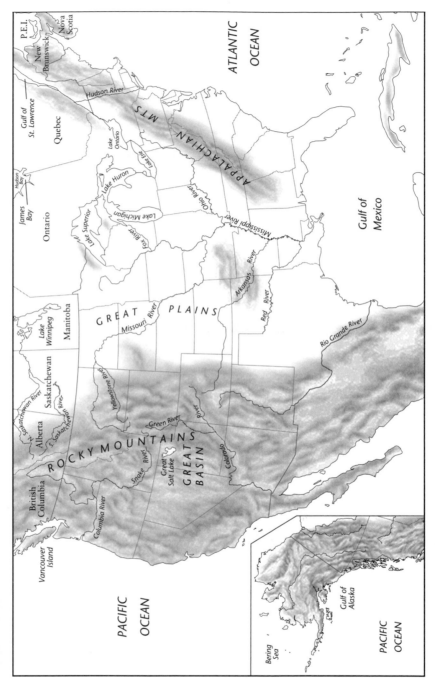

CHAPTER 1

Hopeful Travelers

In late July 1849 Michigan adventurer Cephas Arms crossed South Pass in Wyoming's Wind River Mountains, bound for the California gold fields. The pass not only marked the Continental Divide but also represented for many overlanders the beginning of what they thought was the real West. Settlers headed for Oregon and miners destined for California boomtowns all expected South Pass to be more than mere dirt and rock. In the mind's eye, the pass was a gateway, an entrance grown grander by months of imagination and anticipation. Arms and his companions certainly expected a great moment at the pass. Perhaps they fancied crossing it as a rite of passage, a momentous step toward wealth and independence. But neither the pass nor the moment measured up to their expectations. As Arms confided to his diary, South Pass "hardly deserves the name, it is so little like the idea one forms of a pass."

Cephas Arms was not the first to form ideas that did not quite match landscape realities. Three centuries before the Michigan gold seeker made his way, disappointed, over the pass, Spanish missionary-explorer Fray Marcos de Niza described the Zuni pueblos of present-day New Mexico in extravagant terms. Although Fray Marcos had never seen the place he called Cíbola, he reported that its seven cities held more gold and precious stones than all of Mexico and Peru. A year later, in 1540, when the expedition of Francisco Vásquez de Coronado reached the Zuni town of Hawikuh, Spanish explorers found "a small rocky pueblo, all crumpled up"—and promptly rained curses down on Fray Marcos's head.

The missionary Fray Marcos and the prospector Arms were participants in a long tradition of geographic speculation and conjecture. They were members in a company of hopeful travelers, adventurers certain of what they were going to find even before setting out for distant countries. From earliest times, inquisitive humans wondered about lands beyond their own. Every exploration journey, whatever its objective, began with a trip taken at home. That homebound trip was an interior tour of personal imagination. Explorers always believed they knew much about the lands and peoples to be met along the way. Explorers' minds and maps had few blank places. Sure of what was ahead, each adventurer filled the route with expectations, imaginary mileposts aimed at keeping the enterprise on track. These conjectures, and the expectations that came from them, became part of what historical geographers call *lore*. Such lore might confidently predict a good trail or a navigable river. Lore might promise golden cities or native peoples ready to embrace the Christian gospel. Prospective explorers gathered materials for making conjectures and fashioning lore from many places. Travelers' tales, translations from such classical writers as Aristotle and Ptolemy, and stories from the Bible and other devotional literature provided rich sources as explorers and their advisers created a mental geography for places they had yet to see.

Explorers went into the country with their minds and imaginations already prepared to find what they sought. One recent historian has written that the explorer "knows in advance what he will find." The revealing of America began within a long tradition of geographic conjecture. Fray Marcos and Cephas Arms were inheritors not only of specific geographic ideas but of a whole speculative cast of mind. Dreams about wealth to gain and souls to save were more than flights of fancy. Such thoughts, having been expressed for centuries in maps, letters, pamphlets, and books, powerfully shaped both the expectations and the behavior of those who went in search of distant places. Territories of the mind were as persuasive as anything the eye could see. And the actual experience of seeing places along the way was conditioned by these prejourney expectations.

The mental maps drafted from conjecture and imagination glowed with bright promise and reassuring images. Even those imaginary maps which depicted terror and loss in a great unknown showed paths in and out of such supposedly empty places. Mental maps convinced travelers that they knew faraway places even before making the journey. Armchair cartographers and stay-at-home explorers, for example, joined forces with ambitious kings and zealous evangelists to invent a place that later carried the name *America*.

Conjectural geographers constructed their America and then invested it with a compelling set of European dreams and illusions. Once built with the materials of expectation and desire, America was then revealed by a vast company of hopeful travelers traversing landscapes both real and imaginary. And when unyielding terrain realities collided with cherished illusions, as they did at Hawikuh and South Pass, revelation took on the hard edge of frustration and disappointment. But as it so often happened, disappointments bred new dreams and fresh illusions.

Reading the conjectures, arguments, and reports collected in this chapter, one might easily dismiss some of them on two counts. Modern readers might scoff at St. Brendan's preposterous misadventures with a whale named Jasconius or feel vaguely superior knowing that Sir John Mandeville never saw the people of Sumatra he so vividly described. If we find the authors suspect, we also tend to doubt the intelligence of the intended audience. How could anyone believe what seems to us such nonsense? People of the past often seem to us more gullible than any who live in the present. A thoughtful reading of these documents, however, can bring us around to a fresh appreciation of the texts and of their authors and audiences. These texts provided the raw materials for the European invention and subsequent revelation of America. Because pious writers put St. Brendan out to sea in search of Paradise and Eden, explorers in later years came to expect blessed lands and sacred cities beyond the western sea. Because Marco Polo and Sir John Mandeville reported on an Eastern world of gold and silver, travelers centuries later believed they would find such places in present-day New Mexico and Kansas. And these documents present a vital lesson: that the act of seeing is more cultural than physiological. Indeed, for generations of explorers and travelers, the mind's eye saw farther and clearer than the eyes of the body. Conjecture fed on conjecture, and explorers often found the contours of hope and desire more compelling than what the actual journey had to offer. The documents in this chapter are traces from the distant shores of imagination. They remind us of the struggle to know the world and make sense and order from that knowledge.

The masters of conjecture and imagination never asked "Are we there yet?" but always wanted to know "What does 'there' look like?" and "What does it mean?" Writers and travelers like Marco Polo and Roger Bacon labored to resolve what seemed a paradox. Speculation and exploration made the world appear large yet at the same time brought faraway places close to home. Time and distance, the very ideas of "here" and "there," changed as conjecture expanded mental maps and horizons. From Aristotle to Adam of Bremen, what early geographers wrote was neither simple deception nor malicious deceit. Rather, their conjectures were expressions of hope, illusion, expectation, and considerable self-deception, fired by superheated imaginations. Whether reporting on an elusive spiritual paradise or a kingdom of gold, those who tramped the lands of imagination gave their narratives the ring of truth and the feel of eyewitness accounts. Sometimes, as in the case of St. Brendan's Isle of the Blessed, the places were fabricated with the materials of fantasy and sacred belief. Once built, such places took on lives of their own. If Fray Marcos's golden cities of Cíbola were not in Zuni country, they might lie to the north and east on the plains of Kansas. Each actual journey that did not reveal the desired place only intensified the long-ing for it and made the place seem even more real. In other provinces of the conjectural landscape the places were real enough. It was their meaning and promise that grew ever larger and more tempting. The elephants and camels that trooped through the pages of Marco Polo marched again when Spanish explorers made their way through the Southwest and the Southeast. However the conjectures were built and whatever they promised, they had the power to spark ambition and spur action.

No matter how they were portrayed, distant places had such compelling power because they came from or through the deepest parts of medieval and Renaissance European emotional, intellectual, and material life. Caught in endless rounds of local and regional conflict, some Europeans fondly imag-ined remote places as peaceful havens far from the ravages of war. The shape of the earth and the spiritual condition of other peoples concerned many Christian theologians. And wealth, increasingly measured in the possession of gold and other precious metals, gave substance and attraction to all sorts of geographic speculations.

Those who, centuries after his death, read the ancient philosopher Aristotle's ponderings of the earth's size and shape, made his concerns theirs. Aristotle's revelation of the world as a sphere set boundaries on what had otherwise seemed an endless earth, a world without definition and order. European thinkers embraced Aristotle's conjectural geography and were con-fident that the earth could be known and used for human purposes. Once scholars set out to consider the earth's physical character, it was no great leap to study the difference between the whole world and that part inhabited by humans. Both Ptolemy and Roger Bacon envisioned earths teeming with living beings of all kinds. As Bacon wrote, "The diversity of places is the diversity of things." Europeans wanted to judge all things by their own stan-dards, but they expected to find a world filled with the different, the strange, the diverse. Because the inhabited world seemed to stretch far beyond Christian Europe, conjectural geography proposed an earth inhabited by peoples eager to be evangelized. The missionary impulse proved one of the most powerful motives for exploration in the Americas. Missionary geogra-phers conjured up whole human communities possessing the desire for Christian salvation and yet unreached by even the most dedicated preacher.

Such communities represented opportunity—opportunity not only for missions but also for economic gain. By the fifteenth century, conjectural geography was increasingly capitalist in language and design. No reader of Marco Polo or Mandeville could miss the message. The countries of imagi-nation offered much more than escape from violence or the rewards of spiritual service to the Christian faith. They promised gold and spices, the measure of wealth and power in a world increasingly dominated by the marketplace and its values. And this wealth did not lie in some remote territory, inaccessible to merchants and miners. India, China, Japan, and the islands of the western sea belonged to a world Europeans thought of as *their* world.

In much early European conjectural geography, one message remained unspoken but was always understood. The message was that all geographic visions, whether expressed in scholarly, commercial, or religious language, required a real journey to reach fulfillment. Merchants had to walk the trading paths or sail the seas. Scholars had to see and study strange peoples and places firsthand. Missionaries had to preach and teach from place to place. Conjectural geography was born at home, but it demanded the road for full life. Each sort of vision and each kind of visionary had a restlessness at its heart. There was a war inside each speculation, a battle in the imagination between staying at home and making the journey. Revelation began at home but finally required a purposeful and planned voyage. Revealing America started with homebound conjectures but unfolded in countless journeys.

1. Aristotle Explains Why the Earth Is a Sphere, Third Century B.C.

In the 1560s, some thirty years after the first official French voyages to what is now eastern Canada, Parisian lawyer Etienne Pasquier wrote, "It is a striking fact that our Classical authors had no knowledge of all this America, which we call New Lands." Pasquier's observation reflected both his respect for ancient tradition and his sense that the "New Lands" demanded a fresh image of the world. While the writers of ancient Greece and Rome had not known about the Americas, they had considered the earth's size and shape often and at length. Of those classical geographers, none had greater influence than Aristotle (384–322 B.C.).

From the thirteenth century on, generations of European writers, theologians, and politicians cited Aristotle's works with approval. His words became so much a part of the European vocabulary that some quoted him almost without knowing it. When the Spanish conquistador Hernán Cortés wrote that it was "a universal condition of men to want to know," his words followed Aristotle's injunction to see and to know.

"Concerning the Heavens" was Aristotle's extended discussion of cosmology (the origins of the universe) and cosmography (the nature and shape of the universe). Like others in the ancient world, Aristotle was convinced that the earth was a sphere. Observation and calculation had persuaded him of its roundness. Aristotle and his contemporaries imagined a universe with a round and immovable earth at the center. As historian Jeffrey Burton Russell has explained, "Aristotle's concept became a traditional standard."

Further proof [that the earth is a sphere] is obtained from the evidence of the senses. If the earth were not spherical, eclipses of the moon would not exhibit segments of the shape which they do. As it is, in its monthly phases the moon takes on all varieties of shape—straight-edged, gibbous and concave—but in eclipses the boundary is always convex. Thus if eclipses are due to the interposition of the earth, the shape must be caused by its circumference, and the earth must be spherical. Observation of the stars also shows not only that the earth is spherical but that it is of no great size, since a small change of position on our part southward or northward visibly alters the circle of the horizon, so that the stars above our heads change their position considerably, and we do not see the same stars as we move to the North or South. Certain stars are seen in Egypt and the neighborhood of Cyprus, which are invisible in more northerly lands, and stars which are continuously visible in the northern countries are observed to set in the others. This proves both that the earth is spherical and that its periphery is not large, for otherwise such a small change of position could not have had such an immediate effect. For this reason those who imagine that the region around the Pillars of Heracles joins on to the regions of India, and that in this way the ocean is one, are not, it would seem, suggesting anything utterly incredible. They produce also in support of their contention the fact that elephants are a species found at the extremities of both lands, arguing that this phenomenon at the extremes is due to communication [that is, connection] between the two.

2. Ptolemy Describes His Known World, Second Century A.D.

While Aristotle influenced everyone from theologian Thomas Aquinas to adventurer Hernán Cortés, the cartography of medieval and Renaissance Europe carried the imprint of another ancient geographer. Claudius Ptolemy of Alexandria, an Egyptian deeply influenced

by Greek culture and active in the second century A.D., wrote two
books of enduring significance for European conjectural geography.

Ptolemy in fact did not so much write as compile *Geography* and
Astronomy (sometimes known by its Arabic title *Almagest*). Indeed,
he offered an encyclopedic view of the world. Ptolemy's earth was a
sphere covered by water except for one great connected landmass.
Called the *oikoumene* ("the known or inhabited world"), this mega-
continent comprised three large continents. Christian Europe readily
accepted the notion of a trio of continents—Africa, Asia, and
Europe—for it fit the biblical idea of a world divided among the three
sons of Noah. Ptolemy also asserted that the earth was split into climate zones, each determining everything from skin color and posture
to intelligence and social behavior. Ptolemy's three-continent earth
left little room either on the map or in the imagination for new places,
let alone new continents. And his rigid climatic determinism predis-
posed some of his readers to view other peoples and cultures in nega-
tive ways.

We have divided the inhabited regions into three large divisions as
seemed proper to the ancient writers who examined these areas, and
left us their conclusions in their commentaries, as we ourselves desire to do,
partly from what we have seen and partly from the traditions of others. We
have set ourselves to depict such a map of the whole inhabited earth presenting nothing untried concerning those things which in part are useful and can
well fill the mind by giving it something which is historical, arousing and
exciting it to exercise its powers.

That part of the earth which is inhabited by us is bounded on the east by
the unknown land which borders on the eastern races of Greater Asia,
namely the *Sinae* and the *Seres*, and on the south by the likewise unknown
land which encloses the Indian sea and which encompasses Ethiopia south of
Libya, the country called Agisymba, and on the west by the unknown land
encircling the Ethiopian gulf of Libya and by the Western ocean bordering
on the westernmost parts of Africa and Europe, and on the north by the continuous ocean called the Ducalydonian and Sarmatian which encompasses
the British islands and the northernmost parts of Europe, and by the
unknown land bordering on the northernmost parts of Greater Asia, that is
to say on Sarmatia and Scythia and Serica. The water moreover is much
greater than is the land.

While this depiction of the world appeared in an atlas that also featured a map of the Americas, this particular image preserved a conception of the world with only three continents. Ptolemy, *Geographica Universalis* (Strassburg, 1522).

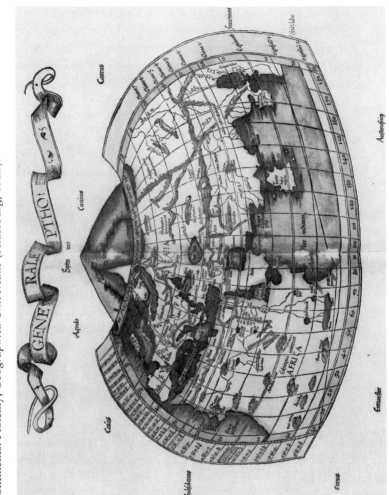

3. Roger Bacon Puzzles Over the Size of the Earth, 1264

For the English philosopher Roger Bacon (1214–1292), revealing the world involved confronting a troubling dilemma. Bacon and his successors wanted to respect the authority and conclusions of earlier writers, whether biblical or classical. At the same time, Bacon recognized that those writers often disagreed on key points. Bacon believed that there was an internal harmony in all truth. Disagreements about the relative size of the continents and the ocean thus forced him to consider other ways to learn about distant places. Although neither an explorer nor a traveler, Bacon increasingly pushed for personal observation as a prime means to gain knowledge.

In the geographic sections of his *Opus Majus*, Bacon posed three important questions about the nature of the habitable world. What are the world's size and shape? Does the heat of the sun preclude human life in what Ptolemy called the "torrid zones"? What is the extent of the ocean, and is it a barrier to travel? Bacon's studies of earlier geographers convinced him that the ends of the earth were closer together and that the sea was not nearly as large as Ptolemy had imagined. Bacon thus invented a world that inquiring travelers could explore. And even more important, he made that inquiry a fundamental part of future geographic revelation.

Now the subject of habitation is considered in two ways; in the first, with respect to the heavens, namely how much can be inhabited on account of the sun and how much not. This question was mentioned previously in a general way, and will be touched upon later. In the second way, the size of the habitable earth in comparison with the water is considered, namely, how far the water hinders. We are now to consider this latter question. Ptolemy in his book on the Arrangement of the Sphere maintains that about a sixth part of the earth is habitable, due to the water, and that all the rest is covered by water. Therefore in the Almagest in the second book he states that habitation is not known except in a quarter of the earth, namely, in that in which we dwell; whose length is from east to west and is one half of an equinoctial circle to the pole, and is one fourth of the colure. But Aristotle maintains at the end of the second book of the Heavens and the World that more than a fourth is inhabited. And Averoes confirms this. Aristotle says

The Americas, from Ptolemy, *Geographica Universalis*. Maps and atlases printed in Europe often carried the name *Ptolemy* as a sign of authority. This map of the Americas was published by Basel University cartographer Sebastian Munster in 1540.

that the sea is small between the end of Spain on the west and the beginning of India on the east. Seneca in the fifth book on Natural History says that this sea is navigable in a very few days if the wind is favorable. And Pliny teaches in his Natural History that it was navigated from the Arabic Sea to Cadiz; whence he states a man fled from his king in fear and entered a gulf of the Red Sea which is called Arabic, which is distant about the space of a year's voyage from the Indian Sea according to Jerome in his letter, as will be explained below. Therefore the width of the earth through which the Red Sea extends is very great; from which fact it is clear that the beginning of India in the east is far distant from us and from Spain, since the distance is so great from the beginning of Arabia toward India. From the end of Spain beneath the earth the sea is so small that it cannot cover three quarters of the earth.

For the things of the world cannot be known except through a knowledge of the places in which they are contained. For place is the beginning of the generation of things, as Porphyry says; because in accordance with the diversity of places is the diversity of things; and not only is this true in the nature of things, but in those of morals and of the sciences, as we see in the case of men that they have different manners according to the diversity of regions and busy themselves in different arts and sciences. He who is ignorant of the places in the world lacks a knowledge not only of his destination, but of the course to pursue.

4. St. Brendan and the Search for Paradise, *c.* 1300

Schoolbook history often suggests that geographers of early medieval Europe imagined the Atlantic to be a hostile place—a boiling, inky-dark sea inhabited by fierce monsters. But the adventures (both real and imaginary) of the Irish monk St. Brendan tell a very different story.

The historical Brendan (484–577) lived in two sixth-century worlds, the world of the Christian monastic way and that of the Irish seafarer. Yet Brendan was neither a missionary seeking souls for the Christian faith nor a fisherman sailing rough seas in a skin boat. Rather, he was a true believer questing for paradise on earth. Like Columbus centuries later, St. Brendan was sure that paradise could be found across the Atlantic.

Although no contemporary account of St. Brendan survives and the extent of his own journeys remains unclear, the stories surrounding him reveal a compelling vision of the Atlantic and land beyond. The unknown authors of the *Life of St. Brendan* and St. Brendan's *Navigation* created a spiritual geography. They fashioned a distant land of peace and prosperity, founded on Europe's landscape and cultural ideals. Clear water, groves of trees, precious stones, fruit, and flowers abounded in this lush Land of Promise beyond the sunset. The legendary St. Brendan seems to have thought that finding paradise was reward enough, but many who later read about his travels were perhaps more attracted by the promise of wealth in their own world than of bliss in paradise.

The St. Brendan literature was vastly popular in the Middle Ages. One recent scholar found that the St. Brendan stories were at least as well known as the Song of Roland and the adventures of King Arthur. The *Life of St. Brendan* first appeared in print about 1471 and was translated into English in 1483. In the section of the *Life* excerpted below, St. Brendan hears about paradise and prepares to make his own Atlantic journey. The *Navigation* exists in more than 120 manuscript copies and received wide circulation in that form. It was not published until the end of the nineteenth century.

---

a. Life of St. Brendan

This version is based on the English text published about 1520, with modern capitalization and punctuation added.

St. Brendan the holy man was a monk and born in Ireland and there he was abbot of a house [the monastery of Clonfert in Galway] wherein were a thousand monks. There he had a full strict and holy life in great penance and abstinence and he governed his monks full virtuously. Then within a short time after there came unto him an holy abbot called Beryne to visit him and each was joyful of the other. Then St. Brendan began to tell the Abbot Beryne of many wonders that he had seen in divers lands. When Beryne heard that of St. Brendan he began to sigh and sore wept and St. Brendan comforted him the best ways he could saying, you come hither for to be joyful with me and therefore for God's love leave your mourning and tell me what marvels you have seen in the great sea ocean that compasseth all the world about and all other waters come out of him which runneth in all parts of the earth.

Then Beryne began to tell St. Brendan and his monks the marvels that he had seen full sore weeping and said I have a son his name is Meruoke and he was a monk of great fame which had a great desire to seek about by ship in divers countries to find a solitary place wherein he might dwell secretly out of the business of this world for to serve God quietly with more devotion. I counseled him to sail in to a land far in the sea beside the mountain of stones which is full well known. And then he made him ready and sailed thither with his monks and when he came thither he liked the place full well where he and his monks served our Lord full devoutly. And then Beryne saw in a vision that this monk Meruoke sailed right far eastward in the sea more than three days sailing and suddenly to his seeming there a dark cloud [appeared] and covered them a great part of the day. They saw no light and as our Lord would the [cloud passed] away and they saw a full fair land and thitherward they drew. In the land was joy and mirth enough and the earth of the land shined as bright as the sun and there were the fairest trees and herbs that ever any man saw and there were many precious stones shining bright and every herb there was full of flowers and every tree full of fruit so that it was a glorious sight and a heavenly joy to be there.

Then there came to them a fair young man and full courteously he welcomed them all and called every monk by his name and said that they were much bound to praise the name of our Lord Jesus that would of his grace show to them the glorious place where is ever day and never night and this place is called paradise terrestre [paradise on earth]. But by this land is another land wherein no man may come and this young man said to them, you have been here half a year without meat, drink, or sleep and they supposed that they had not been there the space of half an hour so merry and joyful they were. The young man told them that this is the place where Adam and Eve dwelled in first and ever should have dwelled there if they had not broken the commandment of God. Then the young man brought them to their ship again and said they might no longer abide there. When they were all shipped [on board the vessel] suddenly this young man vanished away out of their sight and then within a short time by the purveyance of our Lord Jesus they came to the abbey where St. Brendan lived.

Then he [St. Brendan] received them goodly and demanded [of] them where they had been so long. They said, we have been in the land of the blessed before the gates of paradise where as is ever day and never night. They all said that the place is full delectable and for yet all their clothes smelled of that sweet and joyful place. And then St. Brendan purposed soon after to seek [that place] by God's help. Later [he] began to search for a good ship and strong and supplied it for seven years. Then he took his leave of all his brethren and took twelve monks with him. But before they entered into the ship they fasted forty days and lived devoutly and each of them received the sacrament. When St. Brendan with his twelve monks were entered into the ship there came other two of his monks and prayed him that they might sail with him. Then St. Brendan called the sailors to wind up the sail and forth they sailed in God's name.

b. The Paradise of Delights

St. Brendan and his brethren, having received the blessing of the man of God, and having given mutually the kiss of peace in Christ, sailed away towards the south during Lent, and the boat drifted about to and fro, their sustenance all the time being the water brought from the island, with which they refreshed themselves every third day, and were glad, as they felt neither hunger nor thirst. On Holy Saturday they reached the island on their former procurator, who came to meet them at the landing place, and lifted every one of them out of the boat in his arms. As soon as the divine offices of the day were duly performed, he set before them a repast.

In the evening they again entered their boat with this man, and they soon discovered, in the usual place, the great whale, upon whose back they proceeded to sing the praises of the Lord all the night, and to say their Masses in the morning. When the Masses had concluded, Jasconius [the name given to the great whale] moved away, all of them still on its back; and the brethren cried aloud to the Lord: "Hear us, O Lord, the God of our salvation." But St. Brendan encouraged them: "Why are you alarmed? Fear not, for no evil shall befall us, as we have here only a helper on our journey."

The great whale swam in a direct course towards the shore of the Paradise of Birds, where it landed them all unharmed, and on this island they sojourned until the Octave of Pentecost. When that solemn season had passed, their procurator, who was still with them, said to St. Brendan: "Embark now in your boat, and fill all the waterskins from the fountain. I will be the companion and the conductor of your journey henceforth, for without my guidance you could not find the land you seek, the Land of Promise of the Saints." Then, while they were embarking, all the birds of the island, when they saw St. Brendan, sung together in concert: "May a happy voyage under his guidance bring you safely to the island of your procurator." They took with them provisions for forty days, as their course lay to the west for that space of time; during which the procurator went on before them, guiding their way.

At the end of forty days, towards evening, a dense cloud overshadowed them, so dark that they could scarce see one another. Then the procurator said to St. Brendan: "Do you know, father, what darkness is this?" And the saint replied that he knew not. "This darkness," said he, "surrounds the island you have sought for seven years; you will soon see that it is the entrance to it;" and after an hour had elapsed a great light shone around them, and the boat stood by the shore.

When they had disembarked, they saw a land, extensive and thickly set with trees, laden with fruits, as in the autumn season. All the time they were traversing that land, during their stay in it, no night was there; but a light always shone, like the light of the sun in the meridian, and for the forty days they viewed the land in various directions, they could not find the limits thereof. One day, however, they came to a large river flowing towards the middle of the land, which they could not by any means cross over. St. Brendan then said to the brethren: "We cannot cross over this river, and we must therefore remain ignorant of the size of this country." While they were considering this matter, a young man of resplendent features, and very handsome aspect, came to them, and joyfully embracing and addressing each of them by his own name.

He then said to St. Brendan: "This is the land you have sought after for so long a time; but you could not hitherto find it, because Christ our Lord wished first to display to you His divers mysteries in this immense ocean. Return now to the land of your birth, bearing with you as much of those fruits and of those precious stones, as your boat can carry; for the days of your earthly pilgrimage must draw to a close, when you may rest in peace among your saintly brethren. After many years this land will be made manifest to those who come after you, when the days of tribulation may come upon the people of Christ. The great river you see here divides this land into two parts; and just as it appears now, teeming with ripe fruits, so does it ever remain, without any blight or shadow whatever, for light unfailing shines thereon.

5. The Vinland Voyages Reveal the North Atlantic, 986–*c.* 1010

While no student of early European voyages across the Atlantic doubts the fact of Norse journeys to Iceland, Greenland, and the edges of eastern Canada, the scope and meaning of those travels remain charged with controversy. Arguments about the dates and locations of Norse settlements have sometimes obscured what was a unique Scandinavian view of the north Atlantic and a complex set of relations with native peoples.

The selections printed below are arranged in the order of their composition, not in the chronological sequence of the events they describe. Presented this way, they give us a feel for the unfolding Norse understanding of what came to be called North America.

The first selection, drawn from the *History of the Archbishops of Hamburg-Bremen* by the German scholar Adam of Bremen (d. 1076?), reports on Adam's visit to the king of the Danes in 1070. That visit produced the earliest written record of Norse voyages into the Atlantic. Adam's *History*, which had limited circulation in manuscript and was not published until 1595, presents an Atlantic world dotted with fertile islands set in an ice-choked sea. But this was no simple account of daring adventurers in search of new homelands. Adam inserted his own sacred geography, insisting that the "savages" who lived in such remote places could be civilized by the Christian gospel.

The second selection, drawn from the *Saga of the Greenlanders* and composed about 1200, begins with information about the voyage that Norse merchant Biarni Heriulfson made from Iceland in c. 986. Intending to trade at the Norse settlement in Greenland, the merchant missed his port and found instead the Labrador Peninsula of Canada. Heriulfson passed his information on to Eirik the Red and Eirik's son Leif. The narrative continues with Leif Eiriksson's voyage in the year 1000. Most scholars agree that Helluland was the name given to some part of the coast of Baffin Island, while Markland indicated the coast of Labrador. What the Norse meant by the name *Vinland* remains uncertain. Some historians now believe that it was a general geographic term encompassing the region from the present-day Strait of Belle Isle south to Cape Breton Island and perhaps as far south as Cape Cod. Eiriksson's Vinland settlement was in the strait of Belle Isle, probably at L'Anse aux Meadows on the northern tip of Newfoundland.

The last selection, also from the *Saga of the Greenlanders,* tells of violent encounters between the Norse and their native neighbors, whom the contemptuous Norse called *skraelings*. The word *skraeling* appears to mean "weakling" or "barbarian." Native opposition to the Norse presence was an important factor in the European retreat from Vinland. The account also reveals women's significant role in Norse expansion to Vinland. Modern readers of these documents should remember that fifteenth-century Europeans outside Scandinavia knew very little about Norse voyaging.

a. Adam of Bremen Reports on Norse Voyages, 1070

Beyond Norway, which is the farthermost northern country, you will find no human habitation, nothing but ocean, terrible to look upon and limitless, encircling the whole world.

The island, Thule [Iceland], which is separated from the others by endless stretches, is situated far off in the west of the ocean and is, they say, barely known. This Thule is now called Iceland, from the ice which binds the ocean.

In the ocean there are very many other islands of which not the least is Greenland, situated far out in the ocean opposite the mountains of Sweden and the Rhiphaean [Rhaetian] range. To this island they say it is from five to seven days sail from the coast of Norway, the same as to Iceland. The people there are greenish from the salt water, whence, too, that region gets its name. The people live in the same manner as the Icelanders except that they are fiercer and trouble seafarers by their piratical attacks. Report has it that Christianity of late had also winged its way to them.

He [Svien Estridsson, king of the Danes] spoke also of yet another island of the many found in that ocean. It is called Vinland because vines producing excellent wine grow wild there. That unsown crops also abound on that island we have ascertained not from fabulous reports but from the trustworthy relation of the Danes. Beyond that island, he said, no habitable land is found in that ocean, but every place beyond it is full of impenetrable ice and intense darkness.

b. The Voyage of Leif Eiriksson, from the *Saga of the Greenlanders*

The next thing that happened was that Bjarni Herjolfsson came over from Greenland to see earl Eirík, and the earl made him welcome. Bjarni gave an account of those travels of his on which he had seen these lands, and the people thought how lacking in enterprise and curiosity he had been in that he had nothing to report of them, and he won some reproach for this. Bjarni became a retainer of the earl's, and the next summer returned to Greenland.

There was now much talk about voyages of discovery. Leif, son of Eirík the Red of Brattahlid, went to see Bjarni Herjolfsson, bought his ship from him, and found her a crew, so that they were thirty-five in all. Leif invited Eirík his father to lead the expedition too, but Eirík begged off, reckoning he was now getting on in years, and was less able to stand the rigors of bad times at sea than he used to be. Leif argued that of all their family he would still command the best luck, so Eirík gave way to him, and once they were ready for their voyage came riding from home. When he had only a short way to cover to the ship, the horse he was riding on stumbled. Eirík fell off and injured his foot. "It is not in my destiny," said Eirík then, "to discover more lands than this we are now living in. Nor may we continue further this time all together." Eirík returned home to Brattahlid, but Leif rode on to the ship and his comrades with him, thirty-five of them all told. There was a German on the expedition named Tyrkir.

They now prepared their ship and sailed out to sea once they were ready, and they lighted on that land first which Bjarni and his people had lighted on last. They sailed to land there, cast anchor and put off a boat, then went ashore, and could see no grass there. The background was all great glaciers, and right up to the glaciers from the sea as it were a single slab of rock. The land impressed them as barren and useless. "At least," said Leif, "it has not happened to us as to Bjarni over this land, that we failed to get ourselves ashore. I shall now give the land a name, and call it Helluland, Flatstone Land." After which they returned to the ship.

After that they sailed out to sea and lighted on another land. This time too they sailed to land, cast anchor, then put off a boat and went ashore. The country was flat and covered with forest, with extensive white sands wherever they went, and shelving gently to the sea. "This land," said Leif, "shall be given a name in accordance with its nature, and be called Markland, Wood Land." After which they got back down to the ship as fast as they could.

From there they now sailed out to sea with a northeast wind and were at sea two days before catching sight of land. They sailed to land, reaching an island which lay to the north of it, where they went ashore and looked about them in fine weather, and found that there was dew on the grass, whereupon it happened to them that they set their hands to the dew, then carried it to their mouths, and thought they had never known anything so sweet as that was. After which they returned to their ship and sailed into the sound which lay between the island and the cape projecting north from the land itself. They made headway west round the cape. There were big shallows there at low water; their ship went aground, and it was a long way to look to get sight of the sea from the ship. But they were so curious to get ashore they had no mind to wait for the tide to rise under their ship, but went hurrying off to land where a river flowed out of a lake. Then, as soon as the tide rose under their ship, they took their boat, rowed back to her, and brought her up into the river, and so to the lake, where they cast anchor, carried their skin sleeping-bags off board, and built themselves booths [huts]. Later they decided to winter there and built a big house.

There was no lack of salmon there in river or lake, and salmon bigger than they ever saw before. The nature of the land was so choice, it seemed to them that none of the cattle would require fodder for the winter. No frost came during the winter, and the grass was hardly withered. Day and night were of a more equal length there than in Greenland or Iceland. On the shortest day of winter the sun was visible in the middle of the afternoon as well as at breakfast time.

c. Norse and Native People—The First Encounters

That same summer a ship arrived in Greenland from Norway. Her captain was a man named Thorfinn Karlsefni, a son of Thord Horsehead, the son of Snorri Thordarson of Hofdi. Thorfinn Karlsefni was a very well-to-do man, and spent the winter at Brattahlid with Leif Eiriksson. It did not take him long to set his heart on Gudrid; he asked for her hand, and she left it to Leif to answer for her. So now she was betrothed to him and their wedding took place that winter.

There was the same talk and to-do over the Vinland voyages as before, and the people there, Gudrid as well as the rest, put strong pressure on Karlsefni to undertake an expedition. So his voyage was decided on, and he secured himself a ship's company of sixty men and five women. Karlsefni entered into this agreement with his shipmates, that they should receive equal shares of everything they made by way of profit. They took with them all sorts of livestock, for it was their intention to colonize the country if they could manage it. Karlsefni asked Leif for his house in Vinland. He would lend the house, he said, but not give it.

Next, then, they sailed their ship to sea and reached Leifsbudir all safe and sound, and carried their sleep-bags ashore. They soon enjoyed a big and splendid catch, for a fine big whale was stranded there. They went and cut it up, and had no problem with regard to food. The livestock went on up ashore there, but it was soon found that the males grew unmanageable and played havoc all round. They had brought the one bull with them. Karlsefni had timber felled and dressed for his ship, laying the wood out on the rock to dry. They took every advantage of the resources the country had to offer, both in the way of grapes and all kinds of hunting and fishing and good things.

After that first winter came summer. It was now they made acquaintance with the Skraelings, when a big body of men appeared out of the forest there. Their cattle were close by; the bull began to bellow and bawl his head off, which so frightened the Skraelings that they ran off with their packs, which were of grey furs and sables and skins of all kinds, and headed for Karlsefni's house, hoping to get inside there, but Karlsefni had the doors guarded. Neither party could understand the other's language. Then the Skraelings unslung their bales, untied them, and proffered their wares, and above all wanted weapons in exchange. Karlsefni, though, forbade them the sale of weapons. And now he hit on this idea; he told the women to carry out milk to them, and the moment they saw the milk that was the one thing they wanted to buy, nothing else. So that was what came of the Skraelings' trading: they carried away what they bought in their bellies, while Karlsefni and his comrades kept their bales and their furs. And with that they went away.

6. Sir John Mandeville and the Geography of Fantasy, *c.* 1360–1370

Few expressions of conjectural geography got wider circulation from the fourteenth to the eighteenth century than the *Travels* of Sir John Mandeville. Mandeville was the pseudonym of a writer whose name and nationality are unknown. The author in fact invented not only his own name and identity but his journeys as well. He most likely never ventured far from home. Mandeville's *Travels* indeed presents a catalogue of fabulous stories about remote and exotic places.

Although the stories were fabricated, the expectations they generated were quite real. Purporting to be the reports of an eyewitness, the *Travels* swept readers into a world filled with monsters and natural wonders. In the selection below, Mandeville describes the landscape and peoples of Lamary. Lamary was probably Mandeville's name for Sumatra, a large island in the East Indies.

From this country men go by the great sea Ocean through many isles and divers countries, which were long to tell. At the last, after fifty-two days journey, men come to a land which is called Lamary. In that land is great heat; and the custom is there that men and women go all naked and shame not for to show themselves as God made them. And they scorn others that are clad; for they say that God made Adam and Eve naked, and that men should have no shame of that that God made, for nothing that is kindly is foul. They say also that men that use clothes are of another world, or else they believe not in God that made all the world. In that country is no marriage between man and woman; but all the women of that land are common among each man. And they say, if they did otherwise, they did great sin, because God said to Adam and Eve, be fruitful and multiply, and replenish the earth. And no man there says, "This is my wife"; no woman, "This is my husband." And when women are delivered of children, they give them up to whom they will of men that have laid by them. And on the same wise the land is common among each man. For that that a man has one year, another has another year; and each man takes what he desires, now here, now there. For all things are common, as I said before, both grain and all other goods; for there is no thing under lock, and each man is as rich as another. But they have an evil custom among them, for they will more gladly eat men's flesh than any other. Nevertheless, the land is plentiful enough in meat and fish and grain, and also of gold and silver and many other goods. And thither merchants bring children for to sell; and the men of that country buy them. And those that are fat they eat; and those that are not fat they feed until they be fat and then slay them and eat them. And they say it is the best and sweetest meat in the world.

7. Marco Polo and the Image of the East, 1298

In 1298 Venetian merchant and sometime traveler Marco Polo (1254?–1324) was captured by Genoese forces. While a prisoner, Polo met Rusticello of Pisa. Rusticello was an experienced wordsmith, having written several tales of romance and adventure. What he heard from Polo was an amazing story of exploration.

In 1256 merchants Nicolo and Maffeo Polo had set out from Constantinople for Cathay, the lands of the empire of China. The Polos remained in China for nearly a decade, returning to Venice in the late 1260s. In 1271 they embarked again for the East, this time joined by Nicolo's young son Marco. For the next twenty years Marco Polo drank in the wonders of the empire of the Great Khan. When he returned to Venice in 1292, Polo boasted that he had traveled more of the world than any man since the Creation. While the full extent of Polo's travels is difficult to document, there is no doubt that he had gained an understanding of the East unparalleled by any other European of his age.

The book that readers, including Christopher Columbus, came to know as the *Travels* was pieced together by Rusticello from his conversations with Polo and the merchant's own notes. Few books written by a prisoner of war have exerted a greater influence and attracted a wider audience. To fill in gaps in the narrative, Rusticello borrowed liberally from his own work. While some of the *Travels* owed more to Rusticello than to Polo, the message was clear: The world of the East promised vast riches—wealth that was available to any venturesome merchants. This notion of accessible wealth was especially plain in Polo's discussion of Japan, a place he called Cipangu. Polo never actually saw Cipangu, but he was certain that his secondhand account was accurate. Accurate or not, the image of Cipangu was vividly imprinted on the minds of many European geographers and mariners. Polo's image of the lands of Prester John and the legendary giants Gog and Magog was equally memorable. Drawing on biblical as well as more recent sources, Polo fashioned a set of expectations about the peoples of the East—expectations that became part of the baggage carried by many explorers bound for North America.

a.   Polo Describes the Wonders of Cipangu

Cipangu is an Island towards the east in the high seas, 1500 miles distant from the Continent; and a very great Island it is.

The people are white, civilized, and well-favored. They are Idolaters, and are dependent on nobody. And I can tell you the quantity of gold they have is endless; for they find it in their own Islands, and the king does not allow it to be exported. Moreover few merchants visit the country because it is so far from the main land, and thus it comes to pass that their gold is abundant beyond all measure.

I will tell you a wonderful thing about the Palace of the Lord of that Island. You must know that he has a great Palace which is entirely roofed in fine gold, just as our churches are roofed with lead, insomuch that it would scarcely be possible to estimate its value. Moreover, all the pavement of the Palace, and the floors of its chambers, are entirely of gold, in plates like slabs of stone, a good two fingers thick; and the windows also are of gold, so that altogether the richness of this Palace is past all bounds and all belief.

They have also pearls in abundance, which are of a rose color, but fine, big, and round, and quite as valuable as the white ones. In this Island some of the dead are buried, and others are burned. When a body is burned, they put one of these pearls in the mouth, for such is their custom. They have also quantities of other precious stones.

b. Polo and the Peoples of the East

Let us now proceed to another province farther east, called Tenduc, where we shall enter the dominion of Prester John.

Tenduc is a province containing many towns and villages. The chief city is named Tenduc. The people are subject to the Great Khan, for so also are the descendants of Prester John. The province is ruled by a king in the lineage of Prester John, who is a Christian and a priest and also bears the title "Prester John." His personal name is George. He holds the land as a vassal of the Great Khan—not all the land that was held by Prester John, but a part of it. I may tell you that the Great Khans have always given one of their daughters of kinswomen to reigning princes of the lineage of Prester John.

This province produces lapis lazuli in plenty and of good quality, besides excellent camlets of camel hair. The inhabitants live by stockrearing and agriculture. There is also a certain amount of commerce and industry. The rulers, as I have said, are Christians; but there are many idolaters and Mahometans. There is also a class of men called *Argon*, that is to say "half-breeds," who are born of a blend of the two stocks native to Tenduc, the idolaters and the Mahometans. They are a handsome race, more so than the other natives, besides being more intelligent and businesslike.

It is in this province that Prester John had his chief residence when he was lord of the Tartars and of all these neighboring provinces and kingdoms; and it is here that his descendants still live. King George, of whom I have already spoken, is the sixth ruler in descent from Prester John. This is the place which we call in our language Gog and Magog; the natives call it Ung and Mungul. Each of these two provinces was inhabited by a separate race: in Ung lived the Gog, in Mungul the Tartars.

SUGGESTIONS FOR FURTHER READING

Cassidy, Vincent H. *The Sea Around Them: The Atlantic Ocean, A.D. 1250.* Baton Rouge: Louisiana State University Press, 1968.

Grafton, Anthony. *New Worlds, Ancient Texts: The Power of Tradition and the Shock of Discovery.* Cambridge, Massachusetts: Harvard University Press, 1992.

Greenblatt, Stephen. *Marvelous Possessions: The Wonder of the New World.* Chicago: University of Chicago Press, 1991.

Hale, J. R. *Renaissance Exploration*. London: The British Broadcasting Corporation, 1968.

O'Gorman, Edmundo. *The Invention of America*. Bloomington: Indiana University Press, 1961.

Parry, J. H. *The Age of Reconnaissance*. New York: Mentor Books, 1963.

Penrose, Boise. *Travel and Discovery in the Renaissance, 1450–1620*. New York: Atheneum Books, 1962.

Russell, Jeffrey Burton. *Inventing the Flat Earth: Columbus and Modern Historians*. New York: Praeger Books, 1991.

Zerubavel, Eviatar. *Terra Cognita: The Mental Discovery of America*. New Brunswick, New Jersey: Rutgers University Press, 1992.

CHAPTER 2

The Quest
for America

Expectations about America were nurtured and expressed long before
that name appeared on a European map and before any real voyage.
But expectations born of hope and conjecture required outbound journeys. Speculations were transformed into expeditions as Europeans carried their desires and obsessions to distant shores. The voyages of John
Cabot (1497), Lucas Vásquez de Ayllón (1521, 1526), and Giovanni da
Verrazzano (1523–1524) began the European revealing of North
America. These expeditions, however, neither remained long enough
along the coast nor penetrated sufficiently deep into the interior to make
a detailed record. The written records they produced were either frag-
mentary or of limited circulation.

Things changed dramatically in the third decade of the sixteenth century when imperial competition, personal rivalries, and fresh sources of
information all gave exploration renewed energy and direction. In the
1530s, Spanish and French adventurers and their patrons launched
dozens of probes into North America. From the Gulf of St. Lawrence to
Florida, from the Gulf Coast to the Gulf of California, and through the
Southwest to the central Great Plains, European travelers scouted the
land and encountered scores of native tribes and groups. This chapter
examines three of those journeys—the expeditions of Jacques Cartier
(1534, 1535–1536) and Hernando de Soto (1539–1543) and the series
of journeys that came to compose the expedition of Francisco Vásquez
de Coronado (1540–1542).

These enterprises now seem quite different from their successors, different not so much in organization and results as in the "personality" of
the journey. Each expedition had a unique character that reflected the
collective experiences of the participants. An expedition's personality,
moreover, was not only shaped by the cultural past but also constantly
remade by events along the way. Yet the Cartier, de Soto, and Coronado
ventures shared a common attribute. They were all quests, epic searches

out of the pages of medieval romance. It was as if these expeditions had come from the tales of El Cid and King Arthur. They featured pageantry and violence on a grand scale. Fantastic voyages, they brought suffering and death, glory and wonder. Reading the surviving records, we can share in the participants' feelings of surreal terror and awe, astonishment and horror.

For all their dramatic sound and fury, these quests were neither spontaneous adventures nor ill-conceived schemes. Each drew for energy and direction on a body of belief about the land and its promise. This body of belief held a powerful mixture of reasons, conjectures, fantasies, and clichés. Here the geography of conjecture came to play a central role in telling European explorers what they were going to find even before they left home. Hope and illusion were everywhere.

In the long history of North American exploration, no illusion proved more durable than the belief in the Northwest Passage, the dream route that the nineteenth-century poet Walt Whitman called "the passage to India." When Jacques Cartier (1491–1557) sailed up the St. Lawrence River in 1535, he was bound for China. And what stopped his progress were rapids near present-day Montreal later named Lachine, the China Rapids. The ever-elusive passage was part of American landscapes of promise—promise as defined by European aspirations. If early explorers' routes did not lead to the territories described by Marco Polo, they might take daring men to cities of gold and lands of plenty. Hernando de Soto and Francisco Vásquez de Coronado, for example, were fully persuaded that the shape and location of North America promised gold.

The very quest for wealth might be its own reward. Sixteenth-century European men, especially those living in societies that cherished military ideals, sought personal glory and individual distinction by quest and conquest. At the same time, the quest might give the faithful and the zealous the opportunity to serve the Christian God. Sacred quest language permeates sixteenth-century exploration accounts. Biblical stories of exile, wandering, and travel in the wilderness often gave shape to exploration narratives as Europeans borrowed from those accounts to lend structure to their own experiences. Sometimes the borrowed phrases were mere pious clichés; at other times—as in the case of Alvar Núñez Cabeza de Vaca—the rhetoric of faith came from compelling personal experience. And on all these journeys there were flags and other symbols of national power. Imperial European nations, rapidly becoming more modern and more powerful, marched with explorers over each mountain and down every trail.

These sixteenth-century odysseys bring us face-to-face not only with Europeans' complex exploration motives but also with the substance of what was revealed. Modern readers of early exploration accounts are likely to think that the explorers found a pristine world, a landscape untouched since the Creation. Such a vision of early America as Eden appealed to some Europeans, who used it as a way to comment on the faults of their own societies. Modern students sometimes do the same, making sixteenth-century native North America a foil for modern urban-industrial America. The temptation is to construct a fantasy country, a perfect wilderness unspoiled by human hands. But travelers to sixteenth-century North America did not find such a paradise. Instead, they came upon landscapes shaped by Native American hands. Those landscapes were filled with hunting camps, towns, irrigation canals, agricultural fields, fish and game preserves, and places for food storage. Trails for war and commerce ribboned through this world in an intricate web. Everywhere the travelers looked, they saw human creativity as native people actively shaped the physical world and turned it to serve human needs and desires. Reading these narratives, we encounter spaces and places, the handiwork of women and men busy making their part of the world called home.

The Cartier, de Soto, and Coronado journeys featured in this chapter help us to understand and appreciate the process of mutual discovery. What happened throughout each of these ventures was *joint* exploration. One human community that might call itself an exploring party passed through the lands and lives of another, more settled community. That "passing through" was sometimes violent, sometimes peaceful. But whatever its character, each community looked across the cultural divide and struggled to find answers to a common set of questions. Who are these beings? Are they human, however our community defines humanity? Where do they come from, and where are they going? What do they want? Do they mean to do us harm or good? What powers do they possess for good or ill? As these selections show, mutual discovery took many forms. Trade, diplomacy, sacred rituals, personal relationships, and physical touching for healing were all ways to know the other.

We can read these documents as some of the earliest reports on the struggle to know and to reveal. The reports in this chapter are like dispatches from a combat zone. Sometimes the news is all about violence and death by conquest or disease. At other times the news is gentler, revealing a human landscape of awe and perhaps grudging respect. These sixteenth-century journeys changed lives, often in unexpected ways. At the end of his long journey, Cabeza de Vaca and his fellow travelers were "rescued" by a party of Spanish slave hunters. Cabeza de Vaca's Indian escort found it hard to believe that the travelers belonged with the slavers. As Cabeza de Vaca recalled it, the Indians said that the travelers "had come from whence the sun rises, and they [the slavers] whence it goes down; we healed the sick, they killed the sound; that we had come naked and barefooted, while they had arrived in clothing and on horses with lances; that we were not covetous of anything, but all that was given to us we directly turned to give, remaining with nothing; that the others had only the purpose to rob whomsoever they found, bestowing nothing on anyone." Exploration encounters had surely yielded knowledge on both sides of the cultural divide. Cabeza de Vaca, the black slave Esteban, and the Indians must have wondered just where they belonged and into what country they had stumbled.

A. Jacques Cartier and the Kingdom of Canada

Jacques Cartier's first two voyages (1534, 1535–1536) to the shores of eastern Canada produced memorable accounts of the region's peoples and landscapes. The record of Cartier's first voyage initially appeared in Giovanni Battista Ramusio's *Navigationi et viaggi*, published in 1556. In 1867 a more reliable French manuscript was discovered, and it provides the basis for the English translation used here. While scholars agree that this document is not in Cartier's hand, the first-person style and the level of detail point to the captain as the original author. Cartier's role in preparing a record of his second voyage is clearer. Published in Paris in 1545, the *Brief récit* was drafted by Cartier and edited by Jean Poullet, a member of the second expedition. Plants, animals, cornfields, and villages were all carefully described. Both a sense of wonder and a determination to judge all things by European standards vividly shine through in these excerpts.

1. Cartier's Sailors and the Great Auks of Funk Island

In this selection the Great Auk, extinct since 1844, lives again at its roosts on Funk Island off the eastern coast of Newfoundland. Cartier's sailors saw the birds not so much as living things but as food to be taken and consumed. On Funk Island as in the rest of America, Europeans imagined a boundless and inexhaustible plenty.

A nd on [Thursday] the twenty-first of the said month of May we set forth from this [Catalina] harbour with a west wind, and sailed north, one quarter north-east of Cape Bonavista as far as the Isle of Birds [Funk Island], which island was completely surrounded and encompassed by a cordon of loose ice, split up into cakes. In spite of this belt [of ice] our two long-boats were sent off to the island to procure some of the birds, whose numbers are so great as to be incredible, unless one has seen them; for although the island is about a league in circumference, it is so exceeding full of birds that one would think they had been stowed there. In the air and round about are an hundred times as many more as on the island itself. Some of the birds are as large as geese, being black and white with a beak like a crow's. They are always in the water, not being able to fly in the air, inasmuch as they have only small wings about the size of half one's hand, with which however they move as quickly along the water as the other birds fly through the air. And these birds are so fat that it is marvelous. We call them apponats; and our two long-boats were laden with them as with stones, in less than half an hour. Of these, each of our ships salted four or five casks, not counting those we were able to eat fresh.

2. The Cartier Expedition Meets and Trades with the Micmac Indians at Chaleur Bay, 1534

Cartier and his company never expected America to be an empty place, and in the following selection he describes the initial meetings with Micmac Indians at Chaleur Bay on Canada's Gaspé Peninsula. While these French explorers were seeing the Micmacs for the first time, the Indians already had considerable experience with European fishermen. The Micmacs knew all about trading fur for European goods. More than once they had waved furs on sticks, hoping to get something in return. The commentary in this report also reveals something fundamental about the long history of the fur trade. Europeans believed they were exchanging trinkets and trifles for priceless furs. On the other side of the bargain, native people thought they were getting rare iron and textile items while handing over common furs in abundant supply. Not only were the European goods valuable, but some native people believed that the objects carried powerful spirit energy.

The *Voyages* of Jacques Cartier, 1534–1536

The cape on the south shore was named Hope cape for the hope we had of finding here a strait. And on [Saturday] the fourth of the said month [of July], being St. Martin's day, we coasted along the north shore [of Chaleur Bay] in order to find a harbour, and entered a small bay and cove completely open, with no shelter from the wind. We named it St. Martin's cove. We remained in this cove from [Saturday] the fourth until [Sunday] the twelfth [of July]. And while there, we set out on Monday the sixth [of July], after hearing mass, in one of our long-boats, to examine a cape and point of land, that lay seven or eight leagues to the west of us, and to see in which direction the coast ran. And when we were half a league from this point, we caught sight of two fleets of Indian canoes that were crossing from one side [of Chaleur Bay] to the other, which numbered in all some forty or fifty canoes. Upon one of the fleets reaching this point, there sprang out and landed a large number of Indians, who set up a great clamor and made frequent signs to us to come on shore, holding up to us some furs on sticks. But as we were only one boat we did not care to go, so we rowed towards the other fleet which was on the water. And they [on shore] seeing we were rowing away, made ready two of their largest canoes in order to follow us. These were joined by five more of those that were coming in from the sea, and all came after our long-boat, dancing and showing many signs of joy, and of their desire to be friends, saying to us in their language: *Napou tou daman asurtat,* and other words, we did not understand. But for the reason already stated, that we had only one of our long-boats, we did not care to trust to their signs and waved to them to go back, which they would not do but paddled so hard that they soon surrounded our long-boat with their seven canoes. And seeing that no matter how much we signed to them, they would not go back, we shot off over their heads two small cannon. On this they began to return towards the point, and set up a marvellously loud shout, after which they proceeded to come on again as before. And when they had come alongside our long-boat, we shot off two fire-lances which scattered among them and frightened them so much that they began to paddle off in very great haste, and did not follow us any more.

The next day [Tuesday, July 7] some of these Indians came in nine canoes to the point at the mouth of the cove, where we lay anchored with our ships. And being informed of their arrival we went with our two long-boats to the point where they were, at the mouth of the cove. As soon as they saw us they began to run away, making signs to us that they had come to barter with us; and held up some furs of small value, with which they clothe themselves. We likewise made signs to them that we wished them no harm, and sent two men on shore, to offer them some knives and other iron goods, and a red cap to give to their chief. Seeing this, they sent on shore part of their people with some of their furs; and the two parties traded together. The savages showed a marvellously great pleasure in possessing and obtaining these iron wares and other commodities, dancing and going through many ceremonies, and throwing salt water over their heads with their hands. They bartered all they had to such an extent that all went back naked without anything on them; and they made signs to us that they would return on the morrow with more furs.

On Thursday the ninth of the said month [of July] as the wind was favorable for getting under way with our ships, we fitted up our long-boats to go and explore this [Chaleur] bay; and we ran up it that day some twenty-five leagues. The next day [Friday, July 10], at daybreak, we had fine weather and sailed on until about ten o'clock in the morning, at which hour we caught sight of the head of the bay, whereat we were grieved and displeased. At the head of this bay, beyond the low shore, were several very high mountains. And seeing there was no passage, we proceeded to turn back. While making our way along the [north] shore, we caught sight of the Indians on the side of a lagoon and low beach, who were making many fires that smoked. We rowed over to the spot, and finding there was an entrance from the sea into the lagoon, we placed our long-boats on one side of the entrance. The savages came over in one of their canoes and brought us some strips of cooked seal, which they placed on bits of wood and then withdrew, making signs to us that they were making us a present of them. We sent two men on shore with hatchets, knives, beads, and other wares, at which the Indians showed great pleasure. And at once they came over in a crowd in their canoes to the side where we were, bringing furs and whatever else they possessed, in order to obtain some of our wares. They numbered, both men, women, and children, more than 300 persons. Some of their women, who did not come over, danced and sang, standing in the water up to their knees. The other women, who had come over to the side where we were, advanced freely towards us and rubbed our arms with their hands. Then they joined their hands together and raised them to heaven, exhibiting many signs of joy. And so much at ease did the savages feel in our presence, that at length we bartered with them, hand to hand, for everything they possessed, so that nothing was left to them but their naked bodies; for they offered us everything they owned, which was, all told, of little value. We perceived that they are people who would be easy to convert, who go from place to place maintaining themselves and catching fish in the fishing-season for food. Their country is more temperate than Spain and the finest it is possible to see, and as level as the surface of a pond. There is not the smallest plot of ground bare of wood, and even on sandy soil, but is full of wild wheat, that has an ear like barley and the grain like oats, as well as of pease, as thick as if they had been sown and hoed; of white and red currant-bushes, of strawberries, of raspberries, of white and red roses and of other plants of a strong, pleasant odour. Likewise there are many fine meadows with useful herbs, and a pond where there are many salmon. I am more than ever of opinion that these people would be easy to convert to our holy faith.

3. Cartier Reports on Trade and Imperial Politics at Gaspé, 1534

The next selection, also drawn from the account of Cartier's first voyage, gives a glimpse of the complex ways in which native people understood and coped with the French presence. The St. Lawrence Iroquois fishing at Gaspé Bay eagerly sought trade with the newcomers, especially exchanges that would bring useful goods. But when Cartier erected a cross and royal coat of arms—a sign of imperial possession—an elderly chief quickly grasped the meaning of the situation and acted forcefully. The French responded by telling a smooth story about the cross as a navigation aid and then by "detaining" two young Indian men. Those men, Domagaya and Taignoagny, were taken to France to serve as guides and translators for the second Cartier expedition.

On account of the continuous bad weather with over-cast sky and mist, we remained in that harbor and river [Gaspé harbor behind Sandy Beach Point], without being able to leave, until the twenty-fifth [of July]. During that time there arrived a large number of savages, who had come to the river [the Gaspé basin] to fish for mackerel, of which there is a great abundance. They [the Indians] numbered, as well men, women, and children, more than 300 persons, with some forty canoes. When they had mixed with us a little on shore, they came freely in their canoes to the sides of our vessels. We gave them knives, glass beads, combs and other trinkets of small value, at which they showed many signs of joy, lifting up their hands to heaven and singing and dancing in their canoes. This people may well be called savage; for they are the sorriest folk there can be in the world, and the whole lot of them had not anything above the value of five sous, their canoes and fishing-nets excepted. They go quite naked, except for a small skin, with which they cover their privy parts, and for a few old furs which they throw over their shoulders. They are not at all of the same race or language as the first [the Micmacs] we met. They have their heads shaved all around in circles, except for a tuft on the top of the head, which they leave long like a horse's tail. This they do up upon their heads and tie in a knot with leather thongs. They have no other dwelling but their canoes, which they turn upside down and sleep on the ground underneath. They eat their meat almost raw, only warming it a little on the coals; and the same with their fish. On St. Magdalen's day [July 22], we rowed over in our long-boats to the spot on the shore where they were, and went on land freely among them. At this they showed great joy, and the men all began to sing and dance in two or three groups, exhibiting signs of great pleasure at our coming. But they made all the young women retire into the woods, except two or three who remained, to whom we gave each a comb and a little tin bell, at which they showed great pleasure, thanking the captain [Cartier] by rubbing his arms and his breast with their hands. And the men, seeing we had given something to the women that had remained, made those come back who had fled to the woods, in order to receive the same as the others. These, who numbered some twenty, crowded about the captain and rubbed him with their hands, which is their way of showing welcome. He gave them each a little tin ring of small value; and at once they assembled together in a group to dance; and sang several songs. We saw a large quantity of mackerel which they had caught near the shore with the nets they use for fishing, which are made of hemp thread, that grows in the country where they ordinarily reside; for they only come down to the sea in the fishing-season, as I have been given to understand. Here likewise grows Indian corn like pease, the same as in Brazil, which they eat in place of bread, and of this they had a large quantity with them. They call it in their language, *Kagaige*. Furthermore they have plums which they dry for the winter as we do, and these they call, *honnesta*; also figs, nuts, pears, apples and other fruits, and beans which they call, *sahe*. If one shows them something they have not got and they know not what it is, they shake their heads and say, *nouda,* which means, they have none of it and know not what it is. Of the things they have, they showed us by signs the way they grow and how they prepare them. They never eat anything that has a taste of salt in it. They are wonderful thieves and steal everything they can carry off.

On [Friday] the twenty-fourth of the said month [of July], we had a cross made thirty feet high, which was put together in the presence of a number of Indians on the point at the entrance to this harbor, under the cross-bar of which we fixed a shield with three *fleurs-de-lys* in relief, and above it a wooden board, engraved in large Gothic characters, where was written, LONG LIVE THE KING OF FRANCE. We erected this cross on the point in their presence and they watched it being put together and set up. And when it had been raised in the air, we all knelt down with our hands joined, worshipping it before them; and made signs to them, looking up and pointing towards heaven, that by means of this we had our redemption, at which they showed many marks of admiration, at the same time turning and looking at the cross.

When we had returned to our ships, the chief, dressed in an old black bear-skin, arrived in a canoe with three of his sons and his brother; but they did not come so close to the ships as they had usually done. And pointing to the cross he [the chief] made us a long harangue, making the sign of the cross with two of his fingers; and then he pointed to the land all around about, as if he wished to say that all this region belonged to him, and that we ought not to have set up this cross without his permission. And when he had finished his harangue, we held up an axe to him, pretending we would barter it for his fur-skin. To this he nodded assent and little by little drew near the side of our vessel, thinking he would have the axe. But one of our men, who was in our dinghy, caught hold of his canoe, and at once two or three more stepped down into it and made the Indians come on board our vessel, at which they were greatly astonished. When they had come on board, they were assured by the captain that no harm would befall them, while at the same time every sign of affection was shown to them; and they were made to eat and to drink and to be of good cheer. And then we explained to them by signs that the cross had been set up to serve as a landmark and guide-post on coming into the harbor, and that we would soon come back and would bring them iron wares and other goods; and that we wished to take two of his [the chief's] sons away with us and afterwards would bring them back again to that harbor. And we dressed up his two sons in shirts and ribbons and in red caps, and put a little brass chain round the neck of each, at which they were greatly pleased; and they proceeded to hand over their old rags to those who were going back on shore. To each of these three, whom we sent back, we also gave a hatchet and two knives at which they showed great pleasure. When they returned on shore, they told the others what had happened. About noon on that day six canoes came off to the ships, in each of which were five or six Indians, who had come to say good-bye to the two we had detained, and to bring them some fish. These made signs that they would not pull down the cross, delivering at the same time several harangues which we did not understand.

4. Mutual Discovery: Cartier and the People of Hochelaga, 1535

The final selection in this set is drawn from the second Cartier expedition and describes the moment of mutual discovery when the Iroquois people of Hochelaga (present-day Montreal) welcomed Cartier and his company. The report details the town, its setting, and the behavior of the Iroquois and the French toward each other. Modern readers should note that touching was both a way to heal and a means to acquire spiritual power.

We sailed on in as fine weather as one could wish until October 2, when we arrived at Hochelaga, which is about forty-five leagues from the spot where we left our bark. During this interval we came across on the way many of the people of the country, who brought us fish and other provisions, at the same time dancing and showing great joy at our coming. And in order to win and keep their friendship, the Captain made them a present of some knives, beads and other small trifles, whereat they were greatly pleased. And on reaching Hochelaga, there came to meet us more than a thousand persons, both men, women, and children, who gave us as good a welcome as ever father gave to his son, making great signs of joy; for the men danced in one ring, the women in another and the children also apart by themselves. After this they brought us quantities of fish, and of their bread which is made of Indian corn, throwing so much of it into our long-boats that it seemed to rain bread. Seeing this the Captain, accompanied by several of his men, went on shore; and no sooner had he landed than they all crowded about him and about the others, giving them a wonderful reception. And the women brought their babies in their arms to have the Captain and his companions touch them, while all held a merry-making which lasted more than half an hour. Seeing their generosity and friendliness, the Captain had the women all sit down in a row and gave them some tin beads and other trifles; and to some of the men he gave knives. Then he returned on board the long-boats to sup and pass the night, throughout which the Indians remained on the bank of the river, as near the long-boats as they could get, keeping many fires burning all night, and dancing and calling out every moment *aguyase* which is their term of salutation and joy.

At daybreak the next day, the Captain, having put on his armour, had his men marshalled for the purpose of paying a visit to the village and home of these people, and to the mountain which lies near the town. The Captain was accompanied by the gentlemen and by twenty sailors, the remainder having been left behind to guard the long-boats. And he took three Indians of the village as guides to conduct them thither. When we had got underway, we discovered that the path was as well-trodden as it is possible to see, and that the country was the finest and most excellent one could find anywhere, being everywhere full of oaks, as beautiful as in any forest in France, underneath which the ground lay covered with acorns. And after marching about a league and a half, we met on the trail one of the headmen of the village of Hochelaga, accompanied by several Indians, who made signs to us that we should rest at that spot near a fire they had lighted on the path; which we did. Thereupon this headman began to make a speech and to harangue us, which, as before mentioned, is their way of showing joy and friendliness, welcoming in this way the Captain and his company. The Captain presented him with a couple of hatchets and a couple of knives, as well as with a cross and a crucifix, which he made him kiss and then hung it about his neck. For these the headman thanked the Captain. When this was done we marched on, and about half a league thence, found that the land began to be cultivated. It was fine land with large fields covered with the corn of the country, which resembles Brazil millet, and is about as large or larger than a pea. They live on this as we do on wheat. And in the middle of these fields is situated and stands the village of Hochelaga, near and adjacent to a mountain, the slopes of which are fertile and are cultivated, and from the top of which one can see for a long distance. We named this mountain "Mount Royal." The village is circular and is completely enclosed by a wooden palisade in three tiers like a pyramid. The top one is built crosswise, the middle one perpendicular and the lowest one of strips of wood placed lengthwise. The whole is well joined and lashed after their manner, and is some two lances [about thirty-three feet] in height. There is only one gate and entrance to this village and that can be barred up. Over this gate and in many places about the enclosure are species of galleries with ladders for mounting to them, which galleries are provided with rocks and stones for the defence and protection of the place. There are some fifty houses in this village, each about fifty or more paces in length, and twelve or fifteen in width, built completely of wood and covered in and bordered up with large pieces of bark and rind of trees, as broad as a table, which are well and cunningly lashed after their manner. And inside these houses are many rooms and chambers; and in the middle is a large space without a floor, where they light their fire and live together in common. Afterwards the men retire to the above-mentioned quarters with their wives and children. And furthermore there are lofts in the upper part of their houses, where they store the corn of which they make their bread. This they call *carraconny,* and they make it in the following manner. They have wooden mortars, like those used [in France] for braying hemp, and in these with wooden pestles they pound the corn into flour. This they knead into dough, of which they make small loaves, which they set on a broad hot stone and then cover them with hot pebbles. In this way they bake their bread for want of an oven. They make also many kinds of soup with this corn, as well as with beans and with pease, of which they have a considerable supply, and again with large cucumbers and other fruits. They have in their houses also large vessels like puncheons, in which they place their fish, such as eels and others, that are smoked during the summer, and on these they live during the winter. They make great store of these as we ourselves saw. All their food is eaten without salt. They sleep on the bark of trees, spread out upon the ground, with old furs of wild animals over them; and of these, to wit, otters, beavers, martens, foxes, wildcats, deer, stags and others, they make their clothing and blankets, but the greater portion of them go almost naked. The most precious article they possess in this world is *esnoguy,* which is as white as snow. They procure it [wampum] from shells in the river in the following manner. When an Indian has incurred the death-penalty or they have taken some prisoners of war, they kill one and make great incisions in his buttocks and thighs, and about his legs, arms and shoulders. Then at the spot where this *esnoguy* is found, they sink the body to the bottom and leave it there for ten or twelve hours. It is then brought to the surface; and in the above-mentioned cuts and incisions they find these shells, of which they make a sort of bead, which has the same use among them as gold and silver with us; for they consider it the most valuable article in the world. It has the virtue of stopping nose-bleeding; for we tried it. This whole tribe gives itself to manual labor and to fishing merely to obtain the necessities of life; for they place no value upon the goods of this world, both because they are unacquainted with them, and because they do not move from home and are not nomads like those of Canada and of the Saguenay, notwithstanding that the Canadians and some eight or nine other tribes along this river are subjects of theirs.

As we drew near to their village, great numbers of the inhabitants came out to meet us and gave us a hearty welcome, according to the custom of the country. And we were led by our guides and those who were conducting us into the middle of the village, where there was an open square between the houses, about a stone's throw or thereabouts in width each way. They signed to us that we should come to a halt here, which we did. And at once all the girls and women of the village, some of whom had children in their arms, crowded about us, rubbing our faces, arms and other parts of the upper portions of our bodies which they could touch, weeping for joy at the sight of us and giving us the best welcome they could. They made signs to us also to be good enough to put our hands upon their babies. After this the men made the women retire, and themselves set down upon the ground round about us, as if we had been going to perform a miracle play. And at once several of the women came back, each with a four-cornered mat, woven like a tapestry, and these they spread upon the ground in the middle of the square, and made us place ourselves upon them. When this had been done, the ruler and chief of this tribe, whom in their language they call *Agouhanna*, was carried in, seated on a large deer-skin, by nine or ten Indians, who came and set him down upon the mats near the Captain, making signs to us that this was their ruler and chief. This *Agouhanna*, who was some fifty years of age, was in no way better dressed than the other Indians except that he wore about his head for a crown a sort of red band made of hedgehog's [porcupine] skin. This chief was completely paralyzed and deprived of the use of his limbs. When he had saluted the Captain and his men, by making signs which clearly meant that they were very welcome, he showed his arms and legs to the Captain motioning to him to be good enough to touch them, as if he thereby expected to be cured and healed. On this the Captain set about rubbing his arms and legs with his hands. Thereupon this *Agouhanna* took the band of cloth he was wearing as a crown and presented it to the Captain. And at once many sick persons, some blind, others with but one eye, others lame or impotent and others again so extremely old that their eyelids hung down to their cheeks, were brought in and set down or laid out near the Captain, in order that he might lay his hands upon them, so that one would have thought Christ had come down to earth to heal them.

Seeing the suffering of these people and their faith, the Captain read aloud the Gospel of St. John, namely, "In the beginning," etc. making the sign of the cross over the poor sick people, praying God to give them knowledge of our holy faith and of our Saviour's passion, and grace to obtain baptism and redemption. Then the Captain took a prayer-book and read out, word for word, the Passion of our Lord, that all who were present could hear it, during which all these poor people maintained great silence and were wonderfully attentive, looking up to heaven and going through the same ceremonies they saw us do. After this the Captain had all the men range themselves on one side, the women on another and the children on another, and to the headmen he gave hatchets, to the others knives, and to the women, beads and other small trinkets. He then made the children scramble for little rings and tin *agnus Dei* [small figures of a lamb with a cross], which afforded them great amusement. The Captain next ordered the trumpets and other musical instruments to be sounded, whereat the Indians were much delighted. We then took leave of them and proceeded to set upon our return. Seeing this the squaws placed themselves in our way to prevent us, and brought us some of their provisions, which they had made ready for us, to wit: fish, soups, beans, bread and other dishes, in hope of inducing us to partake of some refreshment and eat with them. But as these provisions were not to our taste and had no savour of salt, we thanked them, making signs that we were in no need of refreshment.

B.   Hernando de Soto and the Invasion of La Florida

While four narratives of the Hernando de Soto expedition (1539–1543) are known to have survived, none is more comprehensive and detailed than the account written by the Portuguese Gentleman of Elvas. Despite years of scholarly investigation, the identity of Elvas remains unknown. The narrative was first published in Portugal in 1557 and contains a full account of the entire four-year journey. Based on his own experience, Elvas recounted the march from Espiritu Santo (present-day Tampa Bay) northeast to what is now Lakeland, Florida. The expedition then found a trail heading north-west into the chiefdom of Apalachee and its leading town Anhaica (present-day Tallahassee). The chiefdoms of the Southeast were stable territories with large towns, ritual mound centers, and complex economic systems. After wintering at Anhaica, the de Soto expedition marched into present-day Georgia, in search of great cities of gold.

1.   The Gentleman of Elvas Recounts the Battle of the Lakes, 1539

This first selection describes the Battle of the Lakes at Napituca near present-day Live Oak, Florida. Here Indians put up a strong resistance against Spanish forces. The selection concludes with a graphic description of the long lines of chained Indian slaves the Spanish used to carry expedition baggage.

Modern readers should note that the name *La Florida* means the entire Southeast, while *Florida* usually applies to the peninsula known today as Florida.

We marched five days, passing through some small towns, and arrived at Napituca on the fifteenth day of September, where we found fourteen or fifteen Indians who begged for the release of the cacique [headman] of Caliquen. Having learned from Juan Ortiz [a Spanish guide], to whom a native had made it known, that the Indians had determined to assemble and fall upon the Christians, for the recovery of their chief, the Governor [de Soto], commanded his men to be in readiness, the cavalry to be armed and on horseback, each one so disposed of in his lodge as not to be seen by the Indians, that they might come to the town without reserve. Four hundred warriors, with bows and arrows, appeared in sight of the camp; and going into a thicket, they sent two of their number to demand the cacique. The Governor, with six men on foot, taking the chief by the hand, conversing with him the while to assure the Indians, went towards the place where they were, when, finding the moment right, he ordered a trumpet to be sounded. Directly, they who were in the houses, infantry as well as cavalry, set upon the natives, who, assailed unexpectedly, thought only of their safety. From thirty to forty natives fell by the lance; the rest escaped into two very large ponds, situated some way apart, wherein they swam about; and, being surrounded by the Christians, they were shot at with crossbow and arquebus, although to no purpose, because of the long distance they were off.

At night, one of the lakes was ordered to be guarded, the people not being sufficient to encircle both. The Indians, in attempting to escape in the dark, would come swimming noiselessly to the shore, with a leaf of water-lily on the head, that they might pass unobserved; when those [the Spanish] mounted, at sight of any ruffle on the surface, would dash into the water up to the breasts of the horses, and the natives would retire again. In such way passed the night, neither party taking any rest. Juan Ortiz told them [the Indians] that, as escape was impossible, they would do well to give up; which they did, driven by extreme chillness of the water; and one after another, as cold overpowered, called out to him, asking not to be killed—that he was coming to put himself in the hands of the Governor. At four o'clock in the morning they had all surrendered, save twelve of the principal men, who, as of more distinction and more valiant than the rest, preferred to die rather than yield. Then the Indians of Paracoxi [native people previously captured and enslaved by de Soto] who were going about unshackled, went in after them, and pulled them out by the hair. They were all put in chains, and, on the day following, were divided among the Christians for their service.

While captives, these men determined to rebel, and gave the lead to an interpreter, one reputed brave, that when the Governor might come near to speak with him, he should strangle him; but no sooner was the occasion presented, and before his hands could be thrown about the neck of [de] Soto, his purpose was discovered, and he received so heavy a blow from him in the nostrils, that they gushed with blood. The Indians all rose together. He who could only catch up a pestle from a mortar, as well as he who could grasp a weapon, equally exerted himself to kill his master, or the first one he met;

Spanish Explorations, 1528–1543

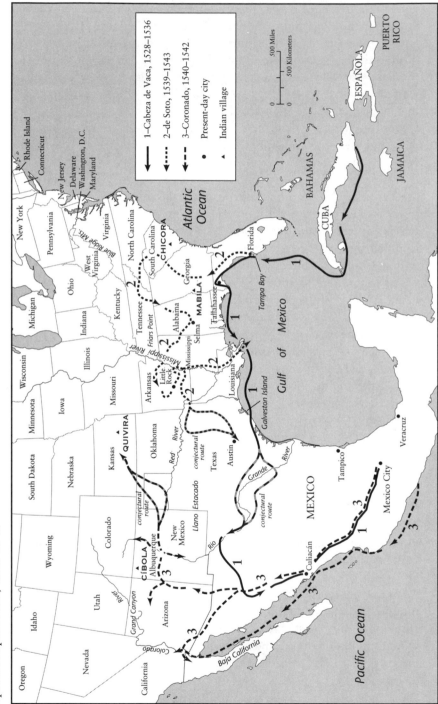

and he whose fortune it was to find a lance, or a sword, handled it in a manner as though he had been accustomed to use it all his days. One Indian, in the public yard of the town, with blade in hand, fought like a bull in the arena, until the lancers put an end to him. Another got up, with a lance, into a maize crib, made of cane, called by the Indians *barbacoa,* and defended the entrance with the uproar of ten men, until he was stricken down with a battle-axe. They who were subdued may have been in all two hundred men. Some of the youngest the Governor gave to those who had good chains and were vigilant; all the rest were ordered to execution, and, being bound to a post in the middle of the town yard, they were shot to death with arrows by the people of Paracoxi.

[On September 23 the Spanish expedition left Napituca and headed west toward Anhaica.]

Two captains having been sent in opposite directions, in quest of Indians, a hundred men and women were taken, one or two of whom were chosen out for the Governor, as was always customary for officers to do after successful raids, dividing the others among themselves and companions. They were led off in chains, with collars about the neck, to carry luggage and grind corn, doing labor proper for servants. Sometimes it happened that, going with them for wood or maize, they would kill a Christian, and flee, with the chain on, which others would file at night with a splinter of stone, in the place of iron, at which work, when caught, they were punished, as a warning to others, and that they might not do the like. The women and youths, when removed a hundred leagues from their country, no longer cared, and were taken along loose, doing the work, and in very little time learning the Spanish language.

2. The Gentleman of Elvas Views the People of Cofitachequi, 1540

By the time the de Soto expedition reached the leading town in the chiefdom of Cofitachequi (near present-day Camden, South Carolina) in the spring of 1540, native people knew about Spanish demands for food, shelter, porters (*tamemes*), and sexual favors. Native leaders struggled to find ways, either by diplomacy or warfare, to cope with this unprecedented invasion. The invaders they encountered were not only visible, in the shape of Spanish soldiers, horses, and dogs, but also invisible, in the form of disease-bearing microorganisms. The invisible disease invasion proved more destructive than any armed Spaniard.

In this selection Elvas recounts the strategy used by an influential woman known to the Spanish as the Lady, or *Cacica*, of Cofitachequi. Playing on de Soto's character as an "inflexible man" who "ever acted as he thought best," she persuaded the Spaniard that greater wealth lay north and west in the province of Chiaha. The quest for Chiaha eventually took de Soto into the Tennessee Valley.

Directly as the Governor [de Soto] arrived, four canoes came towards him, in one of which was a kinswoman of the Cacica, who, coming near, addressed him in these words. "My sister sends me to salute you, and to say, that the reason why she has not come in person is, that she has thought to serve you better by remaining to give orders on the other shore; and that, in a short time, her canoes will all be here, in readiness to conduct you there, where you may take your rest and be obeyed."

The Governor thanked her, and she returned to cross the river. After a little time the Cacica came out of the town, seated in a chair, which some principal men having borne to the bank, she entered a canoe. Over the stern was spread an awning, and in the bottom lay extended a mat where were two cushions, one above the other, upon which she sat; and she was accompanied by her chief men, in other canoes, with Indians. She approached the spot where the Governor was, and, being arrived, thus addressed him. "Be this coming to your shores most happy. My ability can in no way equal my wishes, nor my services become the merits of so great a prince; nevertheless, good wishes are to be valued more than all the treasures of the earth without them. With sincerest and purest good-will I tender you my person, my lands, my people, and make you these small gifts."

The Cacica presented much clothing of the country, from the shawls and skins that came in the other boats; and drawing from over her head a large string of pearls, she threw them about his neck, exchanging with him many gracious words of friendship and courtesy. She directed that canoes should come to the spot, whence the Governor and his people passed to the opposite side of the river. So soon as he was lodged in the town, a great many turkeys were sent to him. The country was delightful and fertile, having good lands between the streams; the forest was open, with abundance of walnut and mulberry trees. The sea was stated to be distant two days' travel. About the place, from half a league to a league off, were large vacant towns, grown up in grass, that appeared as if no people had lived in them for a long time. The Indians said that, two years before, there had been a great pest in the land, and the inhabitants had moved away to other villages. In the *barbacoas* were large quantities of clothing, shawls of thread, made from the bark of trees, and others of feathers, white, gray, vermilion, and yellow, rich and proper for winter. There were also many well-dressed deer-skins, of colors drawn over with designs, of which had been made shoes, stockings, and hose. The Cacica, observing that the Christians valued the pearls, told the Governor that, if he should order some sepulchres [burial places] that were in the town be to searched, he would find many; and if he chose to send to those that were in the uninhabited towns, he might load all his horses with them. They examined those in the town, and found three hundred and fifty pounds' weight of pearls, and figures of babies and birds made of them.

To all it appeared well to make a settlement there, the point being a favorable one, to which could come all the ships from New Spain, Peru, Sancta Marta, and Tierra-Firme, going to Spain; because it is on the way there, is a good country, and one fit in which to raise supplies; but [de] Soto, as it was his object to find another treasure like that of Atahualpa, lord of Peru, would not be content with goods, lands nor pearls, even though many of them were worth their weight in gold. So he answered them that urged him to make a settlement, that in all the country together there was not support for his troops a single month; and should a richer country not be found, they could always return to that who would, and in their absence the Indians would plant their fields and be better provided with maize. The natives were asked if they had knowledge of any great lord farther on, to which they answered, that twelve days' travel thence was a province called Chiaha.

The Governor then resolved at once to go in quest of that country, and being an inflexible man, and dry of word, who, although he liked to know what others all thought and had to say, after once he said a thing he did not like to be opposed, and as he ever acted as he thought best, all bent to his will.

3. Rodrigo Ranjel and Gonzalo Fernández de Oviedo Evaluate the de Soto Expedition, 1546

With hundreds of soldiers and sometimes thousands of Indian porters, the de Soto expedition was a huge community snaking its way through the Southeast. Two powerful forces drove this community—de Soto's own passion for wealth and the constant need to find food and shelter for survival. After the Battle of Mabila (October 1540) at the heavily fortified town of Mabila west or southwest of present-day Selma, Alabama, Spanish expectations about gold might have seemed less likely to be fulfilled. But de Soto was not about to abandon his dream, no matter how nightmarish it proved for others. From the spring of 1541 until his death a year later on the banks of

the Mississippi River, de Soto led his party on a wandering, sometimes aimless journey through present-day Mississippi, Tennessee,
and Arkansas. After de Soto's death, Luis de Moscoso commanded
the survivors on a nearly two-year effort to retreat back to New
Spain. Of the some 600 adventurers in the original party, only 311
lived to reach the Gulf of Mexico in July 1543.

Popular history has sometimes made de Soto's expedition into a
glorious and romantic jaunt through a savage country. De Soto's
Spanish contemporaries knew better. Expedition survivors were some
of de Soto's sharpest critics. In 1546, Spanish official and historian
Gonzalo Fernández de Oviedo met with Rodrigo Ranjel, de Soto's
secretary, to obtain a copy of Ranjel's expedition report. This report,
unfinished at the time of Oviedo's departure from Santo Domingo,
became part of Oviedo's *Historia General y Natural de las Indias*
(1555–1557). Both Ranjel and Oviedo found much to criticize when
they reviewed the history of the expedition. Their comments are
printed here. But many consequences that had been visited on native
peoples escaped their attention, either because they did not understand the meaning of a particular event or because the impact was felt
after the Spanish party moved on. De Soto's invasion disrupted native
political, social, and economic relationships. Peoples scattered in the
face of the Spanish forces. Death from disease was everywhere.
Indians taken as captives or hostages died or could not return home.
Mound building, so important a part of southeastern native cultures,
gradually ceased as diminished populations moved to new territories
and regrouped in new ways. As Ranjel and Oviedo remind us, death
and destruction marched in company with de Soto.

I have wondered many times at the venturesomeness, stubbornness, and
persistency or firmness, to use a better word for the way these baffled conquerors kept on from one toil to another, and then to another still greater;
from one danger to many others, here losing one companion, there three and
again still more, going from bad to worse without learning by experience.
Oh, wonderful God! that they should have been so blinded and dazed by a
greed so uncertain and by such vain discourses as Hernando de Soto was
able to utter to those deluded soldiers, whom he brought to a land where he
had never been, nor put a foot into. He thought that experience in the South
[Peru] was sufficient to show him what to do in the North, and he was
deceived as the history will tell.

The historian [Oviedo] asked a very intelligent gentleman who was with
the Governor, and who went with him through his whole expedition in this

northern country, why, at every place they came to, this Governor and his army asked for those *tamemes* or Indian carriers, and why they took so many women and these not old nor the most ugly; and why, after having given them what they had, they held the chiefs and principal men; and why they never tarried nor settled in any region they came to, adding that such a course was not settlement or conquest, but rather disturbing and ravaging the land and depriving the natives of their liberty without converting or making a single Indian either a Christian or a friend. He replied and said: That they took these carriers or *tamemes* to keep them as slaves or servants to carry the loads of supplies which they secured by plunder or gift, and that some died, and others ran away or were tired out, so that it was necessary to replenish their numbers and to make more; and the women they desired both as servants and for their foul uses and lewdness, and that they had them baptized more on account of carnal intercourse with them than to teach them the faith.

Oh, wicked men! Oh, devilish greed! Oh, bad consciences! Oh, unfortunate soldiers! that you should not have understood the perils you were to encounter, and how wasted would be your lives, and without rest your souls! Give ear, then, Catholic reader, and do not lament the conquered Indians less than their Christian conquerors or slayers of themselves, as well as others, and follow the adventures of this Governor, ill governed, taught in the School of Pedrarias de Avila [conqueror of Nicaragua], in the scattering and wasting of the Indians of Castilla del Oro; a graduate in the killing of the natives of Nicaragua and canonized in Peru as a member of the order of the Pizarros; and then, after being delivered from all those paths of Hell and having come to Spain loaded with gold, neither bachelor nor married, knew not how nor was able to rest without returning to the Indies to shed human blood, not content with what he had spilled; and to leave life as shall be narrated, and providing the opportunity for so many sinners deluded with his vain words to perish after him.

C. Alvar Núñez Cabeza de Vaca's Journey Across America, 1528–1536

No recorded journey through sixteenth-century North America was more filled with wonder and revelation than the one undertaken by Alvar Núñez Cabeza de Vaca (d. 1557) and his three companions Alonso del Castillo, Andrés Dorantes, and the black Moroccan slave Esteban. And few travelers became more adept at the arts of survival than these wayfarers.

The Spanish-born Cabeza de Vaca, sometime leader of the party, had considerable military experience before joining Pánfilo de Narváez's Florida-bound expedition as second-in-command. This exploring enterprise landed at Tampa Bay in the spring of 1528 and soon came to grief. Throughout the fall of that year, Narváez's exhausted explorers sailed makeshift boats along the Gulf Coast until landing at present-day Galveston Island on the Texas coast. For the next six years the survivors—some alone and some in small groups—struggled to stay alive. The first excerpt below, from Cabeza de Vaca's *Relation* (1542), recalls his own efforts during those years. In 1534 he joined Alonso del Castillo, Andrés Dorantes, and Esteban for a two-year journey to Mexico. The party crossed the Rio Grande between Brownsville and Laredo, Texas, and moved into northern Mexico. The footsore travelers were eventually found in July 1536. They had accomplished the first crossing of North America from Atlantic to Pacific waters by a group of nonnative people.

Cabeza de Vaca's *Relation,* the first book devoted wholly to North America, was part geographic description and part personal confession. It was his attempt to chart the progress of unwilling pilgrims in a bewildering world. In fact, both the Spanish Christian Cabeza de Vaca and his Indian hosts explained the universe in remarkably similar ways. It was a universe where the supernatural was ever-present, where spirit forces with many names and faces were always hovering nearby. Cabeza de Vaca depicted his journey as a series of passages, each one taking him from one mysterious place to another. He negotiated those passages by playing several roles—trader, artisan, and healer. When it came to stories of great cities and vast wealth, the *Relation* made only modest claims. Cabeza de Vaca reported discoveries of mere traces of mineral wealth. But traces were enough, and the signs of gold were as good as gold itself.

The selections printed here illustrate Cabeza de Vaca's many roles. As with other European writers of the time, he uses the word *Christian* as a synonym for Spaniards as a national group.

1. Cabeza de Vaca on Trading and the Business of Survival

Cabeza de Vaca quickly understood that the trader's role gave him the security and freedom denied to many captives. As a peddler, he gained valuable information about Gulf Coast peoples and cultures.

I was obliged to remain with the people belonging to the island more than a year, and because of the hard work they put upon me and the harsh treatment, I resolved to flee from them and go to those of Charruco, who inhabit the forests and country of the main, the life I led being insupportable. Besides much other labor, I had to get out roots from below the water, and from the cane where they grew in the ground. From this employment I had my fingers so worn that did a straw but touch them they would bleed. Many of the canes are broken, so they often tore my flesh, and I had to go in the midst of them with only the clothing on I have mentioned.

Accordingly, I put myself to contriving how I might get over to the other Indians, among whom matters turned somewhat more favorably for me. I set to trafficking [trading], and strove to make my employment profitable in the ways I could best contrive, and by that means I got food and good treatment. The Indians would beg me to go from one quarter to another for things of which they have need; for in consequence of incessant hostilities, they cannot traverse the country, nor make many exchanges. With my merchandise and trade I went into the interior as far as I pleased, and traveled along the coast forty or fifty leagues. The principal wares were cones and other pieces of sea-snail, conchs used for cutting, and fruit like a bean of the highest value among them, which they use as a medicine and employ in their dances and festivities. Among other matters were sea-beads. Such were what I carried into the interior; and in barter I got and brought back skins, ochre with which they rub and color the face, hard canes of which to make arrows, sinews, cement and flint for the heads, and tassels of the hair of deer that by dyeing they make red. This occupation suited me well; for the travel allowed me liberty to go where I wished, I was not obliged to work, and was not a slave. Wherever I went I received fair treatment, and the Indians gave me to eat out of regard to my commodities. My leading object, while journeying in this business, was to find out the way by which I should go forward, and I became well known. The inhabitants were pleased when they saw me, and I had brought them what they wanted; and those who did not know me sought and desired the acquaintance, for my reputation. The hardships that I underwent in this were long to tell, as well of peril and privation as of storms and cold. Oftentimes they overtook me alone and in the wilderness; but I came forth from them all by the great mercy of God our Lord. Because of them I avoided pursuing the business in the winter, a season in which the natives themselves retire to their huts and ranches, torpid and incapable of exertion.

I was in this country nearly six years, alone among the Indians, and naked like them. The reason why I remained so long, was that I might take with me the Christian, Lope de Oviedo, from the island; Alaniz, his companion, died soon after; to get the survivor out from there, I went over to the island every year, and entreated him that we should go, in the best way we could contrive, in quest of Christians. He put me off every year, saying in the next coming we would start. At last I got him off, crossing him over the bay, and over four rivers in the coast, as he could not swim. In this way we went on with some Indians, until coming to a bay a league in width, and everywhere deep. From the appearance we supposed it to be that which is called Espiritu Sancto [perhaps La Vaca Bay]. We met some Indians on the other side of it, coming to visit ours, who told us that beyond them were three men like us, and gave their names. We asked for the others, and were told that they were all dead of cold and hunger; that the Indians further on, of whom they were, for their diversion had killed Diego Dorantes, Valdevieso, and Diego de Huelva, because they left one house for another; and that other Indians, their neighbors with whom Captain Dorantes now was, had in consequence of a dream, killed Esquivel and Mendez. We asked how the living were situated, and they answered that they were very ill used, the boys and some of the Indian men being very idle, out of cruelty gave them many kicks, cuffs, and blows with sticks; that such was the life they led.

2. On the Loose in Texas

> Living as itinerant traders, Cabeza de Vaca and his companions wandered from one native camp to another, selling goods and staying one step ahead of starvation.

I have already stated that throughout all this country we went naked, and as we were unaccustomed to being so, twice a year we cast [shed] our skins like serpents. The sun and air produced great sores on our breasts and shoulders, giving us sharp pain; and the large loads we had, being very heavy, caused the cords to cut into our arms. The country is so broken and thickset, that often after getting our wood in the forests, the blood flowed from us in many places, caused by the obstruction of thorns and shrubs that tore our flesh wherever we went. At times, when my turn came to get wood, after it had cost me much blood, I could not bring it out either on my back or by dragging.

I bartered with these Indians in combs that I made for them and in bows, arrows, and nets. We made mats, which are their houses, that they have great necessity for; and although they know how to make them, they wish to give their full time to getting food, since when otherwise employed they are pinched with hunger. Sometimes the Indians would set me to scraping and softening skins; and the days of my greatest prosperity there, were those in which they gave me skins to dress. I would scrape them a very great deal and eat the scraps, which would sustain me two or three days. When it happened among these people, as it had likewise among others whom we left behind, that a piece of meat was given us, we ate it raw; for if we had put it to roast, the first native that should come along would have taken it off and devoured it; and it appeared to us not well to expose it to this risk; besides we were in such condition that it would have given us pain to eat it roasted, and we could not have digested it so well as raw. Such was the life we spent there; and the meagre subsistence we earned by the matters of traffic which were the work of our hands.

3. Cabeza de Vaca Hears News of Northern Kingdoms

No single piece of geographic information gathered by Cabeza de Vaca more fascinated Spanish officials in Mexico City than news that there might be rich empires to the north.

Thus we took our way, and traversed all the country until coming out at the South Sea. Nor was the dread we had of the sharp hunger through which we should have to pass (as in verity we did, throughout the seventeen days' journey of which the natives spoke) sufficient to hinder us. During all that time, in ascending by the river [Rio Grande], they gave us many coverings of cowhide [buffalo hide]; but we did not eat of the fruit. Our sustenance each day was about a handful of deer-suet, which we had a long time been used to saving for such trials. Thus we passed the entire journey of seventeen days, and at the close we crossed the river and traveled another seventeen days.

As the sun went down, upon some plains that lie between chains of very great mountains, we found a people who for the third part of the year eat nothing but the powder of straw, and, that being the season when we passed, we also had to eat of it, until reaching permanent habitations, where there was abundance of maize brought together. They gave us a large quantity in grain and flour, pumpkins, beans, and shawls of cotton. With all these we loaded our guides, who went back the happiest creatures on earth.

Those who there received us, after they had touched us went running to their houses and directly returned, and did not stop running, going and coming, to bring us in this manner many things for support on the way. They fetched a man to me and stated that a long time since he had been wounded by an arrow in the right shoulder, and that the point of the shaft was lodged above his heart, which, he said, gave him much pain, and in consequence, he was always sick. Probing the wound I felt the arrow head, and found it had passed through the cartilage. With a knife I carried, I opened the breast to the place, and saw the point was on a slant and difficult to take out. I continued to cut, and, putting in the point of the knife, at last with great difficulty I drew the head out. It was very large. With the bone of a deer, and by virtue of my calling, I made two stitches that threw blood over me, and with hair from a skin I stopped the flow. They asked me for the arrow head after I had taken it out, which I gave, when the whole town came to look at it. They sent it into the distant country that the people there might view it. In consequence of this operation they had many of their customary dances and festivities. The next day I cut the two stitches and the Indian was well. The wound I made appeared only like a seam in the palm of the hand. He said he felt no pain or sensitiveness in it whatsoever. This cure gave us control throughout the country in all that the inhabitants had power, or deemed of any value, or cherished. We showed them the hawk-bell we brought, and they told us that in the place whence that had come, were buried many plates of the same material; it was a thing they greatly esteemed, and where it came from were fixed habitations. The country we considered to be on the South Sea [the Pacific Ocean], which we had ever understood to be richer than the one of the North.

5.   A Report on Traces of Wealth

When read along with Cabeza de Vaca's news about northern kingdoms, these words about gold and silver were enough to launch the first moves in the Coronado expedition.

From this spot, called the river Petutan, to the river to which Diego de Guzman came, where we heard of Christians, may be as many as eighty leagues; thence to the town where the rains overtook us, twelve leagues, and that is twelve leagues to the South Sea. Throughout this region, wheresoever the mountains extend, we saw clear traces of gold and lead, iron, copper, and other metals. Where the settled habitations are, the climate is hot; even in January the weather is very warm. Thence toward the meridian, the country unoccupied to the North Sea is unhappy and sterile. There we underwent great and incredible hunger. Those who inhabit and wander over it are a race of evil inclination and most cruel customs. The people of the fixed residences and those beyond regard silver and gold with indifference, nor can they conceive of any use for them.

In the time, we traversed from sea to sea; and from information gathered with great diligence, there may be a distance from one to another at the widest part, of two thousand leagues; and we learned that on the coast of the South Sea there are pearls and great riches, and the best and all the most opulent countries are near there.

D. Toward Cíbola: The Coronado Expedition, 1539–1542

Despite Cabeza de Vaca's intriguing report about "populous towns and very large houses" in lands far to the north of Mexico, it took New Spain's Viceroy Antonio de Mendoza more than a year to shape an exploration plan for the area. Although Mendoza was eventually convinced of the existence of rich kingdoms in the north country, what drove him to implement the plan was the desire to move before his rivals—especially Hernán Cortés—could act.

The viceroy decided to launch a small-scale expedition, led by a missionary priest who would attract little or no attention. For that duty Mendoza selected the French Franciscan Fray Marcos de Niza (d. 1558). The Franciscan had recently come to Mexico from missionary assignments in Peru and Guatemala. But while Fray Marcos could command the expedition, success depended on a skilled guide. Of Cabeza de Vaca's original party, only Esteban could be persuaded to serve in that role. After many delays, the small party left the frontier town of Culicán, armed with instructions from the viceroy. These directions said nothing about seven glittering cities or a place called Cíbola.

Most historians now agree that Fray Marcos himself never crossed what is now the United States–Mexico border. Instead, it was Esteban and some Indian companions who ventured north into the Zuni country of present-day western New Mexico. It was a venture that cost Esteban his life at the hands of Zuni warriors.

---

1. The Narrative of Fray Marcos de Niza, 1539

By the summer of 1539, Fray Marcos was back in Mexico City, fashioning a story about cities and wealth beyond anything seen in Mexico. Borrowing from a medieval legend about seven refugee Christian bishops who fled across the Atlantic, the missionary put that story together with the Opata Indian word *cíbola* (meaning "Zuni") to create the Seven Cities of Cíbola. Fray Marcos's fantasy grew larger with each telling, until at least one Spanish official believed Cíbola had not only gold and jewels but elephants and camels as well. Fray Marcos's written report, as well as his own talks with religious leaders, set off a wave of speculation about Cíbola and the northern lands. Out of such speculation and conjecture came the Coronado expedition.

In Fray Marcos's *Narrative,* several terms appear often enough to require definition. The word *jornada* means "one day's journey," at best an imprecise measure of distance. The word *despoblado* is sometimes mistranslated as "desert." It was meant to describe a region with neither a settled population nor permanent agriculture.

This day there came to me three Indians, of those that are called *Pintados* [Indians with tattoos], their faces, chests and arms all decorated; these are in a district to the east and they border on a people who are next to the seven cities. They told me that having heard of me, they had come to see me, and, among other things, they gave me much information concerning the seven cities and the provinces that Esteban's Indian had told me of, in the same manner that Esteban's told me.

And so I traveled that day, the second day of Easter, and two other days, traveling the same *jornadas* as had Esteban, at the end of which I reached the people who had given him information of the seven cities and of the country farther away, which told me that from there it was thirty *jornadas* to the city of Cíbola, which is the first of the seven, and I had the account not only from one, but from many. And very particularly they told me of the grandeur of the houses and the style of them, just as the first one had. They told me that beyond these seven cities are other kingdoms. I wished to know for what they went so far from their homes, and they told me that they went for turquoises and for cowhides [buffalo skins] and other things; and of both they had a quantity in that town.

They told me that the form of clothing of the people of Cíbola is a cotton shirt reaching to the instep of the foot, with a button at the throat and a large tassel that hangs from it; the sleeves of the shirt being of the same width above as below. To me it appeared like the Bohemian [gipsy] dress. They say that they go girt with belts of turquoises, and that over these they wear the shirts. Some wear very good blankets and other cowhides.

Here I found a man, a native of Cíbola. He told me that Cíbola is a large city, that it has many people and streets and plazas, and that in some parts of the city there are some very large houses that have ten stories, and that in these the chiefs assemble on certain days of the year. He said the houses are of stone and lime, in the form that I was told of by those before, and that the porches and fronts of the principal houses are of turquoises.

With these [Indians] and my own Indians and interpreters I pursued my journey until within sight of Cíbola, which is situated on a plain at the skirt of a round hill. It has the appearance of a very beautiful town, the best I have seen in these parts. The houses are of the fashion that the Indians had described to me, all of stone, with their stories and terraces, as it appeared to me from a hill where I was able to view it. The city is bigger than the city of Mexico. At times I was tempted to go to it, because I knew that I ventured only life, which I had offered to God the day I commenced the journey. At the end I feared [to do so], considering my danger and that, if I died, I would not be able to make a report of this country, which to me appears the greatest and best of discoveries.

2. Pedro de Castañeda Recalls the March to Cíbola, 1540

Fray Marcos de Niza's report on Cíbola told Spanish adventurers in Mexico exactly what they wanted to hear. While ventures to Florida had been unrewarding, they believed that still more places like Mexico and Peru must exist. The Cíbola news touched off a round of wild conjecture about the promise of the Seven Cities. This promise offered something for everyone—whether missionary, empire builder, or soldier of fortune.

Eager to steal a march on any rival, Viceroy Mendoza commissioned the governor of New Galicia, Francisco Vásquez de Coronado (1510–1554), to organize and lead a full-scale Cíbola expedition.

Town leaders at Zuni

Funded by private investors, this venture eventually numbered two hundred mounted troops, sixty-odd foot soldiers, and perhaps as many as thirteen hundred Indian auxiliaries. Among the members of the party was Pedro de Castañeda (d. 1554), who became a literate and perceptive observer of the whole journey. Some years after the expedition, Castañeda wrote his "Narrative of an Expedition to Cíbola, undertaken in 1540, in which are Described all those Settlements, Ceremonies and Customs." While other participants recorded specific events during the expedition, Castañeda tried to present the entire journey. Equally important, Castañeda depicted native peoples and the physical landscape in sympathetic terms. The four selections reprinted here give some sense of the complex human drama in this first extended encounter between native peoples and the Spanish in the Southwest.

a. Marching to the Zuni Pueblos

When the general [Coronado] crossed the settled region and reached Chichiticale, where the *despoblado* began, and they could not see anything of any account, he could not help but feel some disappointment, because, although the reports of what lay ahead were alluring, no one had seen it except the Indians who had accompanied the negro [Esteban], and they had already been caught in several lies. The men were all disillusioned to see the famous Chichiticale turned out to be a roofless ruined house, although it appeared that formerly, at the time when it was inhabited, it must have been a fortress. One could easily tell that it had been built by strange people, orderly and warlike, from afar. This house was built of red mud.

From here they proceeded over the *despoblado* and after fifteen days, at a distance of eight leagues from Cíbola, arrived at a river which, because its water was muddy and red, they called Red River. Here it was that they saw the first Indians in that land—two of them—who fled and went to warn the others. On the night of the following day, two leagues from the pueblo, the Indians began shouting from a safe place, and although the men were fore-warned some were so confused that more than one put his saddle on backward. This happened only to beginners, as the veterans quickly mounted their horses and rode out over the field. The Indians, well acquainted with the land, fled, for none could be found.

On the following day, in good formation, the soldiers entered the inhabited land. When they got within sight of the first pueblo, which was Cíbola [probably Hawikuh], the curses that some hurled at Fray Marcos were such that God forbid they may befall him.

It is a small, rocky pueblo, all crumpled up, there being many farm settlements in New Spain that look better from afar. It is a pueblo of three or four stories and has some 200 warriors. The houses are small, have little space and no patios, for one patio serves a whole section. The people of the district had gathered there, for this is a province comprising seven pueblos, some of which are by far larger and stronger pueblos than Cíbola. These people waited in the open within sight of the pueblo, drawn up in squadrons. As they refused to accept peace in response to the requisitions [the *requerimiento*] which the Spaniards made through interpreters, but, on the contrary appeared warlike, the Spaniards gave the "Santiago, after them," and they were quickly routed. Then the soldiers proceeded to take the pueblo, which was no easy task; for, as the entrance was narrow and winding, the general was struck to the ground by a large stone as they were entering and he would have been killed had it not been for Don Garcia López de Cárdenas and Hernando de Alvarado, who threw themselves upon him and carried him away, receiving a good many blows from the stones. However, as nothing could resist the first onrush of the Spaniards, in less than one hour they entered the conquered the pueblo. Here they found provisions, of which there was the greatest need. After that the whole province submitted peacefully.

b. Hernando de Alvarado's Expedition
   to Pecos, 1540

There came to Cíbola some Indians from a pueblo of the province in the interior called Cicuyé [Pecos], distant seventy leagues to the east. Among them came a chieftain whom our men called "Bigotes," because he had long mustaches. He was a young man, tall, well built, and robust in appearance. He told the general [Coronado] they came to serve him in response to the appeal that they should offer themselves as friends and that, if the Spaniards planned to visit their land, they should consider them as their friends. The Indians gave them some presents of dressed skins, shields and headpieces. All this was accepted with much affection. The general gave them glassware, pearl beads, and jingle bells, which they prized very highly as something they had never seen before.

The natives gave information of the cattle [buffalo]. They were made out to be cattle by the picture which one of the Indians had painted on his body, since this could not be determined from the skins, because the hair was so wooly and tangled that one could not tell what the animals were.

The general ordered Hernando de Alvarado and twenty men to go with the Indians and gave him a commission for eighty days, after which he was to come back and report on what they had found. Captain Alvarado set out on the expedition and after five days' travel he came to a pueblo called Acuco [Acoma], built on a rock. It contained some two hundred warriors—robbers who were feared throughout the land. The pueblo was extremely strong because it was built above the entrance to the rock, which was hewn sheer on all sides and so high that it would require a good musket to land a ball on top. There was only one way to go up, a stairway made by hand. This started at a place where the path sloped to the ground. This stairway was wide and had some two hundred steps leading up to the top. Then there was another narrow one, built up against the wall, with about one hundred steps. At the top of this it was necessary to climb up the rocky stairway about three times the height of a man by placing one's toes in the holes in the rock and likewise the hands. At the top there was a protecting wall of large and small stones so that, without exposing themselves, the inhabitants could hurl so many down that no army, however powerful, could reach the top. At the top there was space for planting and growing a large amount of maize. There were cisterns to store snow and water.

These people came down to the valley in a warlike mood, and no amount of entreaties was of any avail with them. They drew lines and tried to prevent our men from crossing them. But, as they saw that they were pressed, they soon gave up the field, I mean, they accepted peace before any harm was done them. They made their peace ceremonies by approaching the horses, taking their sweat, and anointing themselves with it, making crosses with the fingers of their hands. However, their most reliable peace pact consists in crossing their hands, and this peace they keep inviolable. They presented a large number of turkey cocks with very large wattles, much bread, dressed deerskins, piñon nuts, flour, and maize.

Three days' travel farther on Alvarado and his men arrived at a province called Tiguex. The Indians all came out peacefully, seeing that men who were feared in all those provinces were coming with Bigotes. Alvarado sent word to the general from there, asking him to come to spend the winter in that land. The general was highly pleased to learn that the country was improving.

Five days farther on Alvarado reached Cicuyé, a very strong pueblo four stories high. The people came out to meet him and their captain [Bigotes] with demonstrations of joy and took him into the pueblo with drums and flageolets, similar to fifes, of which they had many. They presented the Spaniards with quantities of clothing and turquoises, which are found in abundance in that region.

Here the soldiers rested for a few days. They took as interpreter an Indian slave, a native of the farthest interior of the land extending from there to Florida, which is the region discovered by Don Hernando de Soto. This Indian, whom they named the Turk because he looked like one, told of large towns, which he should not have done. Hernando de Alvarado took him along as a guide, to the cattle. The Turk told so many and such great tales about the riches of gold and silver found in his land that the Spaniards did not care to look for the cattle, and as soon as they saw a few they turned back to report the rich news to the general.

c. Coronado's Interview with the Turk, 1540

He [Coronado] rejoiced greatly at the good news, for the Turk claimed that in his land there was a river, flowing through plains, which was two leagues wide, with fish as large as horses and a great number of very large canoes with sails, carrying more than twenty oarsmen on each side. The nobles, he said, traveled in the stern, seated under canopies, and at the

These people eat raw meat and drink blood, but do not eat human flesh. They are gentle people, not cruel, and are faithful in their friendship. They are very skillful in the use of signs. They dry their meat in the sun, slicing it in thin sheets. When it is dry they grind it, like flour, for storage and for making mash to eat. When they put a handful in an *olla* [a jar] it soon fills it, as the mash swells a great deal. They cook it with fat, which they always try to have with them. When these Indians kill a cow they clean a large intestine and fill it with blood and put it around their necks to drink when they are thirsty. After they cut open the belly of the cow they squeeze out the chewed grass and drink the juice, which remains on top, saying that it contains the substance of the stomach. They cut open the cow at the back and pull off the skin at the joints, using a flint the size of a finger, tied to a small stick, doing this as handily as if they used a fine large tool. They sharpen the flints on their own teeth. It is remarkable to see how quickly they do it.

In these plains there are numerous wolves, with white hair, which follow the cattle. The deer are white spotted and have long hair. When they are killed, their skin can be pulled off easily by hand when warm; they looked like skinned pigs. Hares, which are very plentiful, run about so stupidly that the mounted men kill them with their lances. This is because the hares are used to running among the cattle. They run away from men on foot.

During this time many of the men who went hunting got lost and were unable to return to the camp for two or three days. They wandered from place to place without knowing how to find their way back, even though they could hardly miss the lower or upper ends of the *barranca* [deep gully] in which the camp was located. Every night upon making the check to find if any one was missing, the soldiers fired their artillery, blew their horns, beat their drums, and lit great bonfires. Some of the hunters were so far away and had strayed so much that all these things profited them little, although they helped others. The best method for them to find their way was to go back to the place where they had slaughtered the cattle and to march in one direction and then in another until they came to the *barranca* or until they met some one who could direct them. It must be remarked that since the land is so level, when they had wandered aimlessly until noon, following the game, they had to remain by their kill, without straying, until the sun began to go down in order to get back to their starting point. This could be done only by experienced men; those who were not so had to put themselves under the guidance of others.

Who could believe that although one thousand horses, five hundred of our cattle, more than five thousand rams and sheep, and more than fifteen hundred persons, including allies and servants, marched over those plains, they left no more traces when they got through than if no one had passed over, so that it became necessary to stack up piles of bones and dung of the cattle at various distances in order that the rear guard could follow the army and not get lost. Although the grass was short, when it was trampled it stood up again as clean and straight as before.

I want to tell, also, about the appearance of the bulls [male buffalo], which is likewise remarkable. At first there was not a horse that did not turn away on seeing them, for their faces are short and narrow between the eyes, the forehead two spans wide. Their eyes bulge on the sides, so that, when they run, they can see those who follow them. They are bearded like very large he-goats. When they run they carry their heads low, their beards touching the ground. From the middle of the body back they are covered with very wooly hair like that of fine sheep. From the belly to the front they have very heavy hair like the mane of a wild lion. They have a hump larger than that of a camel. Their horns, which show a little through the hair, are short and heavy. During May they shed the hair on the rear half of their body and look exactly like lions. To remove this hair they lean against some small trees until they shed their wool as a snake sheds its skin. They have short tails with a small bunch of hair at the end. When they run they carry their tails erect like a scorpion. One peculiar thing about them is that when they are calves they are reddish like ours, and with time, as they become older, they change in color and appearance. Furthermore, all the bulls slaughtered were found to have their left ears slit, while these are whole when they are calves. The reason for this we were unable to discover. Excellent garments could be made from their fine wool, although not colored ones, as the wool itself is dark red.

Another remarkable observation was that the bulls roam without the cows in such large herds that there was no one who could count them. They move so far away from the cows that the distance from the place where we began to see them to where we saw the cows was over forty leagues. The land where they roamed was so level and bare that, whenever one looked at them, one could see the sky between their legs. Consequently at a distance they looked like cleared pine trunks with the crowns joining at the top. When a bull stood alone it resembled four such pines. And however close one was to them, one could not see the ground on the other side when looking across their backs. This was because the earth was so round, for, wherever a man stood, it seemed as if he were on the top and saw the sky around him within a crossbow shot. No matter how small an object was placed in front of him, it deprived him of the view of the land. To engulf oneself in the plains would mean to get lost on account of their great vastness and the scarcity of food in the land, although it is true that after reaching the cattle no such privation would follow.

SUGGESTIONS FOR FURTHER READING

Honour, Hugh. *The New Golden Land: European Images of America from the Discoveries to the Present Time.* New York: Pantheon Books, 1975.

Melanich, Jerald T., and Susan Milbrath, eds. *First Encounters: Spanish Explorations in the Caribbean and the United States, 1492–1570.* Gainesville, Florida: University of Florida Press, 1989.

Quinn, David B. *North America from Earliest Discovery to First Settlements: The Norse Voyages to 1612.* New York: Harper and Row, 1977.

Sauer, Carl O. *Sixteenth Century North America: The Land and the People as Seen by the Europeans.* Berkeley: University of California Press, 1971.

Trigger, Bruce. *Natives and Newcomers: Canada's "Heroic Age" Reconsidered.* Kingston, Ontario, Canada: McGill-Queen's University Press, 1985.

Weber, David J. *The Spanish Frontier in North America.* New Haven: Yale University Press, 1992.

CHAPTER 3

Edging into
America,
1590s–1680s

By the end of the sixteenth century, nearly all the major European players in the drama of American exploration had taken places on the continental stage. The Spanish stood nearly at center stage, while the French and English moved on the edges of the arena. But European players neither were the only actors nor dominated the action. Most, if not all, the business on stage involved actions and transactions between and among native peoples and Europeans. If the speaking parts for such players as Samuel de Champlain and Arthur Barlowe now seem larger and more important, they were not so at the time. Champlain listened while Huron chiefs such as Ochasteguin and Atironta talked. Barlowe paid close attention to words spoken by the Roanoke Indian Granganimeo. And the English scientist-explorer Thomas Hariot learned to speak his own lines in Algonkian, tutored by the Indians Manteo and Wanchese.

The years from the 1580s to the 1680s saw a quickening in the pace of American exploration. There were more journeys, more encounters, and more opportunities for mutual discovery. European audiences eager to read about the "New Lands" could choose from a wide variety of books and pamphlets. Maps and prints now gave visual definition to revelation. The journeys taken in this period were driven by ever more intricate sets of motives. By the middle of the seventeenth century, voyages of discovery were no longer inspired by a single goal or vision. Missionary travelers spread the influence of European empires. Fur traders were also soldiers and diplomats. And even the most single-minded of travelers paused to observe and record something of natural history.

Profit was one of the constants, a master motive that moved generations of Europeans to plan and undertake American ventures. While the expectation of wealth remained unchanged, the definition of wealth and the tactics used to get it were changing. For the generation of Coronado, de Soto, and Cartier, wealth was gold, the plunder of conquest. Gold was like ripe fruit ready to be picked with little or no labor. Journeys opened passages to stores of precious metals. Gold was already wealth. It did not, so the explorers thought, require European labor to transform it into something of value. This precapitalist way of thinking never completely vanished from exploration planning, but newer definitions of work and wealth increasingly supplanted visions of Cíbola and El Dorado. These newer formulations centered on trade and commercial agriculture. From modest beginnings along the North Atlantic Coast and the St. Lawrence River, the fur trade quickly became a global enterprise. The fur business demanded new trapping territories and new native partners. These requirements could be satisfied only by geographic expansion. While colonization and agricultural expansion were not essential goals for the fur trade, they were often silent partners. Fur-trade reports generated colonization interest. More important, fur-trade posts often became centers for future European settlement.

If capitalist thinking and planning were increasingly evident in exploration journeys and reports, the rhetoric of missionary zeal remained equally important. Catholic Christianity, locked in a struggle with the forces of Protestantism, looked to the Americas for renewal and fresh converts. Missionary orders such as the Recollets, the Sulplicians, and the Jesuits traveled extensively in New France, while Franciscans and Jesuits made forays into the Southwest. Published accounts such as the *Jesuit Relations* widely reported these spiritual journeys. The evangelical passion to find and save lost souls burned as bright as ever.

Fur and faith were powerful and sometimes interconnected motives in the exploration of North America. Fur traders and missionaries, moreover, were often agents of empire as well as seekers after pelts and souls. Although textbooks sometimes describe the eighteenth century as the age of empire, in North America that age began at the end of the sixteenth century. After the 1580s, rival European powers directed more attention to North America. Explorers advanced the frontiers of empire. Their maps and reports gave direction and legitimacy to the carving up and parceling out of North America. Each journey described in this chapter had political and diplomatic motives and consequences. And each journey, no matter what its declared goal, also challenged the sovereignty of Native American nations.

Curiosity, wonder, imagination, and illusion did not disappear as exploration became larger in scale and grander in design. Geographic illusions, especially the persistent belief in the Northwest Passage, continued to fascinate European travelers. These same travelers still found it possible to believe in the existence of vast inland seas, lost tribes of Jewish Indians, and herds of exotic animals loose on the Great Plains. Exploration was never the simple process of replacing myth and misconception with truth and accuracy. Explorers left home with illusions and often returned with just as many. No matter how practical a particular exploration plan seemed, it was ultimately founded on the same kind of hope that gave birth to Cíbola, Quivira, and the Passage to India.

A. Spain and the Second Revelation of New Mexico

The Spanish survivors of the Coronado expedition may have enjoyed rich memories, but they had empty pockets. Cíbola and Quivira promised only disillusionment and death. In the aftermath of the Coronado debacle, the Spanish government drafted legislation aimed at controlling the excesses of such conquest explorations. The Orders for New Discoveries, given final form in 1573, promoted missionary journeys. Such ventures were allowed only modest military escorts.

No missionary order in New Spain more quickly seized this opportunity than the Franciscans. Many Franciscans had two goals in mind as they looked to the northern countries that had once captivated their brother Fray Marcos. Saving native souls for the Christian faith was their first objective, and close behind it was the conviction that the Kingdom of God could be established among native people.

Missionary zeal and millennial faith prompted Fray Agustín Rodríguez to join with Captain Francisco Sanchez Chamuscado in planning the first formal Spanish expedition into New Mexico since Coronado. The Chamuscado-Rodríguez expedition (1581–1582) spent much of the late summer and early fall of 1581 visiting pueblos in New Mexico. Upon returning in mid-April 1582, Chamuscado was filled with stories about native people who wore cotton clothing and lived in great stone houses.

This news, with its echoes of Fray Marcos and Coronado, spread swiftly throughout northern Mexico. One who heard the reports was

Antonio de Espejo, a successful cattle rancher. Knowing that he could not launch his own independent expedition without violating Spanish laws, Espejo offered his services to the Franciscans as leader of a second missionary party. The Franciscans, worried about missionaries left behind during the first journey, agreed. In command of a small contingent, Espejo left for New Mexico in early November 1582. By the time he returned in September 1583, he and his men had seen much of New Mexico. More important than what Espejo saw, however, was what he said. The Espejo expedition report, prepared by royal official Diego Perez de Luxan, depicted a densely populated country dangling promises of all sorts—spiritual promises for the Franciscans and something more material for promoters, adventurers, and prospective settlers.

The Chamuscado-Rodríguez and Espejo expeditions renewed and refurbished the Spanish image of New Mexico. Fresh reports revived hopes and expectations that had been crushed after Coronado. One of those who heard and believed such news was Gaspar Castaño de Sosa, an enterprising settler, rancher, and slave trader in northern Mexico. Castaño was also the lieutenant governor of the province of New León, with his headquarters at Almandén (now Monclova, in the Mexican state of Coahuila). Lured by the prospect of wealth in land and slaves, Castaño began to plan a journey to New Mexico. Such a colonizing venture clearly broke Spanish law, something that Castaño was evidently ready to hazard. On July 27, 1590, the Castaño expedition—wagons, animals, and some 170 men, women, and children—left Almandén, forded the Rio Grande into present-day Texas, and followed the Pecos River into New Mexico. In early January 1591, the wagon train crossed Glorieta Pass and headed toward present-day Santa Fe.

Castaño's adventures did not escape official attention, and crown officers soon sent Captain Juan Morlete in pursuit. Morlete caught up with Castaño at the Queres pueblo of Santo Domingo, about forty miles north of present-day Albuquerque, where Castaño had established a Spanish colony. Morlete arrested Castaño and put him in chains. The adventurer was later tried, convicted, and sentenced to exile in the Philippines.

Castaño's "Memoria," written by either Castaño or his secretary, Andrés Pérez de Verlanga, is both a record of daily travel and an account of native New Mexico just before massive Spanish invasion.

1. Castaño Reveals a Pueblo World of Plenty

Although pueblo life was well known to many Spanish travelers, Castaño wrote an especially vivid description of the Pecos pueblo. His account takes note of everything from domestic architecture to food and clothing.

The houses in this pueblo [Pecos] are built like military barracks, back to back, with doors opening out all around; and they are four or five stories high. There are no doors opening into the streets on the ground floors; the houses are entered from above by means of portable hand ladders and trap doors. Each floor of every house has three or four rooms, so that each house, as a whole, counting from top to bottom, has fifteen or sixteen rooms, very neat and well whitewashed. Every house is equipped with facilities for grinding corn, including three or four grinding stones mounted in small troughs and provided with pestles; all is whitewashed. The method of grinding is novel, the flour being passed from one grinder to another, as these Indians do not make tortilla dough, although from this flour they do make many kinds of bread, corn-flour gruel, and tamales.

This pueblo had five plazas. It was also provided with such an abundant supply of corn that everyone marveled. There were those who maintained that the total must amount to more than thirty thousand *fanegas* [about 78,000 bushels], since each house had two or three rooms full of it, all of excellent quality. Moreover, there was a good supply of beans. Both corn and beans were of many colors; it seemed that some of the corn was two or three years old. In the houses, the natives also store quantities of herbs, chili, and *calabashes* [gourds], and many implements for working their cornfields.

As for their clothing, we noticed that most of the men, if not all, wore cotton blankets and over these a buffalo skin, since this was the cold season; some covered their privy parts with small pieces of cloth, very elegant and elaborately decorated. The women wore a blanket tied over the shoulder and left open at the side, with a sash the width of a span [about nine inches] wrapped around the waist. Over this blanket they wear another, nicely decorated and very fancy, or a kind of robe made of turkey feathers, as well as many other novel adornments, all of which is quite remarkable for barbarians.

These Indians have a great deal of pottery, red, figured, and black, such as plates, bowls, salt containers, basins, and very beautiful cups. Some of the pottery is glazed. They also have plentiful supplies of firewood, and of lumber for building houses. Indeed, we were given to understand that whenever anyone wanted to build a house, he had the lumber for that purpose ready at hand; and furthermore, clay for adobes was available in quantities. There are two water holes, at the ends of the pueblo, which the natives use for bathing, since they obtain their drinking water from other springs about an harquebus shot away. The Rio Salado [Pecos River] above-mentioned, which flows along the route we followed, is a quarter of a league distant, although the salt water sinks into the ground many leagues back.

All six of these settlements [the Tewa pueblos] had canals for irrigation, which would be incredible to anyone who had not seen them with his own eyes. The inhabitants harvest large quantities of corn, beans, and other vegetables. They dress in the same fashion as the people described above. Some of the settlements are small, though densely populated. The houses are two or three stories high, and all are entered by means of trap doors and portable ladders.

B. The Oñate Expedition to New Mexico, 1595–1609

The reports of the Chamuscado, Espejo, and Castaño de Sosa expeditions revived interest in New Mexico. The old conquistador dream of God, gold, and glory came back to life as Spaniards embraced New Mexico. Here was a country where one journey could serve God and make a profit. In 1583 the crown therefore ordered the viceroy of Mexico to prepare a New Mexico expedition.

Years of bureaucratic infighting and confusion delayed selection of a leader and preparation for the journey. Not until 1595 did Juan de Oñate (1552–1626) sign a contract "to pacify and colonize" the Kingdom of New Mexico. Already a successful politician and entrepreneur, Oñate accepted an agreement that put the full financial burden of the New Mexico venture on him and his fellow investors. In return, he hoped to gain a kingdom for himself and his family.

So many delays plagued Oñate's expedition that not until March 1598 did Oñate's colonists—some 500 strong—make their way toward New Mexico. After a grand ceremony of imperial possession at what is now El Paso, Texas (late April 1598), Oñate entered present-day New Mexico and established his headquarters at a Tewa pueblo along the Rio Grande, renaming the town San Juan. When

San Juan proved inadequate, Oñate moved across the river to San Gabriel. This post served as his central base until the move to Santa Fe in 1608.

The two documents reprinted here reveal Oñate's desire to gain a clearer understanding of the peoples and terrain of the region and the immediate need to supplement dwindling provisions. Problems of food supply prompted the Vincente de Zaldívar (d. 1650?) expedition to the southern Great Plains in 1598. News of great buffalo herds on the southern plains came to Oñate when an Indian named Jusepe arrived at the Spanish camp. Jusepe had been a guide for the ill-fated Humaña expedition. His understanding of Great Plains geography and buffalo hunting set the Zaldívar journey in motion. This part of Zaldívar's report provides a colorful, detailed look at plains Apaches on the southern plains before the advent of the horse. The second selection recounts Oñate's own journey to the plains in 1601. As with the Zaldívar venture, this expedition was prompted by food short-ages. While supplies of meat and corn were on Oñate's mind, he also was fascinated by Quivira. Like Coronado, Oñate headed on to the Kansas plains in the summer and fall of 1601 in search of golden cities and grand kingdoms.

---

1. Vincente de Zaldívar Reports on His Expedition to the Great Plains, 1598

Few Great Plains animals captured more attention from European travelers than the buffalo. In this account, Spanish adventurers try to herd and pen buffalo, with sometimes comic results.

Next day as he [Zaldívar] traveled, many Indians and Indian women came out to meet him, bringing *piñole* [corn meal]. Most of the men go naked, but some are clothed with skins of buffalo and some with blankets. The women wear a sort of trousers made of buckskin, and shoes or leggins, after their own fashion. He gave them presents and told them by means of the interpreter [Jusepe] that Governor Don Juan de Oñate had sent him that they might know that he could protect those who were loyal to his Majesty and punish those who were not. All were friendly and very well pleased.

They asked him for aid against the Jumanos, as they call a tribe of Indians who are painted after the manner of the Chichimecos. The *sargento mayor* [Zaldívar] promised them that he would endeavor to insure peace to them, since he had come to this land for that purpose.

Bidding them goodbye, he left that place and travelled ten more leagues in three days, at the end of which time he saw the first buffalo bull, which, being rather old, wandered alone and ran but little. This produced much merriment and was regarded as a great joke, for the least one of the company would not be satisfied with less than ten thousand head of cattle [buffalo] in his own corral.

Shortly afterward more than three hundred buffalo were seen in some herds. During the next day they traveled about seven leagues, when they encountered as many as a thousand head of cattle. In that place there were found very good facilities for the construction of a corral with wings. [Zaldívar's plan was to corral and slaughter the buffalo like beef cattle.] Orders having been given for its construction, the cattle went inland more than eight leagues. Upon seeing this the *sargento mayor* went on ahead with ten of his soldiers to a river six leagues from there and where the guide had told him that there were great numbers of cattle. But when he reached the river the cattle had left, because just then many Indian herdsmen [hunters] crossed it, coming from trading with the Picuris [a Northern Tiwa pueblo north of present-day Santa Fe] and Taos, populous pueblos of this New Mexico, where they sell meat, hides, tallow, suet, and salt in exchange for cotton blankets, pottery, maize, and some small green stones which they use.

He camped that night at that river, and on the following day, on his way back to the camp, he found a *ranchería* [settlement] in which there were fifty tents made of tanned hides, very bright red and white in color and bell-shaped, with flaps and openings, and built as skilfully as those of Italy and so large that in the most ordinary ones four different mattresses and beds were easily accommodated. The tanning is so fine that although it should rain bucketfuls it will not pass through nor stiffen the hide, but rather upon drying it remains as soft and pliable as before. This being so wonderful, he wanted to experiment, and, cutting off a piece of hide from one of the tents, it was soaked and placed to dry in the sun, but it remained as before, and as pliable as if it had never been wet. The *sargento mayor* bartered for a tent and brought it to this camp, and although it was so very large, it did not weigh over two *arrobas* [about 50 pounds].

To carry this load, the poles that they use to set it up, and a knapsack of meat and their *piñole*, or maize, the Indians use a medium-sized shaggy dog, which is their substitute for mules. They drive great trains of them. Each, girt round its breast and haunches, and carrying a load of flour of at least one hundred pounds, travels as fast as his master. It is a sight worth seeing and very laughable to see them traveling, the ends of the poles dragging on the ground, nearly all of them snarling in their encounters, traveling one after another on their journey. In order to load them the Indian women seize their heads between their knees and thus load them, or adjust the load, which is seldom required, because they travel along at a steady gait as if they had been trained by means of reins.

[After an ill-fated attempt to herd and corral a large number of buffalo, Zaldívar wrote this vivid description of the Great Plains buffalo.]

Its shape and form are so marvellous and laughable, or frightful, that the more one sees it the more one desires to see it, and no one could be so melancholy that if he were to see it a hundred times a day he could keep from laughing heartily as many times, or could fail to marvel at the sight of so ferocious an animal. Its horns are black, and a third of a *vara* long, as already stated, and resemble those of the *bufalo* [meaning Andalusian long-horn cattle]; its eyes are small, its face, snout, feet, and hoofs of the same form as of our cows, with the exception that both the male and female are very much bearded, similar to he-goats. They are so thickly covered with wool that it covers their eyes and face, and the forelock nearly envelops their horns. This wool, which is long and very soft, extends almost to the middle of the body, but from there on the hair is shorter. Over the ribs they have so much wool and the chine [backbone] is so high that they appear hump-backed, although in reality and in truth they are not greatly so, for the hump easily disappears when the hides are stretched.

In general, they are larger than our cattle. Their tail is like that of a hog, being very short, and having few bristles at the tip, and they twist it upward when they run. At the knee they have natural garters of very long hair. In their haunches, which resemble those of mules, they are hipped and crippled, and therefore run, as already stated, in leaps, especially down hill. They are all of the same dark color, somewhat tawny, in parts their hair being almost black. Such is their appearance, which at sight is far more ferocious than the pen can depict. As many of these cattle as are desired can be killed and brought to these settlements, which are distant from them thirty or forty leagues, but if they are to be brought alive it will be most difficult unless time and crossing [breeding] them with those from Spain make them tamer.

2. Juan de Oñate Recounts His Journey to the Great Plains, 1601

The open and treeless grasslands of the Great Plains fascinated
Spanish explorers since Coronado's time. Oñate found the plains both
beautiful and frightening.

Having traveled to reach this place one hundred and eleven leagues, it became necessary to leave the river, as there appeared ahead some sand dunes; and turning from the east to the north, we traveled up a small stream until we discovered the great plains covered with innumerable cattle. We found constantly better roads and better land, such that the carts could travel without hindrance or difficulty, and although we encountered some large ravines and broken hills, nowhere were they any over which the carts had to pass, as the land was in general level and very easy to traverse. We continued in this direction for some days, along two small streams which flowed toward the east, like the one previously mentioned. We wandered from the direction we had been following, though it did not frighten us much, as the land was so level that daily the men became lost in it by separating themselves for but a short distance from us, as a result of which it was necessary to reconnoitre the country from some of the stopping places.

In order to further insure our safety, the governor [Oñate] decided to send ahead the *maese de campo* [Vincente de Zaldívar] with some companions, and, with the lucky star which ever guides him, in a short time he returned, having found many signs of people, and a country full of pasture lands, which was the matter of deepest concern, since they had been lacking for several days, for the fields there were covered with flowers of a thousand different kinds, so thick that they choked the pasture. The cattle of this territory must eat these flowers far better than ours do, because wherever they were there are multitudes of cattle.

At three in the afternoon we arrived within an arquebus shot of this *ranchería,* and at some ponds that were there. From there the governor and the religious [Franciscans Francisco de Velasco and Pedro de Vergara] went with more than thirty armed horsemen to reconnoitre the people and the *ranchería,* and they, all drawn up in regular order in front of their *ranchos,* began to raise the palms of their hands towards the sun, which is a sign of peace among them. Assuring them that peace was what we wanted, all the people, women, youths, and small children, came to where we were; and they consented to our visiting their houses, which all consisted of branches an *estado* and a half long, placed in a circle, some of them being so wide that they were ninety feet in diameter. Most of them were covered with tanned hides, which made them resemble tents. They were not a people who sowed or reaped, but they lived solely on the cattle. They were ruled and governed by chiefs, and like communities which are freed from subjection to any lord, they obeyed their chiefs but little. They had large quantities of hides which, wrapped about their bodies, served them as clothing, but the weather being hot, all the men went about nearly naked, the women being clothed from the waist down. Men and women alike used bows and arrows, with which they were very dexterous.

C. On the Eastern Edge: The English at Roanoke and Jamestown

While Spanish soldiers, settlers, and missionaries were attempting to reestablish their presence in New Mexico, English adventurers made their first hesitant steps along the South Atlantic Coast. England lagged well behind Spain in what one historian has called "the invasion of America." England's efforts to keep up with its rivals were hampered by dynastic wars, internal political instablity, religious controversy, and a textile-export economy that looked east across the English Channel to markets in western Europe.

Walter Ralegh (1554–1618) emerged as a leading figure in a small group of expansionists eager for Elizabethan England to share in America's wealth. Between 1584 and 1590, Ralegh was involved in organizing a series of voyages to the Carolina coast. Because these ventures eventually centered on establishing an English colony on Roanoke Island off the coast of present-day North Carolina, they are known collectively as the Roanoke voyages. While these journeys failed to create a permanent English presence on the Atlantic Coast, they did produce a valuable store of maps, drawings, and reports.

1. Arthur Barlowe Meets the Roanoke Indians, 1584

This selection comes from the report of the 1584 reconnaissance voyage led by Philip Amadas and Arthur Barlowe. Their expedition left England in April 1584 with two ships. Amadas was an experienced sailor; Barlowe had served as a soldier with Ralegh in Ireland. The expedition report, written by Barlowe, details relations between the English explorers and Roanoke Indians on Hatarask Island. Because the report was intended for publication to encourage interest in Ralegh's 1585 expedition, some scholars believe that details about tensions between the English and their native hosts were edited out.

This island had many goodly woods, full of deer, conies [rabbits], hares, and fowl, even in the midst of summer, in incredible abundance. The woods are not such as you find in Bohemia, Muscovy, or Hercynia, barren and fruitless, but the highest and reddest cedars of the world. We remained by the side of this island two whole days, before we saw any people of the country. The third day we spied one small boat rowing towards us, having in it three persons. This boat came to the island's side, and there two of the people remaining, the third came along the shore side towards us, [and] he walked up and down the point of land next unto us. Then [we] rowed to the land, whose coming this fellow attended, never making any show of fear or doubt. And after he had spoken of many things not understood by us, we brought him with his own good liking, aboard the ship, and gave him a shirt, a hat, and some other things, and made him taste of our wine, and our

The Barlow and Amadas Expedition to Roanoke, 1584

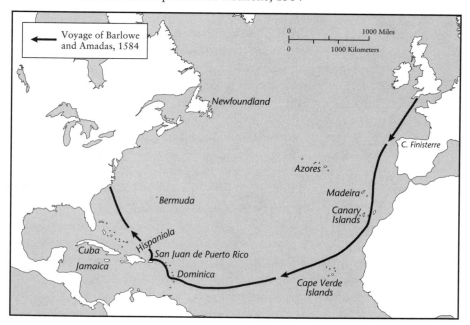

meat, which he liked very well. And after having viewed both barks [ships], he departed, and went to his own boat again, which he had left in a little cove or creek adjoining. As soon as he was two bow shot into the water, he fell to fishing, and in less than half an hour, he had loaded his boat as deep, as it could swim, with which he came again to the point of land, and there he divided his fish into two parts, pointing one part to the ship, and the other to the pinnace [the smaller of the English vessels]. Which after he had (as much as he might) returned the former benefits received, he departed out of our sight.

The next day there came unto us many boats, and in one of them the king's brother, accompanied with forty or fifty men, very handsome, and goodly people, and in their behavior as mannerly, and civil, as any of Europe. His name was Granganimeo, and the king is called Wingina, the country Wingandacoa (and now by her Majesty, Virginia). The manner of his coming was in this sort. He left his boats altogether, as the first man did a little from the ships by the shore, and came along to the place over against the ships, followed with forty men. When he came to the place, his servants spread a long mat upon the ground, on which he sat down, and at the other end of the mat, four others of his company did the like. The rest of his men stood round about him, somewhat afar off. When we came to the shore to him with our weapons, he never moved from his place, nor any of the other four, nor never mistrusted any harm to be offered from us, but sitting still, he beckoned us to come and sit by him, which we performed. And being sat, he made all signs of joy, and welcome, striking on his head, and his breast, and afterwards on ours, to show we were all one, smiling, and making show the best he could, of all love, and familiarity. After he had made a long speech unto us, we presented him with divers things, which he received very joyfully, and thankfully. None of his company dared to speak one word all the time. Only the four which were at the other end, spoke one in the others ear very softly.

After we had presented his brother with such things as we thought he liked, we likewise gave somewhat to the other [the *werowances*, or men of rank] that sat with him on the mat. Presently he arose, and took all from them, and put it into his own basket, making signs and tokens, that all things ought to be delivered unto him, and the rest were but his servants and followers. A day or two after this, we fell to trading with them, exchanging some things that we had for chammoys [dressed deerskins], buffe [perhaps buffalo skins], and deerskins. When we showed him all our packet of merchandize, of all things that he saw, a bright tin dish most pleased him, which he presently took up, and clapped it before his breast, and after made a hole in the brim thereof, and hung it about his neck, making signs, that it would defend him against his enemies' arrows. Those people maintain a deadly and terrible war with the people and king adjoining. We exchanged our tin dish for twenty skins, worth twenty crowns, or twenty nobles, and a copper kettle for fifty skins worth fifty crowns. They offered us very good exchange for our hatchets, and axes, and for knives, and would have given any thing for swords, but we would not part with any. After two or three days, the king's brother came aboard the ships, and drank wine, and ate of our meat, and of our bread, and liked exceedingly thereof. And after a few days passed, he brought his wife with him to the ships, his daughter, and two or three little children. His wife was very well favored, of mean [short] stature, and very bashful. She had on her back a long cloak of leather, with the fur side next to her body, and before her a piece of the same. About her forehead she had a broad band of white coral, and so had her husband many times. In her ears she had bracelets of pearls, hanging down to her middle.

The king's brother had a great liking of our armor, a sword, and divers other things which we had and offered to lay a great box of pearls in trade for them. But we refused it for this time, because we would not make them know that we esteemed thereof, until we had understood in what places of the country the pearl grew.

He was very just of his promise, for many times we delivered him merchandise upon his word, but ever he came within the day, and performed his promise. He sent us every day a brace or two of fat bucks, conies, hares, fish, the best of the world. He sent us divers kinds of fruits, melons, walnuts, cucumbers, gourds, pease, and divers roots, and fruits very excellent good, and of their country corn, which is very white, fair, and well tasted, and grows three times in five months. In May they sow, in July they reap, in June they sow, in August they reap, in July they sow, in September they reap. Only they cast the corn into the ground, breaking a little of the soft turf with a wooden mattock, or pickaxe. Ourselves proved the soil and put some of our pease into the ground, and in ten days they were fourteen inches high. They have also beans very fair, of divers colors, and wonderful plenty, some growing naturally, and some in their gardens. The soil is the most plentiful, sweet, fruitful, and wholesome of all the world.

2. Thomas Hariot Reports Indian Responses to the English Presence, 1585

Thomas Hariot brought to English exploration the keen mind of a mathematician and the sharp eye of a naturalist. Hariot had a knack for languages and the ability to grasp cultural values other than his own. A tutor in the Ralegh household, he specialized in "the mathematical sciences." Hariot may have been with the 1584 Amadas-Barlowe expedition and certainly played a key role in the 1585 voyage to Roanoke. Hariot's *Brief and True Relation of the New Found Land of Virginia* (1588) drew on both his personal observations and the time he spent in England with Manteo and Wanchese, two young Roanoke Indians taken back to England at the end of the Amadas-Barlowe journey. In this selection, Hariot analyzes the impact of European diseases on the Roanoke people, as well as native speculation about the nature and identity of the English visitors.

The *werowance* with whom we dwelt [was] called Wingina, and many of his people would be glad many times to be with us at our prayers, and many times call upon us both in his own town as also in others where he sometimes accompanied us, to pray and sing psalms, hoping thereby to be partaker of the same effects which we by that means also expected.

Twice this *werowance* was so grievously sick that he was like to die, and as he lay languishing, doubting of any help by his own priests, and thinking he was in such danger for offending us and thereby our God, sent for some of us to pray and be a means to our God that it would please him either that he might live, or after death dwell with him in bliss, so likewise were the requests of many others in the like case.

On a time also when their corn began to wither by reason of a drought which happened extraordinarily, fearing that it had come to pass by reason that in some thing they had displeased us, many would come to us and desire us to pray to our God of England, that he would preserve their corn, promising that when it was ripe we also should be partakers of the fruit.

There could at no time happen any strange sickness, losses, hurts, or any other cross [accident] unto them, but that they would impute to us the cause or means thereof for offending or not pleasing us.

One other rare and strange accident, leaving others, will I mention before I end, which moved the whole country that either knew or heard of us, to have us in wonderful admiration.

There was no town where we had any subtle device practiced against us, we leaving it unpunished or not revenged (because we sought by all means possible to win them by gentleness) but that within a few days after our departure from every such town, the people began to die very fast, and many in short space. In some towns about twenty, in some forty, in some sixty, and in one six score [120], which in truth was very many in respect to their numbers. This happened in no place that we could learn but where we had been where they used some practice against us, and after such time. The disease also was so strange, that they knew neither what it was, nor how to cure it; the like by report of the oldest men in the country never happened before, time out of mind.

Some therefore were of opinion that we were not born of women, and therefore not mortal, but that we were men of an old generation many years past then risen again to immortality.

Some would likewise seem to prophesy that there were more of our generation yet to come, to kill theirs and take their places, as some thought the purpose was by that which was already done.

Those that were immediately to come after us they imagined to be in the air, yet invisible and without bodies, and that they by our entreaty and for the love of us did make the people to die in that sort as they did by shooting invisible bullets into them.

3. Francis Magnel Offers a Sailor's Recollection of Jamestown, 1607–1610

The efforts of the Virginia Company of London to plant a trading post and colony along the Atlantic Coast at Jamestown beginning in 1607 produced several formal exploration accounts, including those written by John Smith and William Strachey. Less well known is the modest but important contribution taken from Irish sailor and adventurer Francis Magnel in 1610. Magnel was a mariner on the first Jamestown voyage.

After leaving Jamestown, by a series of misadventures, Magnel ended up in Madrid in the summer of 1610. There Spanish officials, increasingly worried about English activities along the Atlantic Coast, questioned Magnel. His account has the feel of backroom gossip. Hoping to please his Spanish questioners, Magnel sometimes exaggerated his own importance. He also managed to endow Jamestown with more soap and wine than the infant settlement ever had! Magnel had been in Jamestown as an employee, and what he heard about Indians and the fabled Northwest Passage mixed firsthand observation with popular folk belief. Magnel's recollections provide a rare look into the world of everyday imagination.

In this region there are many iron, copper, and other mines, from which they [the English] took samples to England, and the English do not want it known what kind of mines they are until after they are well reinforced in Virginia. And the relator [Magnel] took a sample from these mines to England which weighed eighty pounds, and found it to contain three *reales* [a coin valued at six pence] of gold by weight and five of silver, and four pounds of copper. There are many large pearls in that land, and a great quantity of coral, and in the mountains they find stones very much like diamonds, and for the purpose of finding more of these mines and purifying the ore, the King of England has sent many artisans who understand this business, as well as other workmen trained in all the mechanical arts, to live there. Many kinds of dyes are found there, some of which they sell in England at forty *reales* the pound. The English make a great deal of soap there, which they take to their country. In the rivers there are a great many salmon, sole, and other fish, and as great and good a quantity of cod as in Newfoundland. There is an infinite number of deer in the land, turkeys, swans, and all kinds of fowl. Many wild grapes are natural to the land, from which the English make a wine very similar to that of Alicante, in the opinion of the relator, who has tried one or two. Also there is a great quantity of beans, pease, corn, almonds, walnuts and chestnuts, and above all a lot of flax, which grows wild, without any cultivation. They have a great abundance of skins for very rich furs, especially sable martens, and the [Indian] King has houses full of them, and they are his wealth. The English take from there [Virginia] many drugs and other necessities for apothecary shops. The land is very pleasant and level, and very fertile, with many big rivers; the air is healthy, and the climate like here in Spain, although a little colder in winter.

The natives of Virginia assure the English that they will easily take them to the South Sea [the Pacific Ocean] by three routes. The first route by which they will take them is by land, where it is no more than ten days' journey from the [upper] end of that river [the James River] where the English have their fort to the South Sea, as the natives affirm. The second route is [this]: a journey of a day and a half from the inland end of that river there is another equally big river which flows into the South Sea. The third route is, twelve leagues from the entrance of that river where the English are, to the northwest, there are four other rivers, which one of those English Captains [John Smith] reached in a pinnace, who says that one of those rivers is of very great importance, and the natives affirm that fourteen leagues beyond the four rivers to the northwest there is another big river which reaches far inland until it joins another big river which comes from [flows into]

summer of 1615 that the French trader made a personal journey to Huron country.

Champlain visited Huronia at a time of growing prosperity for the village people. The Huron economy had expanded to encompass both commercial agriculture (corn for export to other native trading partners) and the fur business. For some fifteen years, from 1615 to 1630, Hurons enjoyed the benefits of contact with European industrial society without suffering serious disruptions. That stability was severely challenged and finally destroyed during the next two decades as disease, troublesome encounters with Jesuit missionaries, and devastating raids launched by Iroquois warriors shattered Huronia.

1. Samuel de Champlain Portrays Huron Life, 1615

The following selection, taken from Champlain's *Voyages and Discoveries in New France from the Year 1615 to the End of the Year 1618* (1619), describes some of the aspects of Huron life that the explorer saw during the summer of 1615. While Champlain could be an astute observer, there was much he either missed or misunderstood. For example, he thought that all the Hurons were Attignawantans, not fully grasping that this was but one of the four principal Huron tribes. Bound by European definitions of work and gender, Champlain also misinterpreted the nature and amount of work done by Huron men and women.

The country of the nation of the Attignawantans contains eighteen villages, six of which are enclosed and fortified by palisades of wood in triple rows, bound together, on the top of which are galleries, which they provide with stones and water; the former to hurl upon their enemies and the latter to extinguish the fire which their enemies may set to the palisades. The country is pleasant, most of it cleared up. It has the shape of Brittany, and is similarly situated, being almost surrounded by the *Mer Douce* [Lake Huron]. They [the Hurons] assume that these eighteen villages are inhabited by two thousand warriors, not including the common mass, which amounts to perhaps thirty thousand souls.

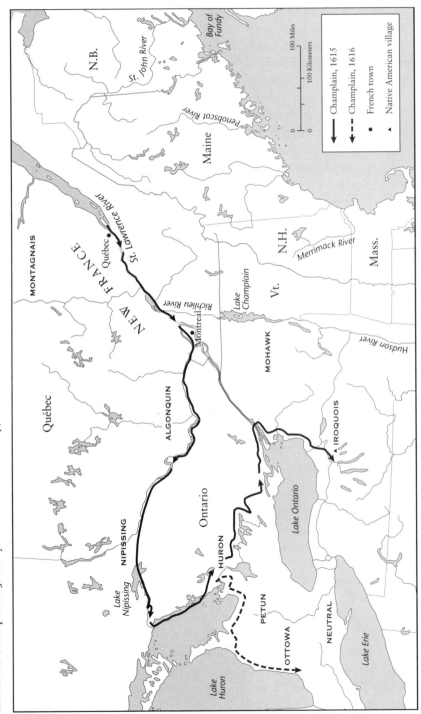

Samuel de Champlain's Journey to the Huron Country, 1615–1616

Their cabins are in the shape of tunnels or arbors, and are covered with the bark of trees. They are from twenty-five to thirty fathoms [about 90 to 100 feet] long, more or less, and six [about 25 to 30 feet] wide, having a passage-way through the middle from ten to twelve feet wide, which extends from one end to the other. On the two sides there is a kind of bench, four feet high, where they sleep in summer, in order to avoid the annoyance of the fleas, of which there were great numbers. In winter they sleep on the ground on mats near the fire, so as to be warmer than they would be on the platform. They lay up a stock of dry wood, with which they fill up their cabins, to burn in winter. At the extremity of the cabins there is a space, where they preserve their Indian corn, which they put into great casks made of the bark of trees and place in the middle of their encampments. They have pieces of wood suspended, on which they put their clothes, provisions, and other things, for fear of the mice, of which there are great numbers. In one of these cabins there may be twelve fires, and twenty-four families. It smokes excessively, from which it follows that many receive serious injury to the eyes, so that they lose their sight towards the close of life. There is no window nor any opening, except that in the upper part of their cabins for the smoke to escape.

In regard to their dress, they have various kinds and styles made of the skins of wild beasts, both those which they capture themselves, and others which they get in exchange for their Indian corn, meal, porcelain [shell beads], and fishing nets from the Algonkins, Nipissings, and other tribes, which are hunters having no fixed abodes. All their clothes are of one uniform shape, not varied by any new styles. They prepare and fit the skins very well, making their breeches of deer-skin rather large, and their stockings of another piece, which extend up to the middle and have many folds. Their shoes are made of the skins of deer, bears, and beaver, of which they use great numbers. There are those among those nations who are much more skilful than others in fitting the skins, and ingenious in inventing ornaments to put on their garments. It is our Montagnais and Algonkins, above all others, who take more pains in this matter. They put on their robes bands of porcupine quills, which they dye a very fine scarlet color. They value these bands very highly and detach them so that they may serve for other robes when they wish to make a change. They also make use of them to adorn the face, in order to give it a more graceful appearance whenever they wish particularly to decorate themselves.

Most of them paint the face black and red. These colors they mix with oil made from the seed of the sunflower, or with bear's fat or that of some other animals. They also dye their hair, which some wear long, others short, others on one side only. The women and girls always wear their hair in one uniform style. They are dressed like men, except that they always have their

Indian deer-hunting techniques as illustrated in Champlain's *Voyages.*

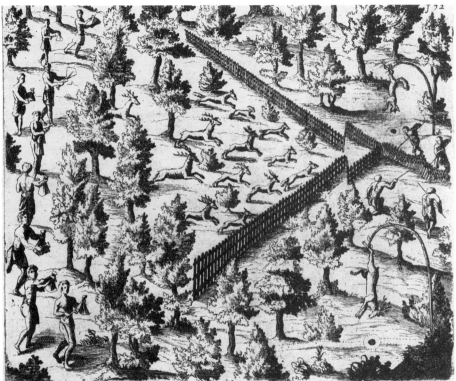

robes gathered about them, which extend down to the knee. They are not at all ashamed to expose the body from the middle up and from the knees down, unlike the men, the rest being always covered. They are loaded with quantities of porcelain, in the shape of necklaces and chains, which they arrange in front of their robes and attach to their waists. They also wear bracelets and earrings. They have their hair carefully combed, dyed, and oiled. Thus they go to the dance, with a knot of their hair behind bound up with eel-skin, which they use as a cord. Sometimes they put on plates a foot square, covered with porcelain, which hang on the back. Thus gaily dressed and habited, they delight to appear in the dance, to which their fathers and mothers send them, forgetting nothing that they can devise to embellish and set off their daughters. I can testify that I have seen at dances a girl who had more than twelve pounds of porcelain on her person, not including the other bagatelles with which they are loaded and bedecked.

All these people have a somewhat jovial disposition, although there are many of them who have a sad and gloomy look. Their bodies are well proportioned. Some of the men and women are well formed, strong, and robust.

There are among these tribes powerful women of extraordinary height. These have almost the entire care of the house and work; namely, they till the land, plant the Indian corn, lay up a store of wood for the winter, beat the hemp and spin it, making from the thread fishing nets and other useful things. The women harvest the corn, house it, prepare it for eating, and attend to household matters. Moreover they are expected to attend their husbands from place to place in the fields, filling the office of pack mule in carrying the baggage, and to do a thousand other things. All the men do is to hunt for deer and other animals, fish, make their cabins, and go to war. Having done these things, they then go to other tribes with which they are acquainted to traffic and make exchanges. On their return, they give themselves up to festivities and dances, which they give to each other, and when these are over they go to sleep, which they like to do best of all things.

2. René de Bréhant de Galinée Expresses Admiration for Indian Canoes, 1669

Even before Huronia's collapse, French merchants were looking to the Great Lakes for new trading partners. Their search was thwarted by the power of the Iroquois raiders who made commerce on the lakes a hazardous enterprise. In 1666, Alexandre de Prouville, the newly appointed viceroy of New France, led a large invasion force into the Mohawk Valley and forced a temporary halt to the raids. Three years later, in 1669, the intendant of New France, Jean Baptiste Talon, organized a modest expedition to survey and map the Great Lakes. Suspicious of growing Jesuit influence in the region, Talon selected his explorers from the Order of St. Sulplice. Francois Dollier de Casson (d. 1701) and René de Bréhant de Galinée were given command of the party, and they set out in the summer of 1669. Their journey reached as far as the Jesuit mission at Sault Ste. Marie. The section of Galinée's report reprinted below reveals the essential role Indian canoes played in the expansion of New France.

Navigation above Montreal is quite different from that below. The latter is made in ships, barks, launches, and boats, because the River St. Lawrence is very deep, as far up as Montreal; but immediately above

Montreal one is confronted with a rapid or waterfall amidst numerous large rocks, that will not allow a boat to go through, so that canoes only can be used. These are little birch-bark canoes, about twenty feet long and two feet wide, strengthened inside with cedar floors and gunwales, very thin, so that one man carries it with ease, although the boat is capable of carrying four men and eight or nine hundred pounds' weight of baggage. There are some made that carry as many as ten or twelve men with their outfit, but it requires two or three men to carry them.

This style of canoes affords the most convenient and the commonest mode of navigation in this country, although it is a true saying that when a person is in one of these vessels he is always, not a finger's breadth, but the thickness of five or six sheets of paper, from death. These canoes cost Frenchmen who buy them from Indians nine or ten crowns in clothes, but from Frenchmen to Frenchmen they are much dearer. Mine cost me eighty livres. It is only the Algonkin-speaking tribes that build these canoes well. The Iroquois use all kinds of bark except birch for their canoes. They build canoes that are badly made and very heavy, which last at most only a month, while those of the Algonkins, if taken care of, last five or six years.

You do not row in these canoes as in a boat. In the latter the oar is attached to a rowlock on the boat's side; but here you hold one hand near the blade of the oar and the other at the end of the handle, and use it to push the water behind you, without the oar touching the canoe in any way. Moreover, it is necessary in these canoes to remain all the time on your knees or seated, taking care to preserve your balance well; for the vessels are so light that a weight of twenty pounds on one side more than the other is enough to overturn them, and so quickly that one scarcely has time to guard against it. They are so frail that to bear a little upon a stone or to touch it a little clumsily is sufficient to cause a hole, which can, however, be mended with resin.

The convenience of these canoes is great in these streams, full of cataracts or waterfalls, and rapids through which it is impossible to take any boat. When you reach them you load canoe and baggage upon your shoulders and go overland until the navigation is good; and then you put your canoe back into the water, and embark again. If God grants me the grace of returning to France, I shall endeavor to take over one of these canoes, to show it to those who have not seen them. I see no handiwork of the Indians that appears to me to merit the attention of Europeans, except their canoes and their rackets [snow shoes] for walking on snow. There is no conveyance either better or swifter than that of the canoe; for four good canoemen will not be afraid to bet that they can pass in their canoe eight or ten rowers in the fastest launch that can be seen.

I have made a long digression here upon canoes because, as I have already said, I have found nothing here more beautiful or more convenient. Without them it would be impossible to navigate above Montreal or in any of the numerous rivers of this country.

3. Marie Guyart Martin, Marie de l'Incarnation, Writes About French Exploration in the Western Great Lakes and Hudson Bay, 1671

Marie Guyart Martin (1599–1672), known to her Ursuline sisters as Marie de l'Incarnation, seems an unlikely member of any company of explorers. Widowed early in her marriage, she sent her young son Claude to live with friends and then joined the Ursulines. After arriving in Quebec in 1639, she never traveled beyond the confines of her own cloistered world. But as superior of the Ursuline Community, Marie de l'Incarnation was in a unique position to hear about journeys far to the north and west. The Ursulines had close ties to the Jesuits, and Marie de l'Incarnation also had sources of information within Quebec's political establishment. Her letters always carried the latest news, and the one reprinted here, dated August–September 1671, is no exception. The letter contains references to most of the major French explorations then under way.

Marie de l'Incarnation knew much about the Jesuits' wide-ranging travels, especially those taken by Father Claude Allouez and Father Charles Albanel. At the time she was writing, Father Allouez was in present-day Wisconsin, preaching among the Fox Indians. Marie de l'Incarnation believed that the expansion of the French empire in North America was part of the larger will of God. She praised the diplomatic mission of Simon François Daumont, Sieur de St. Lusson, to Sault Ste. Marie in 1671 to proclaim French sovereignty over what is now nearly a third of North America. Marie de l'Incarnation also had a remarkable grasp of the growing tensions between England and France at Hudson Bay. She had heard about Jean Bourdon's reputed voyage to the bay in 1656–1657 and evidently knew a great deal about Father Albanel's important Hudson Bay reconnaissance that began in the summer of 1671. English initiatives did not escape her. She worried about the growing influence of the Hudson's Bay Company (chartered in 1670) and the role of company official Charles Bayly as a merchant and imperial agent.

Last autumn Monsieur the Intendant [Talon] sent a gentleman to the Outaouak [Ottawas] to acknowledge all those countries and take possession of them for the King. He is to be two years in this quest, during which time he will accompany the Fathers on their mission in order to recognize all these countries.

The Reverend Father Allouez has pressed on to a very much more distant nation. The ways were very rough and difficult, but at the end he found a nation that is marvellously peopled and the most beautiful that can be imagined. The Savages, who received him as an angel, listened to him and thanked him heartily for bringing them news they had never heard before—namely, that there is a God, a paradise, a hell, and other like things—and also for having procured them the friendship of the French, who they heard were so good to everyone. Thereupon the Father had Monsieur St. Lusson appear and told them he had been sent to them by the great chief of the French, of whom they had heard so much good.

These good Savages had sent to the neighboring nations to inform them that the French wished to make an alliance with them. At this news ambassadors came from ten or twelve nations, and the Father, who was serving as interpreter for the deputy [St. Lusson], made them a delightful speech about the greatness and majesty of the King of France, who wished to take them under his protection, provided they were willing to become his faithful subjects. All consented to this with shouts of joy and approval, and then the Cross was set up [at Sault Ste. Marie] as the trophy of our religion, which the King and all his faithful subjects adored. Opposite to it was placed a pole to which the arms of France were attached, and thus they took possession of all these countries for His Majesty.

For several years the French have been seeking an overland passage to the great Bay of the North [Hudson Bay]. Divers routes have been attempted, but in vain, because great mountains appeared to the north, which cut off the avenues. By a very special providence the Savages of that country came to the number of forty canoes to trade with the French, who welcomed them warmly, as did also the Savages of these regions. There is no doubt that God inspired them to make this journey for their salvation.

Several years ago a worthy man [Jean Bourdon], one of our friends, tried to find the passage, more through a desire for the conversion of these people than for temporal profits. Although it was summer, the sea was filled with ice, for which reason it is called the Glacial Sea [Hudson Strait]. He had a good bark, without which he would have been lost. As he journeyed, he came to a port, where there were a great many Savages, who flattered him and his men with words to oblige some one of them to go to them. A young man was so bold, or rather so innocent, as to disembark. As soon as the

This Jesuit map of Lake Superior (1672) reveals the extent of missionary and fur-trade exploration in the Great Lakes.

barbarians saw him, they ground their teeth like angry dogs; they seized him, stabbed him, and would have killed and eaten him if his shipmates had not quickly come to his aid. Seeing so many reefs and so much ice, which left him only a little path open for navigation, and also perceiving the malignity of these peoples, the leader [Bourdon] turned back and escaped by a miracle.

I tell you this to show you the providence of God in that these peoples, who were formerly so ferocious, have come of themselves with inconceivable mildness and benignity. The Reverend Father Albanel has gone with them to carry the Faith to this people; he knows the Montagnais tongue, which is that of this people, to perfection. Monsieur the Intendant has sent Frenchmen with the Father to take possession of these great countries, which, apart from the Faith, which is the principal end, will be very advantageous for commerce.

We have just learned that some of those that were journeying towards the great Bay of the North [Hudson Bay] have retraced their steps, bringing news that some Savages they encountered informed them that two large vessels and three pinnaces from England [the Hudson's Bay Company expedition of 1670, led by Charles Bayly with Pierre Esprit Radisson and Medard Chouart, Sieur des Groseilliers, as traders] with the intention of taking possession of the harbor and the country, that the vessels had gone back again, laden with pelts, and that the pinnaces were going to spend the winter there. This is a bad business for temporal affairs, perhaps even for spiritual affairs, since the country is coming under the domination of infidels [the English Protestants]. If vessels had been sent from France, as was advised, we might not have suffered this loss. Those that set out from here on this journey of discovery may still plant the Cross and the *fleur de lys* [the symbol of France] in the teeth of the English. Let us pray for this great affair.

4. Louis Jolliet and Father Jacques Marquette Describe Their Voyage Down the Mississippi, 1673

Of all the French exploring probes sent into the American interior, none remains better known centuries after than the Jolliet-Marquette expedition. The journey down the Mississippi taken by fur trader Louis Jolliet (1645–1700) and Jesuit missionary Jacques Marquette (1637–1675) combined religious, commercial, and imperial motives.

In June 1672, Jean-Baptiste Colbert, Louis XIV's principal minister, wrote that "there is nothing more important for that land [New
France], and for the service of his Majesty than the discovery of the
passage into the South Sea." The dream of a passage to India was
plainly alive and well, at least among French imperial planners. Three
months later, Jolliet and Marquette were commissioned by officials in
New France to sail the Mississippi in search of the passage. Many in
the French colony believed that the Mississippi trended west either
directly to the Pacific or to a great inland ocean known as *La Mer de
l'Ouest,* the Sea of the West. Others thought that the Mississippi
might head east to enter English Virginia.

During the summer of 1673, Jolliet and Marquette led a canoe
party down the Mississippi as far as the mouth of the Arkansas River.
By mid-July they had concluded that the great river ran directly south
and was not the elusive Northwest Passage. Despite their failure to
find the passage, the explorers refused to give up the dream. Having
seen the mouth of the Missouri earlier in July, Marquette and Jolliet
were now convinced that this river would prove to be the great passage to the Pacific.

The two selections that follow illustrate both the power of illusion
and the abilities of the explorers to comprehend the complex geography of the lower Mississippi River. Records of the expedition were
compiled by Father Claude Dablon and published in 1681.

---

a. Speculations on the Course of the Missouri River

Pekitanoui [the Missouri River] is a river of considerable size, coming
from the northwest, from a great distance; and it discharges into the
Mississippi. There are many villages of savages along this river, and I hope
by its means to discover the Vermilion or California sea [known today as the
Sea of Cortez or the Gulf of California.]

Judging from the direction of the course of the Mississippi, if it continue
the same way, we think that it discharges into the Mexican gulf. It would be
a great advantage to find the river leading to the southern sea, toward
California; and, as I have said, this is what I hope to do by means of
Pekitanoui, according to the reports made to me by the savages. From them I

have learned that, by ascending this river for 5 or 6 days, one reaches a fine prairie, 20 or 30 leagues long. This must be crossed in a northwesterly direction, and it terminates at another small river—on which one may embark, for it is not very difficult to transport canoes through so fine a country as that prairie. This second river flows toward the southwest for 10 or 15 leagues, after which it enters a lake, small and deep, which flows toward the West, where it falls into the sea. I have hardly any doubt that it is the Vermilion Sea, and I do not despair of discovering it some day.

b. Conjectures on the Course of the Mississippi River

Monsieur Jolliet and I held another council, to deliberate upon what we should do—whether we should push on, or remain content with the discovery which we had made. After attentively considering that we were not far from the Gulf of Mexico, we judged that we could not be more than 2 or 3 days' journey from it; and that, beyond a doubt, the Mississippi River discharges into the Florida or Mexican Gulf, and not to the east in Virginia, whose seacoast is at 34 degrees latitude—which we had passed, without, however, having as yet reached the sea—or to the west in California, because in that case our route would have been to the west, or the west-southwest, whereas we had always continued toward the south. We further considered that we exposed ourselves to the risk of losing the results of this voyage, of which we could give no information if we proceeded to fling ourselves into the hands of the Spaniards who, without doubt, would at least have detained us as captives. Moreover, we saw very plainly that we were not in a condition to resist savages allied to the Europeans [the Spanish], who were numerous, and expert in firing guns, and who continually infested the lower part of the river. Finally, we had obtained all the information that could be desired in regard to this discovery.

E. La Salle and the Creation of a Greater New France, 1679–1687

No French explorer had a more star-crossed career in North America than René-Robert Cavelier, Sieur de La Salle (1643–1687). Having arrived in New France in 1666, La Salle was soon immersed in

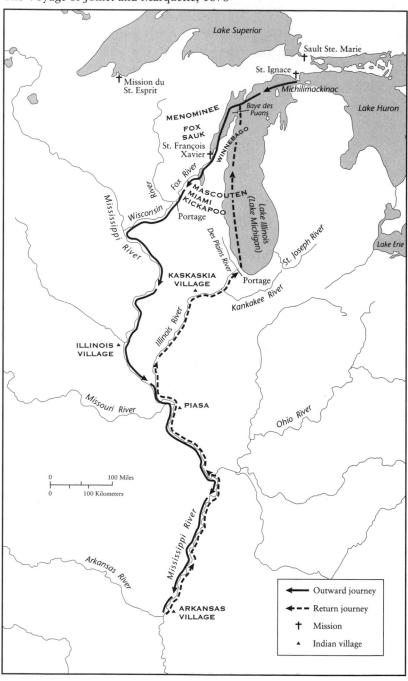

The Voyage of Jolliet and Marquette, 1673

schemes to find the Northwest Passage. In 1669 he joined the Dollier-Galinée expedition, but evidently he did not go as far as Sault Ste. Marie with the party. In fact, his travels between 1669 and 1673 remain shrouded in mystery, though one thing is certain: La Salle fell under the spell of Louis de Buade, comte de Frontenac, the expansion-minded governor general of New France. By 1679, La Salle had fashioned an impressive plan for an extensive Great Lakes fur-trade empire. That empire depended on trading posts deep into the Illinois country and the use of sailing ships on the Great Lakes. The ship *Le Griffon* was the first in that fleet, and when it was lost on Lake Michigan in September 1679, La Salle decided to walk overland from his post at Fort Crevecoeur on the Illinois River to the French establishment at Niagara. His march, made during February and March of 1680, gave La Salle additional information about the country of the Great Lakes and its potential as part of the French empire. La Salle's thoughts on that subject, which blended actual experience with fantasy and conjecture, were included in his "Description of the Illinois Country, 1680" sent to Frontenac in November 1680.

The Great Lakes was only one part of what La Salle hoped would be a vast French domain in North America. The travels of Jolliet and Marquette, as well as those of other French traders, had convinced La Salle that the Mississippi and the Gulf of Mexico were essential for a greater New France. In 1682, La Salle organized his Mississippi expedition, a journey down the river to the Gulf.

By April 1682, La Salle had reached the Gulf of Mexico. His expedition directly challenged Spanish claims, a challenge that Spain was slow to meet. Confident that he knew the precise location of the mouth of the Mississippi, La Salle next planned a large-scale expedition to the Gulf of Mexico, intending to plant a colony in the region. In midsummer 1684 La Salle's expedition—four ships and several hundred soldiers and colonists—lost its way along the Gulf and landed at Matagorda Bay near present-day Port Lavaca, Texas. The expedition gradually collapsed, and in mid-March 1687 the explorer was killed by his own men. One of those who recorded these Gulf Coast events was Henri Joutel, whose *Journal of the Last Voyage Perform'd by Monsieur de La Salle to the Gulph of Mexico* was published in English in 1714. This portion of his account describes the tensions between the French explorers and their Gulf Coast native neighbors.

1. La Salle Describes the Illinois Country, 1680

By the time La Salle wrote this "Description of the Illinois Country" in 1680, it was clear to many traders and royal officials that the Great Lakes was the key to French expansion in North America. In this selection, La Salle portrays Lake Michigan as the center of a vast waterway system connecting eastern Canada to the western country. La Salle was not immune to the lure of the Northwest Passage, claiming that it was possible to reach the sea by water routes from French posts on the Illinois River.

The Niagara River is not navigable for ten leagues [about 20 to 30 miles] from the falls to the entrance into Lake Erie, it being impossible to bring up a vessel, at least without enough men to handle the sail, to haul at the bow, and to warp at the same time, and even with such great caution one cannot hope to be successful always. The entrance into Lake Erie is so obstructed with shallow bars that, in order not to risk losing the vessel every voyage, it is necessary to leave it in a river six leagues away along the lake, which is the nearest harbor or anchorage. There are in Lake Erie three large peninsulas, of which two jut out more than ten leagues. There are sand bars which one may run afoul of before seeing them unless one takes great precautions.

A change of wind is necessary to enter the straits between Lake Erie and Lake Huron, where there is more water and a strong current. Great difficulties confront one at the Straits of Michillimackinac in entering from Lake Huron into the Lake of the Illinois [Lake Michigan]. The wind there is usually counter to the current, and the channel is narrow on account of the bars which extend out from the two shores. There are very few or no anchorages in Lake Huron, and no more harbors than in the Lake of the Illinois along the north, west, and south shores. There are a great number of islands in both lakes. Those of the Illinois are a hazard on account of the sand bars which are off them. This lake is not deep and is subject to terrific winds from which there is no shelter, and the bars border upon the approaches to the islands; but it is possible that with more frequent voyages the dangers will be lessened and the ports and harbors better known as has happened in the case of Lake Frontenac [Lake Ontario], on which navigation is now safe and easy.

The haven [bay] which one enters in order to go from the Lake of the Illinois to the Divine River [the Desplains River] is not at all suitable for

This fanciful depiction of La Salle's Gulf Coast fleet appeared in Louis Hennepin, *Nouveau Voyage d'un Pays plus Grand que l'Europe* (1698).

Avantures mal-heureuses du Sieur de la Salle.

navigation as there are no winds in the roadstead [the present-day Chicago lakefront] nor any passageway for a vessel, not even for a canoe, at least in a great calm. The prairies over which communication is maintained are flooded by the great volume of water flowing down from the neighboring hills whenever it rains. It is very difficult to make and maintain a canal that does not immediately fill up with sand and gravel; one need only dig into the ground to find water; and there are some sand dunes between the lake [Lake Michigan] and the prairies. And, although a canal would be possible with a great deal of expense, it would be useless because the Divine River is not navigable for forty leagues, the distance to the great village of the Illinois [Indians]. Canoes cannot traverse it during the summer, and even then there are long rapids this side of that village.

Mines have not yet been found although pieces of copper have been found in a number of places where the water is low. There is excellent stone [for building] and coal. The Indians relate having sold some yellow metal from the village, but from their description it was too pure to have come from a gold mine.

The buffalo are becoming scarce here since the Illinois [Indians] are at war with their neighbors; both kill and hunt them continually.

It is possible to go by water from Fort Crevecoeur [on the present-day Illinois River] to the sea. New Mexico is not over twenty days' journey distant to the west of this fort. The Oto [Indians], who have come to see Monsieur de La Salle, have brought with them a piebald [horse] belonging to some Spaniards whom they killed in their country only ten days' journey distant from this fort; one could go from the one to the other by the river. These Indians relate that the Spanish who make war against them use lances more than muskets.

There is some very fine wood for shipbuilding along the seven or eight rivers flowing into the Colbert [the Mississippi], the least of which has a course of 300 leagues without falls.

Monsieur de La Salle has seen the Indians of three nations through which de Soto passed, namely, Chickasaw, Casqui, and Aminoya. From them these people go to Mexico; they assure us that they have a very good water route from Crevecoeur to their homes.

It is important that this exploration be carried out because the river on which the Chickasaw live, and which is probably the Sakakoua [the Yazoo], has its source near Carolina, where the English are, 300 leagues to the east of the river Colbert in French Florida near Apalachee; when the English would be able to come by ship to the Illinois, to the Miami [Indians], and close to the Baye des Puans [present-day Green Bay, Wisconsin], and the country of the Sioux, and secure thereby a great portion of our trade.

2. Henri Joutel Chronicles Tensions Between Indians and French Explorers, 1684

Textbook wisdom has it that French explorers and Native Americans always enjoyed mutual respect and understanding. Somehow, so the story goes, the French escaped suffering from the same kind of cultural arrogance that pervaded the lives of so many other Europeans in North America. A close look at French-Indian encounters tells a different story, though. When relations were peaceful, it was usually the result of common interest in trade, diplomacy, or war. None of those bonds united La Salle's party with its native neighbors. The results of contact were confusion and trouble on both sides of the cultural divide. As Joutel explains in this episode, young French adventurers were "more hot than wise."

When we had gathered all, as well what had been taken out of the shipwrecked vessel as what could be picked up in the sea, the next thing was to regulate the provisions we had left proportionably to the number of men we were; and there being no biscuit, meal was delivered out, and with it we made a pudding with water, which was none of the best; some large beans and Indian corn, part of which had taken wet; and every thing was distributed very equitably. We were much incommoded for want of kettles, but Monsieur de Beaujeu gave Monsieur de La Salle one, and he ordered another to be brought from the ship *La Belle*, by which means we were well served.

We were still in want of canoes. Monsieur de La Salle sent to the camp of the Indians to barter for some, and they who went there observed, that those people had made their advantage of our shipwreck, and had some bales of Normandy blankets, and they saw several women had cut them in two and made skirts of them. They also saw bits of iron of the ship that was cast away, and returned immediately to make their report to Monsieur de La Salle, who said we must endeavor to get some canoes in exchange, and resolved to send there again the next day. Monsieur du Hamel, ensign to Monsieur de Beaujeu, offered to go up in his boat, which Monsieur de La Salle agreed to, and ordered Messieurs Moranget, his nephew, Desloges, Oris, Gayen, and some others to bear him company.

No sooner had those gentlemen, who were more hot than wise, landed, but they went up to the camp of the Indians, with their arms in their hands, as if they intended to force them, whereupon several of those people fled. Going into the cabins, they found others, to whom Monsieur du Hamel endeavored to signify by signs, that he would have the blankets they had found restored; but the misfortune was, that none of them understood one another. The Indians thought it their best way to withdraw, leaving behind them some blankets and skins, which those gentlemen took away, and finding some canoes in their return they seized two, and got in, to bring them away.

But having no oars, none of them knowing how to manage those canoes, and having only some pitiful poles, which they could not tell the right use of, and the wind being also against them, they made little way; which the Sieur du Hamel, who was in his boat perceiving, and that night drew on, he made the best of his way, abandoned them and returned to the camp.

Thus night came upon them, which obliged those inexperienced canoe men, being thoroughly tired, to go ashore to take some rest, and the weather being cold, they lighted a fire, about which they laid them down and fell asleep; the sentry they had appointed doing the same. The Indians returning to their camp, and perceiving our men had carried away two canoes, some skins and blankets, took it for a declaration of a war, resolved to be revenged, and discovering an unusual fire, presently concluded that our men had halted there. A considerable number of them went to the place, without making the least noise, found our careless people fast asleep, wrapped up in their blankets, and shot a full volley of their arrows upon them all together on a sudden, having first given their usual shout before they fall on [the enemy].

The Sieur Moranget awaking with the noise, and finding himself wounded, started up and fired his piece successfully enough, some others did the like, whereupon the natives fled. The Sieur Moranget came to give us the alarm, though he was shot through one of his arms, below the shoulder, and had another slanting wound on the breast. Monsieur de La Salle immediately sent some armed men to the place, could not find the Indians, but when day appeared, they found the Sieurs Oris and Desloges dead upon the spot, the Sieur Gayen much hurt, and the rest all safe and sound.

This disaster, which happened the night of the fifth of March [1685], very much afflicted Monsieur de La Salle; but he chiefly lamented Monsieur Desloges, a sprightly youth who served well; but in short, it was their own fault, and contrary to the charge given them, which was to be watchful and upon their guard. We were under apprehensions for Messieurs Moranget and Gayen, lest the arrows be poisoned. It afterwards appeared they were not, however Monsieur Moranget's cure proved difficult, because some small vessel was cut.

SUGGESTIONS FOR FURTHER READING

Bishop, Morris. *Champlain: The Life of Fortitude*. London: Macdonald and Co., 1949.

Bridenbaugh, Carl. *Jamestown, 1544–1699*. New York: Oxford University Press, 1981.

Hamilton, Raphael N. *Marquette's Explorations: The Narratives Reexamined*. Madison: University of Wisconsin Press, 1970.

Kupperman, Karen O. *Settling with the Indians: The Meeting of Indian and English Cultures in America, 1580–1640*. Totowa, New Jersey: Rowman and Littlefield, 1984.

Quinn, David B. *Set Fair for Roanoke: Voyages and Colonies*. Chapel Hill: University of North Carolina Press, 1985.

Simmons, Marc. *The Last Conquistador: Juan de Oñate and the Settling of the Far Southwest*. Norman: University of Oklahoma Press, 1991.

Vaughan, Alden T. *American Genesis: Captain John Smith and the Founding of Virginia*. Boston: Little, Brown, 1975.

CHAPTER 4

The Clash of Empires

Long before the age of Columbus and the beginnings of the European invasion of the continent, North America saw struggles for power and place. With the arrival of the first European explorers, the land became even more both a battleground and a prize. From the sixteenth century on, explorers and travelers advanced royal and imperial ambitions. In the eighteenth century these ambitions, and the conflicts triggered by them, grew and intensified. The idea of territorial empire pervaded nearly every aspect of European public life, from science and politics to business and religion. Missionaries and merchants, naturalists and diplomats all embraced the promise of empire. Such a promise meant more contestants in the race for empire. It also set new journeys in motion, expeditions farther from old centers of occupation on the edges of the continent and deeper into the interior. More than ever, explorers and adventurers sought to reveal an America they intended to conquer and possess.

As the North American stage for Europeans grew wide and the cast of characters large, the motives for this ever-expanding drama became more complex. Eighteenth-century journeys of discovery and exploration were driven by a tangle of passions, illusions, and calculations hard to describe and even harder to separate from one another. One such master passion in this age of empire was war and imperial rivalry. Beginning in the late 1680s and continuing throughout the next century, Great Britain and its allies fought a series of four wars against France. Each of these European conflicts had an American counterpart. The last of the four struggles, sometimes known inaccurately in American history as the French and Indian War (1756–1760), fundamentally changed the balance of power in North America. After France's loss of Canada in the war, Britain emerged as the most powerful nation in eastern North America. Indian nations now faced a dangerous, land-hungry neighbor.

These eighteenth-century conflicts differed notably from earlier episodes of warfare. War was now the business of highly organized nation-states, not of dynasties or bands of rival nobles. This was modern war—armed conflict mounted by professional armies for territory, commercial gain, and global status. Explorers were advance scouts, the vanguard in such campaigns. Exploration reports made certain regions or resources appealing and perhaps worth the cost of conflict. Explorers mapped future battlefields, secured Indian allies, and evaluated new territories. The eighteenth century made explorers—whether they wore uniforms or not—part of the rush for empire.

The idea of empire was everywhere within eighteenth-century voyages. But a close look at that idea and those voyages reveals other motives at work as well. The fur trade remained a constant reason for journeys west beyond the Great Lakes and on to the Great Plains. The eighteenth-century fur trade was less a matter of individual traders on solitary treks and more the bureaucratic operations of international companies like the Hudson's Bay Company, the North West Company, and various French commercial houses. Insofar as these corporate giants worked closely with national governments, imperial and business policy often overlapped.

In the English colonies, land speculation played a key role in prompting journeys of discovery. Like the fur trader, the land surveyor and the company agent represented both corporate enterprise and national ambition. By the middle of the eighteenth century, the western real estate business was in the hands of such companies as the Ohio Company, the Loyal Land Company, and the Greenbrier Company. Their speculative ventures focused attention west of the Ohio River on lands claimed by the French and by many Indian nations. The imperial contest for the Ohio country put surveyors and speculators at the center of a violent struggle. The reports, pamphlets, broadsides, and maps produced by land-company explorers revealed the country and intensified the struggle.

If the eighteenth century was the age of imperial and commercial expansion, it was also the age of scientific observation. Science in this era was not an abstract pursuit, remote from matters of politics and business. Literate Europeans infrequently used the word *science,* and the term *scientist* did not enter English usage until 1834. Instead, scholars and journalists alike talked about *natural history.* Natural history required its students—professional and amateur alike—to observe, collect, and classify all aspects of the visible natural world. This approach fit the larger requirements of eighteenth-century Enlightenment philosophy, which emphasized the power of human reason and the importance of organized knowledge. Most important for exploration, the Enlightenment put great value on useful knowledge. Naturalist-explorers studied plants and animals, hoping to transform nature into natural resources. Beginning with the Pacific voyages of Captain James

The Vérendrye Expeditions, 1738–1743

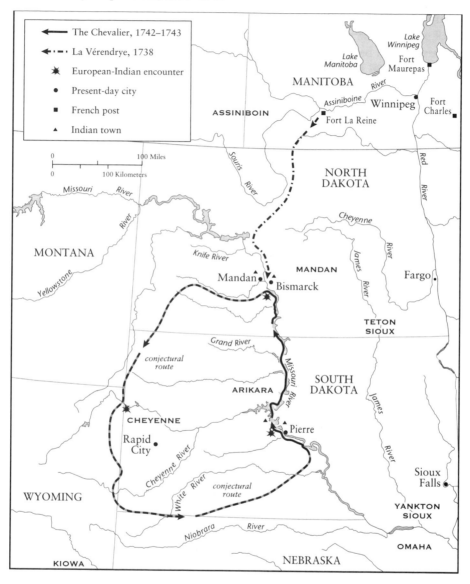

This tribe is of mixed blood, white and black. The women are rather handsome, particularly the light-colored ones; they have an abundance of fair hair. The whole tribe is very industrious. Their dwellings are large and spacious, divided into several apartments by wide planks. Nothing is lying about; all their belongings are placed in large bags hung on posts; their beds are made in the form of tombs and are surrounded by skins. Their fort is very well provided with cellars, where they store all they have in the way of grains, meat, fat, dressed skins and bearskins. They have a great stock of these things, which form the money of the country. The more they have the richer they consider themselves.

B. Russian America

The notion that the country was revealed by Europeans moving from east to west is a powerful and pervasive idea in American history. This angle of vision and sense of direction lend great authority to French and English accounts, but they overlook or discount others. Russian explorers, merchants, bureaucrats, and missionaries journeyed to the northwestern reaches of North America as part of a three-century-long spread eastward through Siberia. This expansion was driven by the fur trade, missionary zeal, and Russian imperial aspirations.

No Russian merchant more aggressively and ambitiously extended the fur trade than Grigorii I. Shelikhov (1747–1795). Shelikhov arrived in eastern Siberia in the early 1770s, attracted by the lure of wealth in the fur business. There he met and married Natal'ia Alekseevna (d. 1810), a well-to-do widow. Along with Ivan Golikov, Grigorii and Natal'ia built the Shelikhov-Golikov Company, later known as the American Company. In 1783, the Shelikhovs made the first in a series of important exploring and trading voyages to Kodiac Island. After her husband's death in 1795, Natal'ia ran the fur-trading company and oversaw its successful merger (1799) as part of the state-chartered Russian-American Company. Her August 1798 report summarizes Russian expansion in the North Pacific and illustrates the connections between trade, religion, and imperial expansion.

1. Natal'ia Alekseevna Shelikova Explains the Successes of the American Company, 1798

Written in part to defend the American Company's accomplishments, this report details the substantial business empire, involving not only commercial establishments but also religious schools and missions, built in the north Pacific by Russian traders.

The late Shelikhov, my husband, on his visit to America with three ships in the years 1784, 1785, and 1786, having civilized the Alaska natives, Kodiac and Afognak islanders, likewise various tribes on the American mainland from Kenai Bay or Cook River to 57 degrees north latitude to Ltua Bay, made more than 120,000 souls Russian subjects, but only those who themselves voluntarily desired this. Trade has been established with those peoples, and a fur trading company founded. And all that has been grounded on firm and reliable rules.

Upon his return from there, Shelikhov instructed his company assistants to carry out the operations noted below. As a result, the following has been done:

1. The Alaska peninsula has been further surveyed and a very short and convenient passage has been found across it on the north side to Bristol Bay

These drawings of Aleut people by Louis Choris (1816) illustrate the changes produced by contact with Russian traders and missionaries. The Aleut man still wears traditional hunting garb, while the woman is dressed in European-style clothing with a Christian cross around her neck.

habitans des îles Aléoutiennes.

without going around the cape and through the dangerous strait between it and Unimak Island. The Alaska natives have become better known and more subordinated.

2. In Kenai Bay, which Cook [Captain James Cook] called a river bearing his name, an outpost of Russian *promyshlenniki* [fur hunters] has been set up for trading. They have civilized the inhabitants and carried on trade and every kind of communication with them.

3. An outpost has also been set up in Chugach Bay, and in 1794 three ships were built there from local materials as an experiment: one excellent frigate, the *Phoenix*, of 24 guns, and two smaller ships, the *Pegasus* and the *Oleg*. Acquaintance has been made with many natives, and trade contacts established.

4. A small fortress was constructed at Cape St. Elias on Montagu or Siukliu Island.

5. On Kodiac a school has been established in which American boys learn, in the Russian language, reading, writing, arithmetic, and navigation. Ten boys were sent to Irkutsk and instructed on various musical instruments, and sent back to Kodiac in 1793, to the delight of the local residents, who have a liking for gaieties.

6. Some exploration has been carried out on the mainland in Iakutat [Yakutat] and Ltua Bays, where the natives are more primitive. There was little success in civilizing them up to 1795, but the situation is not hopeless, for they engage in barter without fear. Ltua Bay is a little beyond 55 degrees north latitude, in the vicinity of the English settlement of Nootka, and should be the boundary of the Russian dominions in America.

7. In all these bays and in other places, copper markers with the inscription "Land of the Russian Dominions" have been buried in the ground for political reasons.

8. Many of the subject Americans and islanders have been baptized without a priest, and many have adopted the way of life of the Russian people; and from distant places whole tribes have moved near to places where the Russian trading posts are located, defending these from attack by their own peoples, who have the hateful habit of robbing and killing each other over the smallest trifles.

9. When, therefore, the local inhabitants had become adherents of the Russians and of our law, my husband in 1793 requested missionaries from the supreme leadership, of whom a whole party, under the command of an archimandrite, was sent there at the expense of the company. In the winter of 1794 and the spring of 1795, they baptized on Kodiac more than 8000 souls, and remarried a large number of Americans, as well as marrying

apologized for not having come in greater numbers, saying they had feared that they would be in the way. They are divided into various tribes or bands, named Naitanes, Yarambicas, etc., ruled by chiefs or captains, among whom the one called Euea, who has presented himself before your Lordship, is generally recognized. They have no fixed habitation, neither do they plant crops, but live in continual motion, never stopping in a place except while it abounds in cattle [buffalo]. This obliges them to divide themselves into an infinite number of little bands for the purpose of seeking better pastures for their horses, and cattle for their own food. This explains why they separate from their chiefs, following out their individual whims, and doing damage which the others can neither prevent or remedy when it comes to their notice.

2. José Mariano Moziño Considers Northwest Coast Indian Life and Work, 1792

> Like other Enlightenment scholars and explorers, Moziño believed that daily occupations revealed much about cultural habits and values. He also recognized the ways in which European goods, especially iron fishing hooks, had changed the native people's methods of harvesting the sea.

Fishing is the branch of industry to which general necessity has forced these inhabitants to apply themselves. Consequently, they know well the seasons in which each kind of fish is abundant and the particular method that should be employed in catching it. In former days they had only fishhooks which they made from shells; but at present these have been abandoned because of the great collection they have made of iron ones. Their nets are small and cannot be used except for catching the smallest fish.

They have another instrument, twenty feet long, four or five inches wide, and one-half inch thick, which is fitted with teeth more than two inches long for two-thirds of its length, the other part being left free to serve as a handle. Herring, and in general any fish coming in schools, remain imprisoned here as in a trap. Sardines are the fish found in greatest abundance, and their catch offers the most entertaining spectacle. A great many canoes join together and, forming a semicircle, close in the mouth of the port and all the places where these fish might escape. [The fishermen] vibrate long, thick poles underneath the water to frighten the fish and, gradually drawing their canoes closer together, each time form a smaller circle until they have corralled the fish in a very small cove, from which they pull them out quickly and in great numbers with nets, little baskets, and rakes. They even gather them in their hands from the places where they are most thickly collected. At the conclusion of the fishing, the *tais* [headman], or someone appointed by him, distributes a considerable portion to each village. In shallow channels they drive in stakes which are tied with cattail leaves and serve as traps to imprison the fish.

Among all the types of fishing, none is more admired than that for the whale. A small canoe, with a keel of scarcely fifteen feet and a two-and-one-half-foot beam, manned by three or four men, goes out to catch the most enormous animal that nature produces. The inventive genius of man is always revealed in proportion to his needs, and that of these savages in the matter with which we are dealing is not inferior to that of the most civilized nations.

They thrust into the whale, with great force, a sharp harpoon attached to a long and heavy shaft so that it will pierce more deeply. This shaft is then recovered by means of a rope, and at the same time they slacken another [rope], tied at one end to the harpoon and at the other to an inflated bladder, which floats over the water like a buoy, marking the place to which the wounded animal has fled during the short time in which it stays alive. There is no catch which the natives solemnize more, nor from which they obtain greater profit. The chief himself is present during the distribution, and when this is done he gives a splendid banquet to all the villages.

I did not see the methods by which they capture sea otters. Because they have become so scarce, it is a very rare thing to encounter one in any of that bay. Having observed that the majority of skins are without holes, I suspect that they kill them with sticks, watching closely for the chance of finding them asleep on the large rocks; or they catch them with slip nooses which are usually called snares.

Hunting provides them with land animals and shore birds. For this purpose nothing is worth more to them today than the gun, and it is very clear that this has replaced, only to their advantage, the ancient use of the arrow.

Since their dances often represent this kind of activity, I observed in one of them the preparation of nets and also the imitation of animals plunged into a pit covered over with slender canes that could be broken by the weight of the body. I have seen complete heads of bears and deer well prepared for being placed over their own heads. This made me think that they follow the same strategy with which the Californians guarantee their shots by disguising themselves with the appearance of the beast they are trying to kill.

The sedentary arts consist solely of spinning and weaving, and constitute the daily occupation of the women. In spinning, they have no equipment other than their muscles and fingers to unite the fibers of cedar [bark], wool, and otter hair. With these they first form a thick strand, which they afterward narrow and lengthen, winding it onto a small bar about one foot long which they turn above a small plank with the same dexterity and agility as our Indian women use in their *malacates* [a Mexican spindle or bobbin].

The looms for weaving textiles are very simple. They hang the warp from a horizontal cane at a height of four and one-half feet from the ground, and with only their fingers, moving with swiftness, flexibility, and extraordinary deftness, they make up for all the tools that would make this work less cumbersome. They have patterns for making hats and capes; they begin both of them with a closely woven center, and weave the ends of the threads around the edges. For sleeping mats they use no more equipment than do our Indians of Xochimilco. The mats are too coarse, either because the cattails do not lend themselves to finer work, or perhaps because they do not take much trouble in weaving them. Cured leather of all kinds is very good; the skins remain extremely soft and can be folded as easily as those of the most skillful tanners.

They work very little with metals. They cut copper into narrow strips, bend back the edges, and curve them to form bracelets and so forth; or without bending them they make the small cylinders which they hang from their ears and the ends of their hair. They lack whetstones upon which to sharpen their iron instruments, and thus are content to make a point [arrowhead] by the force of their blows. They drill perfectly well the small snailshells and the blunted tips of Venus [dentalium] shells, of which they make the same use our ladies do of pearls. Their writing and painting are very crude. Not only are these arts not in their infancy among them; to speak with exactness, they do not exist even in embryo.

D. Britain Beyond the Ohio

The English colonies stretching out along the Atlantic coast from what is now Maine to the Carolinas had few of the advantages in the rush for empire that their powerful rivals enjoyed. Westward to the Alleghenies, English expansion was blocked by the mountains and the lack of water highways. But more important than geography was the presence of native peoples determined to resist any encroachment on tribal territories. And until 1760, New France stood in the way of a greater Britain in America.

Despite these problems, English and colonial adventurers, speculators, and merchants were drawn first to the Ohio country and later to
the western Great Lakes. What attracted them was the promise of
profit in land and fur. And this promise also offered the vision of a
triumphant British empire in North America. Land lay at the heart of
the English colonial enterprise, and it was the lure of lands beyond
the Ohio River that drew speculators from Virginia and England
together to form the Ohio Company in 1747. With George
Washington's brother Lawrence as the company's first manager, the
investors secured royal permission to take up 200,000 acres of land
west of the Alleghenies. The following year (1750), the company
hired Christopher Gist (1706–1759), an experienced frontier scout, to
report on its new domain. The instructions prepared for Gist, reprinted here as the first selection, were much like those written later
for Lewis and Clark and other American explorers. Gist's patrons
envisioned profit from two enterprises—settlement and the Indian
trade. With those twin (but sometimes opposing) aims in mind, they
directed Gist to pursue several missions—everything from discovering routes and passes to describing vegetation and soil quality to
recording the details of native life.

In the fall of 1750, Gist set out from what is now Green Spring,
Maryland, on a long scouting trip that took him across the
Appalachians, along the Ohio River, and up the Miami River into
what is now western Ohio. Following company orders, he paid careful attention to the Ohio country terrain. Once he reached the great
Miami Indian settlement and trading post located near present-day
Piqua, Ohio, Gist took note of native customs, especially with an eye
to the potential role the Miamis might play in an expanding English
empire. The selection reprinted here reveals not only Gist's evaluation
of the physical landscape and its opportunities for English settlement
but also the powerful presence of Miami Indians and their skilled
diplomat-chief La Demoiselle.

Whereas Christopher Gist and his Ohio Company employers saw
profit and paradise just across the Alleghenies, Robert Rogers
(1731–1795) and Jonathan Carver (1710–1780) were caught up in a
visionary scheme far more grand. The scheme made them think they
could see much farther, perhaps even to China. Rogers had opened
his career as leader of a band of guerrilla fighters known as Rogers'
Rangers. Once the struggles against France and its Indian allies had
concluded, Rogers considered larger questions of British imperial destiny and American continental geography. As he imagined it, North

America was split in half by a single height of land—a continental divide—running north and south. The watersheds on each side of the divide were ribboned with rivers, and he assumed that at least one of those was the fabled Passage to India. Explorers and traders might paddle up the Mississippi to its source, portage a narrow divide, and come upon the headwaters of a mighty river bound for the Pacific. Rogers called this river of the West the Ouragon. A generation later, some would call it the Columbia.

Rogers selected Jonathan Carver, a former militia captain from Massachusetts, to test his image of the West. In 1766–1767 Carver made his way up the Mississippi and Minnesota rivers as far as present-day Mankato, Minnesota, but found neither the continental divide nor the great river Ouragon. This journey, however, did produce one of the most influential exploration accounts of the age. First published in London in 1778, *Travels Through the Interior Parts of North America* offered readers not only high adventure but a set of geographic expectations about routes to the Northwest. The Rogers-Carver ideas about westward-flowing rivers, especially the Ouragon, would come alive when Thomas Jefferson planned the Lewis and Clark expedition. The selections reprinted here describe Carver's meeting with the Sioux on the Minnesota River, his ideas about the continental divide, and secondhand news about the Mandan Indians.

The end of French power in New France not only opened the way for Carver and other explorers but also gave English fur traders their first opportunities to exploit the rich Great Lakes trading world. Alexander Henry the Elder (1739–1824) was one of the first to seize that opportunity. Born in New Jersey, Henry entered the Albany fur trade early in his life. In 1760, at the end of hostilities with France, Henry sought a piece of the western fur business. For the next sixteen years he was one of the "pedlars from Quebec," searching out new fur regions between Lake Superior and Lake Winnipeg. Henry recounted these memorable times in his *Travels and Adventures in Canada and the Indian Territories Between the Years 1760 and 1776*, first published in 1809. Years of western travel and conversation with Indians had made Henry a keen student of geography and fur-trade strategy. The short selection reprinted here is based on his talks with Chipewyan Indians in July 1776. Those discussions convinced Henry that Lake Athabasca lay at the heart of a vast river system running up to the eastern face of the Rockies. A quick portage over the mountains would bring merchants to the Pacific and the rich sea-otter trade. In the 1770s, Henry was in no position to test his ideas, but two decades later he taught his young partner, John Jacob Astor, all about such routes and their promise for great wealth.

Robert Rogers, Jonathan Carver, and Alexander Henry the Elder all represented the English thrust into the West. But no trader and promoter marched farther and had wider influence at the end of the eighteenth century than Connecticut-born Peter Pond (1740–1807). A restless ambition drove Pond to be first a soldier and later a merchant seaman. In 1765 he became a fur trader, moving quickly into the fur-rich regions of what are now the Canadian provinces of Manitoba and Saskatchewan. In 1778, Pond crossed the height of land at Methye Portage in what is today northern Saskatchewan and became the first European trader in the Athabasca country. Like Henry, Pond listened to Indian accounts of mountains and rivers. Some years later—at least by 1784—he learned about Captain James Cook's explorations along the Northwest Coast. Pond was now convinced that the rivers he heard Indians describe were the true Northwest Passage. Throughout the 1780s he pressed both the British and the American governments to subsidize an expedition to test his theories. While Pond drew several maps to illustrate his geographic conception of the West, only the one reprinted here was ever published. Appearing in England's prestigious *Gentleman's Magazine* (March 1790), this map expresses Pond's confident geography—a geography that promised both wealth and imperial power. Pond's map strongly influenced the planning of Captain George Vancouver's expedition (1791–1795) to the Northwest Coast. But Pond's influence reached far beyond one maritime journey. If Henry's student was John Jacob Astor, Pond had an even more important pupil. At the end of the 1780s, Pond's apprentice in matters of geography and exploration was Alexander Mackenzie. Guided by Pond's ideas, Mackenzie led the first European transcontinental crossing of North America north of Mexico.

1. The Ohio Company Instructs Christopher Gist, 1750

The Ohio Company understood that exploration was a carefully planned undertaking. In these directions written for Christopher Gist, company directors urged their explorer to pay special attention to the quality of land and the availability of water. Gist's exploration instructions conveyed not only travel directions but also the image of a settlement and agricultural future for lands beyond the Ohio River.

Y ou are to go out as soon as possible to the Westward of the great mountains, and carry with you such a Number of Men, as You think necessary, in Order to search out and discover the Lands upon the River Ohio,
and other adjoining Branches of the Mississippi down as low as the great
Falls [present-day Louisville, Kentucky] thereof: You are particularly to
observe the Ways and Passes thro all the Mountains you cross, and take an
exact Account of the Soil, Quality, and Product of the Land, and the
Wideness and Deepness of the Rivers, and the several Falls belonging to
them, together with the Courses and Bearings of the Rivers and Mountains
as near as you conveniently can: You are also to observe what Nations of
Indians inhabit there, their Strength and Numbers, who they trade with, and
in what Commodities they deal.

When you find a large Quantity of good level Land, such as you think
will suit the Company, you are to measure the Breadth of it, in three or four
different Places, and take the Courses of the Rivers and Mountains on which
it binds [bounds] in order to judge the Quality: You are to fix the Beginning
and Bounds in such a Manner that they may be easily found again by your
Description; the nearer in the Land lies, the better, provided it be good and
level, but we had rather go quite down the Mississippi than take mean broken Land. After finding a large Body of good level Land, you are not to stop,
but proceed farther, as low as the Falls of the Ohio, that we may be
informed of that Navigation; And you are to take an exact Account of all the
larger Bodies of good level Land, in the same manner as above directed, that
the Company may the better judge where it will be most convenient for them
to take their Land.

You are to note all the Bodies of good Land as you go along, tho there is
not a sufficient Quantity for the Company's Grant, but you need not be so
particular in the Mensuration of that, as in the larger Bodies of Land.

You are to draw as good a Plan as you can of the Country you pass thro:
You are to take an exact and particular Journal of all your Proceedings, and
make a true Report thereof to the Ohio Company.

2. Christopher Gist Recalls His Meeting with La Demoiselle and the Miami Indians, 1751

As Gist makes plain in this diary entry, diplomacy, exploration, and
land speculation were often part of the same enterprise.

C rossed the little Miami River, and altering our Course we went SW 25
miles, to the Big Miami River, opposite the Twigtwee Town [Twigtwee

Councils and treaty-making sessions were important opportunities for Native American and European diplomats to gather and discuss common problems. This highly stylized engraving shows Ohio Indians and British officials meeting sometime in the mid-1760s.

was the name English traders used to describe the Miami Indians. French merchants called this town Pickawillany]. All the way from the Shannoah Town [Lower Shawnee Town near present-day Portsmouth, Ohio] to this Place (except the first 20 miles which is broken) is fine, rich level Land, well timbered with large Walnut, Ash, Sugar Trees, Cherry Trees etc. It is well watered with a great number of little Streams and Rivulets, and full of beautiful natural Meadows, covered with wild Rye, blue Grass and Clover, and abounds with Turkeys, Deer, Elks and most Sorts of Game particularly Buffaloes, thirty or forty of which are frequently seen feeding in one Meadow: In short it wants Nothing but Cultivation to make it a most delightfull Country—The Ohio and all the large Branches are said to be full of fine Fish of several Kinds, particularly a Sort of Cat Fish of prodigious Size; but as I was not there at the proper season, I had not an Opportunity of seeing any of them—The Traders had always reckoned it 200 miles, from the

Shannoah Town to the Twigtwee Town, but by my Computation I could make it no more than 150—The Big Miami being high, We were obliged to make a Raft of old logs to transport our Goods and Saddles and swim our horses over—After Firing a few Guns and Pistols, and smoking in the Warriors Pipe, who came to invite Us to the Town (according to their Custom of inviting and welcoming Strangers and Great Men), We entered the Town with English Colours before Us, and were kindly received by their King [La Demoiselle, sometimes known as Old Britain] who invited Us into his own House, and set our Colours upon the Top of it—The Firing of Guns held about a Quarter of an Hour, and then all the white Men and Traders that were there, came and welcomed Us to the Twigtwee Town—This Town is situate on the Northwest side of the Big Miami River about 150 miles from the mouth thereof; it consists of about 400 Families, and daily increasing. It is accounted one of the strongest Indian Towns upon this part of the continent—The Twigtwees are a very numerous People consisting of many different Tribes under the same form of Government. Each Tribe has a particular Chief or King, one of which is chosen indifferently out of any Tribe to rule the whole Nation, and is vested with greater Authorities than any of the others—They are accounted the most powerful People to the Westward of the English Settlements, and much superior to the six Nations [the Iroquois Confederacy] with whom they are now in Amity. Their Strength and Numbers are not thoroughly known, as they have but lately traded with the English, and indeed have very little Trade among them. They deal in much the same commodities with the Northern Indians. There are other Nations or Tribes still further to the Westward daily coming in to them, and 'tis thought their Power and Interest reaches to the Westward of the Mississippi, if not across the continent. They are at present very well affected to the English, and seem fond of an Alliance with them—They formerly lived on the farther side of the Wabash, and were in the French Interest, who supplied them with some few Trifles at a most exorbitant Price—they were called by the French Miamees; but they have now revolted from them, and left their former habitations for the sake of trading with the English; and notwithstanding all their Artifices the French have used, they have not been able to recall them.

3. Jonathan Carver Considers the Mystery of the River of the West, 1766–1768

Although the exploration enterprise launched by Robert Rogers and Jonathan Carver failed to accomplish its mission, Carver's book, and the maps printed along with the text, had wide circulation and enduring influence. In the following brief selections, printed below, Carver reports on native people, western river systems, and the Rocky Mountains.

a. Carver and the Eastern Sioux

As soon as I had reached the land, two of the chiefs presented their hands to me, and led me, amidst the astonished multitude, who had most of them never seen a white man before, to a tent. Into this we entered, and according to the custom that universally prevails among every Indian nation, began to smoke the pipe of Peace. We had not sat long before the crowd became so great, both around, and upon the tent, that we were in danger of being crushed by its fall. On this we returned to the plain, where, having gratified the curiosity of the common people, their wonder abated, and ever after they treated me with great respect.

From the chiefs I met with the most friendly and hospitable reception; which induced me, as the season was so far advanced, to take up residence among them during the winter. To render my stay as comfortable as possible, I first endeavored to learn their language. This I soon did, so as to make myself perfectly intelligible, having before acquired some slight knowledge of the language of those Indians that live on the back of the settlements; and in consequence met with every accommodation their manner of living would afford. Nor did I want for such amusements as tended to make so long a period pass cheerfully away. I frequently hunted with them; and at other times beheld with pleasure their recreations and pastimes.

Sometimes I sat with the chiefs, and whilst we smoked the friendly pipe, entertained them, in return for the accounts they gave me of their wars and excursions, with a narrative of my own adventures and a description of all the battles fought between the English and the French in America, in many of which I had a personal share. They always paid great attention to my details, and asked many pertinent questions relative to the European methods of making war.

I held these conversations with them in a great measure to procure from them some information relative to the chief point I had constantly in view, that of gaining a knowledge of the situation and produce, both of their own country, and those that lay to the westward of them. Nor was I disappointed in my designs; for I procured from them much useful intelligence. They likewise drew for me plans of all the countries with which they were acquainted; but as I entertained no great opinion of their geographical knowledge, I placed not much dependence on them, and therefore think it unnecessary to give them to the public. Such as I afterwards found confirmed, by other accounts, or by my own observation, I made a part of the map prefixed to this work. They draw with a piece of burnt coal, taken from the hearth, upon the inside bark of the birch tree; which is as smooth as paper, and answers the same purposes, notwithstanding it is of a yellow cast. Their sketches are made in a rude manner, but they seem to give as just an idea of a country, although the plan is not so exact, as an experienced draftsman could do.

b. The Image of Western Rivers

From the intelligence I gained from the Naudowessie [Sioux] Indians, among whom I arrived the 7th of December [1766], and whose language I perfectly acquired during a residence of five months; and also from the accounts I afterwards obtained from the Assiniboins, who speak the same tongue, being a revolted band of the Naudowessies; and from the Killistinoes, neighbors of the Assiniboins, who speak the Chipeway language, and inhabit the heads of the River Bourbon [the Nelson River]; I say from these nations, I have learned that the four most capital rivers on the continent of North America, *viz.* the St. Lawrence, the Mississippi, the River Bourbon, and the Oregon or the River of the West have their sources in the same neighborhood. The waters of the three former are within thirty miles of each other; the latter, however, is rather farther west.

This shows that these parts are the highest lands in North America; and it is an instance not to be paralleled on the other three quarters of the globe, that four rivers of such magnitude should take their rise together, and each, after running separate courses, discharge their waters into different oceans at the distance of two thousand miles from their sources.

c. The Mandan Indians
   and the Shining Mountains

A little to the northwest of the heads of the Missouri and the St. Pierre [the Minnesota River], the Indians further told me, that there was a nation rather smaller and whiter than the neighboring tribes, who cultivate the ground, and (as far as I could gather from their expressions) in some measure, the arts. To this account they added that some of the nations, who inhabit those parts that lie to the west of the Shining Mountains [the Rocky

Mountains], have gold so plenty among them that they made their most common utensils of it. These mountains (which I shall describe more particularly hereafter) divide the waters that fall into the South Sea [the Pacific] from those that run into the Atlantic.

That range of mountains, of which the Shining Mountains are a part, begin at Mexico, and continuing northward on the back, or to the east of California, separate the waters of those numerous rivers that fall either into the Gulf of Mexico, or the Gulf of California. From thence continuing their course still northward, between the sources of the Mississippi and the rivers that run into the South Sea, they appear to end in about forty-seven or forty-eight degrees of north latitude; where a number of rivers arise, and empty themselves either into the South Sea, in Hudson's Bay, or into the waters that communicate between these two seas.

Among these mountains, those that lie to the west of the River St. Pierre, are called the Shining Mountains, from an infinite number of crystal stones, of an amazing size, with which they are covered, and which, when the sun shines full upon them, sparkle so as to be seen at a very great distance.

This extraordinary range of mountains is calculated to be more than three thousand miles in length, without any very considerable intervals, which I believe surpasses any thing of the kind in the other quarters of the globe. Probably in future ages they may be found to contain more riches in their bowels, than those of Indostan and Malabar, or that are produced on the Golden Coast of Guinea; nor will I except even the Peruvian Mines. To the west of these mountains, when explored by future Columbuses or Raleighs, may be found other lakes, rivers, and countries, full fraught with all the necessaries or luxuries of life; and where future generations may find an asylum, whether driven from their country by the ravages of lawless tyrants, or by religious persecutions, or reluctantly leaving it to remedy the inconveniences arising from a superabundance of inhabitants; whether, I say, impelled by these, or allured by hopes of commercial advantages, there is little doubt but their expectations will be fully gratified in these rich and unexhausted climes.

4. Alexander Henry the Elder Hears About Waterways to the Pacific, 1776

At a time when European geographers and exploration planners were intent on finding the Northwest Passage, Alexander Henry believed that he had discovered the passage. In this brief selection from his book *Travels and Adventures in Canada,* Henry recounts what he heard from Indian sources. This information, blended with his own ideas about the passage, became the geographic strategy for subsequent explorations.

O ur customers were from Lake Arabuthcow [Athabasca], of which, and the surrounding country, they were the proprietors, and at which they had wintered. They informed us, that there was, at the further end of that lake, a river, called Peace River, which descended from the Stony or Rocky Mountains, and from which mountains the distance to the *salt lake,* meaning the Pacific Ocean, was not great; that the lake emptied itself by a river, which ran to the northward, which they called *Kiratchinini Sibi,* or Slave River, and which flows into another lake, called by the same name; but, whether this lake was or was not the sea, or whether it emptied itself or not into the sea, they were unable to say. They were at war with the Indians who live at the bottom of the river, where the water is salt. They also made war on the people beyond the mountains, toward the Pacific Ocean, to which their warriors had frequently been near enough to see it. Though we conversed with these people in the Cree language, which is the usual medium of communication, they were Chepewyans or Rocky Mountain Indians.

5.   Peter Pond, Map of the Northwest, 1790

Peter Pond's late-eighteenth-century "Map of the Northwest, 1790," which is shown on the opposite page, tells a compelling story about paths to the Pacific Ocean. In drafting the map, Pond drew on firsthand experience, information collected from Indians, and the available body of geographic lore. Accepting the geographic wisdom of the time, Pond sketched the Rocky Mountains as a single, narrow range relatively close to the Pacific Coast. Although he had not seen it, Pond sketched a direct river connection between the Great Slave Lake and the Pacific Ocean by way of the ghost waterway, Cook's River. Peter Pond's map was both an image of the West and a strategy for building a western empire.

Peter Pond, Map of the Northwest, 1790

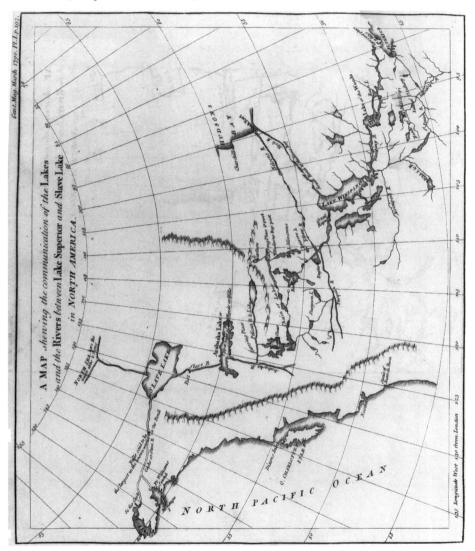

SUGGESTIONS FOR FURTHER READING

Axtell, James. *The Invasion Within: The Contest of Cultures in Colonial North America*. New York: Oxford University Press, 1985.

Cook, Warren L. *Flood Tide of Empire: Spain and the Pacific Northwest, 1543–1819*. New Haven: Yale University Press, 1973.

Eccles, W. J. *The Canadian Frontier, 1534–1760*. New York: Holt, Rinehart and Winston, 1969.

Gibson, James R. *Imperial Russia in Frontier America*. New York: Oxford University Press, 1976.

McConnell, Michael N. *A Country Between: The Upper Ohio Valley and Its Peoples, 1724–1774*. Lincoln: University of Nebraska Press, 1992.

Smith, Barbara S., and Redmond J. Barnett, eds. *Russian America: The Forgotten Frontier*. Tacoma: Washington State Historical Society, 1990.

White, Richard. *The Middle Ground: Indians, Empires, and Republics in the Great Lakes Region, 1650–1815*. Cambridge, England: Cambridge University Press, 1991.

CHAPTER 5

In Search of the Passage to India

In his "Passage to India" (1868), the poet Walt Whitman celebrated the engineering marvels of the age, among them the Suez Canal, the trans-Atlantic telegraph cable, and the soon-to-be-completed transcontinental Pacific railroad. But he understood that behind these wonders of technology lay something far more dynamic, far more powerful than any earth-moving machine or steam locomotive. This was the force of dream and imagination, a force that, the poet recognized, could draw strength from illusion and misconception. Whitman believed that all human achievement sprang from what he called "beams of the spirit" and "unloos'd dreams." And few dreams were more compelling than the drive to join Europe to Asia by way of America—to find the Northwest Passage, Whitman's "passage to India."

For Whitman, the passage provided a metaphor, a means to think about uniting humankind on one "vast terraqueous globe." Whitman was enough of a student of the North American past to recognize that "the marriage of continents, climates and oceans" had grown from the exploration experience of generations of Europeans and Americans. From Columbus, Cartier, and Coronado to Rogers, Carver, and Pond, dozens of explorers and travelers had searched for the passage. Each explorer and cartographer had marked a route that matched personal circumstances and national ambitions. Cartier's way to India had run up the St. Lawrence, while La Vérendrye had ridden on a quest for the Sea of the West. In Whitman's work, an intrepid company of "captains, voyagers, [and] explorers" fashioned a geography of the mind, a continent laced with ghost rivers and phantom seas. No matter where the traveler began—whether from St. Louis or Montreal or a lonely post in Canada's Athabasca country—Marco Polo's Cathay seemed just a motion away.

By the end of the eighteenth century, most European and American geographers had settled on one image of the American West, an image compelling in its simplicity and promising in what it offered to adventurers on the road to the Pacific. Like other Enlightenment scholars, geographers and cartographers believed that the world was a neatly balanced machine, something like a well-oiled clock. The idea of balance most appealed to them. They imagined the earth in symmetrical terms, each terrain feature or body of water matched by similar features and bodies. When geographers looked at North America, the idea of symmetrical landforms had significant (and misleading) results. The mountains of the West, they assumed, must be like those in the East. If the Appalachians had just a few long ridges and were pierced by many passes or water gaps, western mountains must have the same character. Geographers also applied the idea of balance in nature to North America's river systems. Encouraged by what they believed were accurate observations recorded by Jonathan Carver and other travelers, they maintained that the continent's great rivers all had sources closely situated to one another. Some waterways flowed east, and others ran west. With a voyage up one river and a short portage across a narrow set of mountains, the explorer could sail down another river to the Pacific. Not only did geographers balance mountains and rivers, they balanced the entire continent as well. The idea of a continental divide, first presented by French cartographers and then advanced by the likes of Robert Rogers and Jonathan Carver, precisely fit the grand idea of balance. The divide was conceived as a single, nearly straight line running north and south. In the mind's eye, there were rivers and passes everywhere in the West, all promising plain paths to the Pacific.

Few maps better express these dreams and expectations than Samuel Lewis's "Louisiana," prepared for Lewis's and Aaron Arrowsmith's *A New and Elegant Atlas of North America* (Boston, 1804). Lewis's map shows the Rockies as a single chain of mountains running north and south. Lewis's Rockies, like Thomas Jefferson's Blue Ridge Mountains, had many gaps or passes. And in this case a fortunate break occurred right at the imagined headwaters of the Missouri River. Lewis's map not only summarized the dominant geographic elements of this western vision but also made an unmistakable political and cultural statement. The West was an empty space, unformed by any civilized people. The West could be anything Europeans dreamed. The new American nation could make empty spaces into useful places. The West could be a trader's paradise or a farmer's eden. Native American nations were no more than strange names easily moved on the map from place to place and perhaps in the end completely replaced by an American population.

Jacques Clamorgan (*c.* 1734–1814) probably never saw the Lewis map, but he spent much of the 1790s pursuing the promises offered by the map's vision. Born in the West Indies, Clamorgan was a successful New Orleans merchant before heading up the Mississippi to St. Louis. St. Louis in the 1790s was already the center for an expanding fur trade. Ambitious and daring to a fault, Clamorgan quickly emerged as one of the city's most energetic merchants. In October 1793 he joined with other St. Louis entrepreneurs to found the Company of Explorers of the Upper Missouri. Sometimes known simply as the Missouri Company, the venture obtained a royal monopoly on the upper Missouri. Clamorgan's enterprise pursued two goals—profit and imperial defense. Company investors expected a good return on beaver pelts, and the Spanish government saw Clamorgan's traders as a means to fend off British commercial threats from North West Company and Hudson's Bay Company posts on the northern plains.

In the early summer of 1794, Clamorgan launched a major trading expedition up the Missouri. Led by Jean Baptiste Truteau, the traders got no farther than the Arikara Indian villages at the mouth of the Grand River in present-day South Dakota. The selection reprinted here contains portions of the detailed instructions Clamorgan prepared for his traders. While the Truteau expedition did not aim to cross the continent, Clamorgan knew that control of the Missouri and the northern Great Plains was essential to reach the more distant shore.

The Spanish search for the road to the Pacific became better organized and more focused when Clamorgan joined forces with James Mackay (1759–1822) and John Thomas Evans (1770–1799). Mackay was a Scottish trader and explorer who had begun his North American career in the Canadian fur trade. In 1787 he was part of a North West Company trading party that visited the Mandan Indians. Convinced that he would reap grander fortunes in St. Louis, Mackay traveled to Spanish Louisiana in 1793 and became a Spanish citizen. Soon he was Clamorgan's most able field agent. Mackay's ambitions went far beyond the Missouri, and it was probably his influence that made the Pacific a key Missouri Company goal.

John Thomas Evans brought to the Clamorgan-Mackay enterprise personal courage and a very large measure of self-deception. In the 1790s, Welsh men and women on both sides of the Atlantic were fired by the passions of literary and political nationalism. For many, the focus of that passion was the search for Madoc, the lost son of Prince Owain Gwynedd of Wales. The Madoc story, told time and again by poets and politicians, claimed that 300 years before Columbus, young Madoc sailed to North America and established a tribe of Welsh Indians. Over the years the location of this lost tribe shifted. By the end of the eighteenth century, some believed that the Mandan Indians were these people. John Evans was an agent of that belief and sailed up the Missouri seeking Welsh brothers and sisters among the earth-lodge people.

In August 1795, Evans, Mackay, and a party of more than thirty traders headed up the Missouri from St. Louis. Mackay and Evans established a trading post (Fort Charles) among the Omaha Indians in present-day Dakota County, Nebraska. The selection reprinted here is Mackay's letter to Clamorgan detailing the journey upriver and the establishment of trade relations with the Oto Indians. In November, Mackay sent Evans up the Missouri to contact the Mandans. Despite his best efforts, the Welsh adventurer got no farther on this reconnaissance than the confluence of the Missouri and the White rivers in present-day central South Dakota. Like so many other St. Louis traders, Evans was stopped by the Teton Sioux. The Sioux bands were intent on preserving their control of European goods entering the northern plains. While some plains native peoples like the Otos and Mandans were ready to do business with St. Louis, the Sioux saw the traders from the south as potential rivals and possible enemies.

Over the winter of 1795–1796, Mackay and Evans fashioned a new exploration strategy, which promised wealth for the Missouri Company and a northern path for Spanish power to thwart any imperial rivals. Whether consciously or not, Mackay and Evans borrowed ideas from such early French explorers as La Vérendrye and later travelers like Carver and Pond. The agents of the Missouri Company planned to discover a northwest passage, using the Missouri River and similar waterways on the west side of the continental divide. The plan's geography and strategy are made plain in the selection reprinted here—Mackay's instructions for Evans. On his second journey up the Missouri, Evans reached the Mandan villages, only to be embroiled in dangerous encounters with French traders working for the North West Company. These brushes with danger, as well as Indian information about the distance to the Pacific, convinced Evans that he could not accomplish the passage to India. The intrepid Welshman wintered with the Mandans and returned to St. Louis in the summer of 1797. While the Mackay-Evans travels produced little profit for Clamorgan's company, the information gathered and recorded in maps and notes eventually fell into the hands of Meriwether Lewis and William Clark.

Explorers and traders in Spanish employ were not the only European travelers at the end of the eighteenth century in search of the western sea. Alexander Mackenzie (1764–1820) both traveled farther than Mackay and Evans and accomplished the goal of finding a path to Pacific waters. Perhaps even more important, Mackenzie publicized his expeditions and ideas in

Voyages from Montreal (1801), one of the most influential exploration accounts of the nineteenth century.

Having immigrated to Canada from Scotland in 1774, Mackenzie soon entered the fur trade. The young and ambitious Scot quickly became connected to the expansion-minded North West Company. Mackenzie spent the winter of 1787–1788 with Peter Pond, from whom he learned lessons in both geography and imperial strategy. Pond's own reputation—he was implicated in one if not two murders of fellow traders—kept him from leading an expedition to find a passage to the Pacific. The opportunity fell to Mackenzie. Believing that the passage lay on a line northwest of Fort Chipewyan in present-day Saskatchewan, Mackenzie and a small party followed what is now the Mackenzie River in the northerly direction. By July 12, 1789, the first Mackenzie expedition had reached the edge not of the Pacific Ocean but of the Arctic Ocean.

Convinced that he needed better cartographic and surveying skills to make a successful search for the passage, Mackenzie spent time in England acquiring such knowledge. In the fall of 1792, he returned to Fort Chipewyan, ready for a second reconnaissance. With a party of six voyagers and two Indians, Mackenzie set off up Peace River, and he eventually reached the Dean Channel of the Pacific in late July 1793.

Alexander Mackenzie was the first European to cross the continent north of Mexico, but to the dismay of his company backers, he did not locate a useful commercial highway for the rapidly expanding fur business. While his fur-trade patrons were disappointed, Mackenzie moved on to grander ideas. As he made clear in the selection from *Voyages from Montreal* reprinted here, Mackenzie saw the Pacific Northwest in very complex terms. Always more than a trader and explorer, Mackenzie saw himself as an imperial planner, an agent of an expanding British domain. He imagined the valley of the Columbia River as the westernmost extension of that domain. Within the valley there were to be farms and villages, schools and churches—all the institutions of English life.

By the time Thomas Jefferson (1743–1826) read Mackenzie's *Voyages from Montreal* in the summer of 1802, the third president of the United States had already spent considerable time pondering the young republic's future in the West. Now and again during the 1780s and 1790s Jefferson had flirted with the idea of sponsoring expeditions to the West, but nothing ever came of such casual musings. Growing tensions with Spain over passage on the Mississippi, fears about the potential return of France to Louisiana, and reading Mackenzie changed all that. More than any other single thing, it was Mackenzie's ideas about English settlement in the West that troubled

ing with his Indian wife and their children, he struggled to make sense of the tangled courses of the Columbia and other western rivers. A skilled cartographer and diligent journal keeper, Thompson kept notes on Native American life in the northern Rockies that remain an invaluable ethnographic source.

The selection reprinted here is from Thompson's "Narrative," a manuscript prepared late in his life and based on his detailed journals. In the spring of 1807, Thompson and his family left Rocky Mountain House (located west of present-day Red Deer, Alberta) to explore the course of the Columbia River. In late June the Thompsons crossed the continental divide at Howse Pass northwest of present-day Banff and reached the Columbia River. Not recognizing it as the Columbia, Thompson called it the Kootenay. Ascending the Kootenay to near Lake Windermere, Thompson built Kootenay House. The selection reprinted here describes the winter of 1807–1808 at Kootenay House, including a vivid account of salmon spawning on the upper Columbia River.

Generations of explorers and travelers searched in vain for the Passage to India. While these adventurers eliminated one river and trail after another as the passage, the idea of a path across the continent remained as alive as ever. Some passage proponents continued to talk about the route as a way to link Asian, American, and European markets. Others saw the passage as an essential part of the economic growth of North America's vast interior.

Thomas Hart Benton (1782–1858), senator from Missouri, spent thirty years in Congress advocating American expansion and the search for the passage. After a visit to Monticello in late 1824, Benton believed that he was Thomas Jefferson's chosen successor as chief spokesman for empire in the West. When Benton's daughter Jessie married John Charles Frémont, Benton used all his power to advance Frémont's explorations.

In the following excerpt, taken from a speech delivered in 1849, Benton testified to the continuing appeal of the Passage to India. Benton's passage to India promised both the wealth from a global economy and prosperity in the American West.

1. Samuel Lewis, "Louisiana," 1804

Published on the eve of the Lewis and Clark expedition, the map shown on the opposite page exemplified the American image of the West. Samuel Lewis filled the West with navigable rivers, moved the continental divide some 800 miles to the west, and effectively erased the coastal range of mountains. In its most simplified form, this map was what Jefferson's explorers had in their minds when they went up the Missouri in 1804.

Samuel Lewis, "Louisiana," 1804

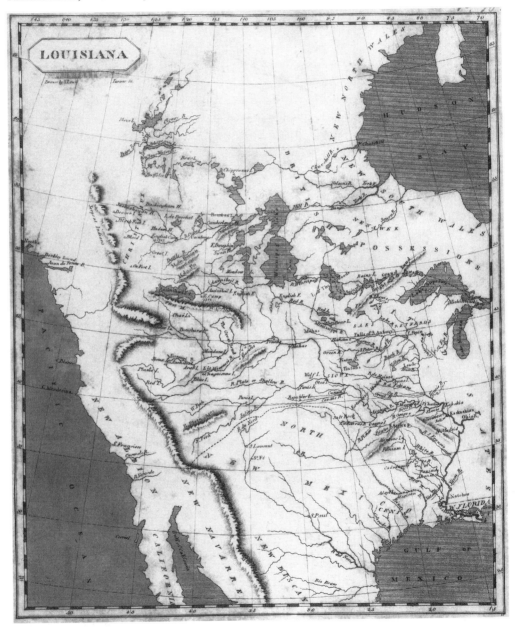

2. Jacques Clamorgan Directs Jean Baptiste Truteau to Build a Commercial Empire on the Missouri River, 1794

While most St. Louis fur-trade promoters in the 1790s did business contentedly in present-day Missouri, Jacques Clamorgan was driven by a larger dream. He envisioned a fur-trade empire with the Missouri River serving as the key part of a passage across the continent to the Pacific Ocean. In these travel directions for trader Jean Baptiste Truteau, Clamorgan revealed his own belief in that vision.

Señor Truteau on leaving this town shall proceed, with all possible foresight, to his destination, the Mandan nation, on the Upper Missouri to make there a settlement or establish an agency for the company.

He shall cause to be constructed, upon his arrival among the Mandans, a building, thirty feet long and fifteen feet wide, built of logs placed one upon another in English fashion, the corners joined and fitted by a kind of mortise; on the inside he shall have a partition made in order that one part may serve as a storeroom and the other as a lodging.

He shall cause to be constructed a fort, one hundred feet by eighty, which shall be so arranged as to enclose the buildings above mentioned, on the highest place in the (small) village, and as near as possible to the Missouri, so that the water may be near; he shall do this under the pretext of giving protection to the women and children in case of attack. There shall be only one door to enter the enclosure, which shall be opposite the space or yard between the two buildings. The stakes of the fort shall project seven feet above the ground, if possible, with strips of wood fastened above by nails; the stakes of the garden shall be only five feet.

Señor Truteau shall take with him little trees, fruit seeds or stones, and other seeds in order to have an orchard and garden.

It shall be the aim of Señor Truteau to keep the Indians in their simplicity of character, giving them counsel and advice only favorable to our commerce, animating them to increase their hunting and to improve their furs and skins in a suitable manner, well flayed to give them form and renown.

He shall fix a very high price on everything, keeping in mind that the prices of the armament are excessive and that without this precaution, the Company would sustain a loss.

He shall obtain all the knowledge and information possible concerning the separation, distance, and direction of the nations which he may see or of which he may hear, referring to the plan which I deliver to him in order that he may know his whereabouts, and to change or correct the location of the nations and rivers, adding those that are found and not yet on the plan.

He shall inform himself of the distance to the Rocky Mountains which are located west of the source of the Missouri.

He shall attempt to have friendly relations with the Indians who live on the other side of the Rocky Mountains, on which there are numerous nations, known under the name Serpientes [Shoshones] and to find out from them, if they have any knowledge of the Sea of the West and if the waters of the rivers on the other side of the Rocky Mountains flow westward.

3.   James Mackay Reports to Jacques Clamorgan from the Oto Indian Village at the Mouth of the Platte River, 1795

Like his Canadian contemporaries, Alexander Mackenzie and David Thompson, James Mackay combined geographic discovery and commercial enterprise. This letter details business strategy and plans for further exploration.

I arrived here the fourteenth of this month after a forty-four days' march. The bad weather and one of my pirogues [large dugout canoe or open boat] of my convoy, which has continually filled with water, delayed me, and will delay me in reaching the Mahas [Omahas].

I must recommend to you never to load your barges too much and always to have at the head some leaders of ability. I ought not to have to tell you, nor to forewarn you, of the indispensable necessity of having a person possessed of a great talent with the Indians remain at the post of the Mahas at the head of your operations. You know that this is a place of importance for the new commerce and for communication with the Mandans.

If the company is to continue its commerce in this distant country, it is absolutely indispensable to have the village of the Otos in your power. Otherwise, your pirogues will be more or less pillaged each year. I have promised them that you will have a fort built among them next year, in order to protect them against their enemies; and that they would have many guns for their hunt; for they complained of not having a fourth of that which they have need. In these two types of promises, I hope that you will not make me out a liar, seeing that the first, under the guise of favoring them, will serve to hold them in check, and that the second is absolutely inseparable from our interests. I have contracted this obligation with them, on condition that they behave well towards the agents that you will send them and toward the boats which might ascend to the Mandans. They have decided on the spot where they wish the fort to be built—at the entrance of the Platte River, where they intend to place their village. This situation will be advantageous. The agent that I have placed there for the trade with them will apprise you of their conduct, and of means of subjecting them to our interests. If it should occur that the Otos do not keep their word and behave themselves badly, deprive them of all help the next year. We will gain much from this by showing them that their need depends absolutely on the good will of the company, and that, in default of us, they must no longer count on the aid of other traders, each accustomed to lie to them in pursuance of his own interests. But if their conduct is honest remember well to carry out my promise. You can not conceive the difficulties one has in passing through this nation, in spite of the presents we must give them. The chiefs have no command, and this nation is so rough that one has trouble to move them, even in their own interest. They complain that Motardi, Quenell and other traders who have come among them for several years, have spoken so much deceit, have cheated so much, and have made them so many promises of which not one has ever been fulfilled, that they wish to believe nothing now without seeing. To tell the truth, they are in a kind of anarchy which will lead them to become dangerous enemies of all the commerce of the Upper Missouri. This danger will increase if this post continues to be open as usual each year to all types of traders who are only interested in the present, and do not worry about the future.

I am satisfied enough with the equipment of my whole convoy, but I wish you had given me better interpreters for the Maha. Many of those people at St. Louis who think they understand the Indians and who on that basis, wish to be sent out to the Indians, when they arrive here, are only children. We need some good, shrewd interpreters.

If the government does not grant the Otos to you as the key to our distant interests, it is absolutely necessary to purchase that trade from those men who might be its proprietors, if, however, you think that we might be able to sustain the increase of expense. Otherwise, we must withdraw as well as we can from the career of discoveries, and give up now, rather than later, our ruinous enterprise.

4. James Mackay Sends John Thomas Evans to the Western Sea, 1796

Seven years before Thomas Jefferson prepared comprehensive exploration directions for Meriwether Lewis, James Mackay drafted similar instructions for John Thomas Evans. Like Jefferson, Mackay understood exploration in broad terms and urged Evans to study plants, animals, and native cultures on his way to the Pacific.

From the time of your departure from this fort until your return to the place where I will be living on the Missouri, you will keep a journal of each day and month of the year to avoid any error in the observations of the important journey which you are undertaking. In your journal you will place all that will be remarkable in the country that you will traverse; likewise the route, distance, latitude and longitude, when you can observe it, also the winds and weather. You will keep another journal in which you will make note of all the minerals; vegetables; timber; rocks; flint-stone; territory; production; animals; game; reptiles; lakes; rivers; mountains; portages, with their extent and location; and the different fish and shellfish which the waters may contain. You will insert in the same journal all that may be remarkable and interesting, particularly the different nations; their numbers, manners, customs, government, sentiments, language, religion, and all other circumstances relative to their manner of living.

You will take heed not to fall in with some parties of savages, where there are neither women nor children, as they are almost always on the warpath. It would not be prudent to appear at any nation if you can avoid it, unless it be in their villages; and in spite of this be well on your guard. You will never fire any guns except in case of necessity; you will never cut any wood except with a knife unless it should be strictly necessary; you will never build a fire without true need, and you will avoid having the smoke seen from afar, camping if possible in the valleys. You will not camp too early and will always leave before daybreak; you will always be on guard against ambushes and will always have your arms in good condition, changing the tinder evening and morning, and you will never separate them from you or place them in the hands of savages. When you see some nations, raise your flag a long way off as a sign of peace, and never approach without speaking to them from a distance. When you enter a village, stop and ground your arms at a small distance until they come to receive and conduct you. Appear always on guard and never be fearful or timid, for the savages are not generally bold, but will act in a manner to make you afraid of them. If, however, they see that you are courageous and venturesome they will soon yield to your wishes. You will recollect that the pipe is the symbol of peace and that when they have smoked with you there is no longer any danger; nevertheless you must beware of treason.

Say to the savages whom you will meet on your route that the white people, who come to meet them, speaking of our Company, still have many

ing spring up with these foreigners any jealousy which would be prejudicial to the success of your journey. You will not neglect any interesting observation on the sea-shore and, although there may be some things which do not appear to merit the least attention, nevertheless, in the journey of this nature, everything is sometimes of great importance. Do not fail to measure the rise of the sea in its ebb and flow.

As soon as you will have visited the sea-shore sufficiently, you will return from it immediately, with as much vigilance as you can to this place, or to the spot where I may be at the time, either among the Mandans or elsewhere. You will take steps to return by a different route from that which you have taken on your way out if you believe it practical; but mind that if you find the route by which you will have passed rather straight and easy for traveling by water in a canoe or other craft, it will be wiser to return by the same route, and, in case there are portages to make from one river to another or from one rapids to another, see whether the place permits the forming of a settlement.

In your orders be strict with your detachment and take care that no offense is committed against the nations through which you pass, especially by the connection that they may seek to have with the women, a thing which is ordinarily the origin of dissatisfaction and discord with the savages.

Take care, above all, to bring with you a collection of the products of the sea-shore: animals, vegetables, minerals, and other curious things that you find, especially some skins of sea-otters and other sea animals and shell-fish which cannot be found in any fresh water. A portion of each will be an unquestionable proof of your journey to the sea-shore; but, if you can find there any civilized people who wish to give you an affidavit of your journey in whatever language they speak, this will be an additional proof of the validity of your journey.

5. Alexander Mackenzie Lays Plans for British Control of the West, 1801

Readers of *Voyages from Montreal* found not one book but two. The first was a pedestrian account of Mackenzie's two expeditions in search of a commercially useful route to the Pacific. The second book, tacked onto the end of the travel narrative, presented Mackenzie's plans for British domain in the West. This excerpt represents the core of that strategy.

The discovery of a passage by sea, Northeast or Northwest from the Atlantic to the Pacific Ocean, has for many years excited the attention of governments, and encouraged the enterprising spirit of individuals. The non-existence, however, of any such practical passage being at length determined, the practicability of a passage through the continents of Asia and America becomes an object of consideration. The Russians, who first discovered that, along the coasts of Asia no useful or regular navigation existed, opened an interior communication by rivers, and through that long and wide-extended continent, to the strait that separates Asia from America, over which they passed to the adjacent islands and continent of the latter. Our situation, at length, is in some degree similar to theirs; the non-existence of a practicable passage by sea, and the existence of one through the continent, are clearly proved; and it requires only the countenance and support of the British Government, to increase in a very ample proportion this national advantage, and secure the trade of that country to its subjects.

[Mackenzie then proposed a commercial monopoly uniting the North West Company and the Hudson's Bay Company.]

By these waters [the Nelson River] that discharge themselves into Hudson's Bay at Port Nelson, it is proposed to carry on the trade to their source, at the head of the Saskatchewan River, which rises in the Rocky Mountains, not eight degrees of longitude from the Pacific Ocean. The Tacoutche or Columbia River flows also from the same mountains, and discharges itself likewise in the Pacific. Both of them are capable of receiving ships at their mouths, and are navigable throughout for boats.

The distance between these waters [the Columbia and Nelson rivers] is only known from the report of the Indians. If, however, this communication should prove inaccessible, the route I pursued, though longer, in consequence of the great angle it makes to the North, will answer every necessary purpose. But whatever course may be taken from the Atlantic, the Columbia is the line of communication from the Pacific Ocean, pointed out by nature, as it is the only navigable river in the whole extent of Vancouver's [Captain George Vancouver] minute survey of that coast: its banks also form the first level country in all the Southern extent of continental coast from Cook's entry, and, consequently, the most Northern situation fit for colonization, and suitable to the residence of a civilized people. By opening this intercourse between the Atlantic and Pacific Oceans, and forming regular establishments through the interior, and at both extremes, as well as along the coasts and islands, the entire command of the fur trade of North America might be obtained, from latitude 48 North to the pole, except that portion of it which the Russians have in the Pacific. To this may be added the fishing in both seas, and the markets of the four quarters of the globe. Such would be the field for commercial enterprise, and incalculable would be the produce of it, when supported by the operations of that credit and capital which Great Britain so pre-eminently possesses. Then would this country begin to be remunerated for the expenses it has sustained in discovering and surveying the coast of the Pacific Ocean, which is at present left to American adventurers, who without regularity or capital, or the desire of conciliating future confidence, look altogether to the interest of the moment. They, therefore, collect all the skins they can procure, and in any manner that suits them, and having exchanged them at Canton for the produce of China, return to their own country. Such adventurers, and many of them, as I have been informed, have been very successful, would instantly disappear from before a well-regulated trade.

6. Thomas Jefferson Prepares Meriwether Lewis for the Pacific Expedition, 1803

Jefferson believed that exploration was not so much travel to strange lands as a journey guided by carefully prepared questions. His instructions for Lewis were designed as a series of questions, ranging from botany and zoology to geography and ethnography.

Your situation as Secretary to the President of the U.S. has made you acquainted with the objects of my confidential message of January 18, 1803 to the legislature; you have seen the act they passed, which, tho' expressed in general terms, was meant to sanction those objects, and you are appointed to carry them into execution.

Instruments for ascertaining, by celestial observations, the geography of the country through which you will pass, have been already provided. Light articles for barter and presents among the Indians, arms for your attendants, say for from 10 to 12 men, boats, tents, and other travelling apparatus, with ammunition, medicine, surgical instruments and provisions you will have prepared with such aids as the Secretary at War can yield in his department; and from him also you will receive authority to engage among our troops, by voluntary agreement, the number of attendants above mentioned, over whom you, as their commanding officer, are invested with all powers the laws can give in such a case.

As your movements while within the limits of the U.S. will be better directed by occasional communications, adapted to circumstances as they arise, they will not be noticed here. What follows will respect your proceedings after your departure from the United States.

Your mission has been communicated to the ministers here from France, Spain, and Great Britain, and through them to their governments; and such assurances given them as to it's objects, as we trust will satisfy them. The country of Louisiana has been ceded by Spain to France, and possession by this time probably given, the passport you have from the minister of France, the representative of the present sovereign of the country, will be a protection with all it's subjects; and that from the minister of England will entitle you to the friendly aid of any traders of that allegiance with whom you may happen to meet.

The object of your mission is to explore the Missouri river, and such principal stream of it, as, by it's course and communication with the waters of the Pacific ocean, whether the Columbia, Oregon, Colorado or any other river may offer the most direct and practicable water communication across this continent for the purposes of commerce.

Beginning at the mouth of the Missouri, you will take careful observations of latitude and longitude, at all remarkable points on the river, and especially at the mouths of rivers, at rapids, at islands, and other places and objects distinguished by such natural marks and characters of a durable kind, as that they might with certainty be recognized hereafter. The courses of the river between these points of observation may be supplied by the compass, the log-line, and by time, corrected by the observations themselves. The variations of the compass too, in different places, should be noticed.

The interesting points of the portage between the heads of the Missouri, and of the water offering the best communication with the Pacific ocean, should also be fixed by observation, and the course of that water to the ocean, in the same manner as that of the Missouri.

Your observations are to be taken with great pains and accuracy, to be entered distinctly and intelligibly for others as well as yourself, to comprehend all the elements necessary, with the aid of the usual tables, to fix the latitude and longitude of the places at which they were taken, and are to be rendered to the war office, for the purpose of having the calculations made concurrently by proper persons within the U.S. Several copies of these as well as of your other notes should be made at leisure times, and put into the care of the most trust-worthy of your attendants, to guard, by multiplying them, against the accidental losses to which they will be exposed. A further guard would be that one of these copies be on the paper of the birch, as less liable to injury from damp than common paper.

The commerce which may be carried on with the people inhabiting the line you will pursue, renders a knolege of those people important. You will therefore endeavor to make yourself acquainted, as far as a diligent pursuit of your journey shall admit, with the names of the nations and their numbers;

> the extent and limits of their possessions;
>
> their relations with other tribes of nations;
>
> their language, traditions, monuments;
>
> their ordinary occupations in agriculture, fishing, hunting, war, arts, and the implements for these;
>
> their food, clothing, and domestic accomodations;
>
> the diseases prevalent among them, and the remedies they use;
>
> moral and physical circumstances which distinguish them from the tribes we know;
>
> peculiarities in their laws, customs, and dispositions;
>
> and articles of commerce they may need or furnish, and to what extent.

And, considering the interest which every nation has in extending and strengthening the authority of reason and justice among the people around them, it will be useful to acquire what knolege you can of the state of morality, religion, and information among them; as it may better enable those who may endeavor to civilize and instruct them, to adapt their measures to the existing notions and practices of those on whom they are to operate.

Other objects worthy of notice will be the soil and face of the country, its growth and vegetable productions, especially those not of the U.S., the animals of the country generally, and especially those not known in the U.S., the remains or accounts of any which may be deemed rare or extinct; the mineral productions of every kind; but more particularly metals, limestone, pit coal, and saltpetre; salines and mineral waters, noting the temperature of the last, and such circumstances as may indicate their character; volcanic appearances; climate, as characterized by the thermometer, by the proportion of rainy, cloudy, and clear days, by lightening, hail, snow, ice, by the access and recess of frost, by the winds prevailing at different seasons, the dates at which particular plants put forth or lose their flower, or leaf, times of appearance of particular birds, reptiles or insects.

Although your route will be along the channel of the Missouri, yet you will endeavor to inform yourself, by enquiry, of the character and extent of the country watered by its branches, and especially on its Southern side. The North river or Rio Bravo which runs into the gulph of Mexico, and the North river, or Rio Colorado which runs into the gulph of California, are understood to be the principal streams heading opposite to the waters of the Missouri, and running Southwardly. Whether the dividing grounds between the Missouri and them are mountains or flat lands, what are their distance from the Missouri, the character of the intermediate country, and the people inhabiting it, are worthy of particular enquiry. The Northern waters of the Missouri are less to be enquired after, because they have been ascertained to a considerable degree, and are still in a course of ascertainment by English traders, and travellers. But if you can learn anything certain of the most Northern source of the Missisipi, and of its position relatively to the lake of the woods, it will be interesting to us.

Two copies of your notes at least and as many more as leisure will admit, should be made and confided to the care of the most trusty individuals of your attendants. Some account too of the path of the Canadian traders from the Missisipi, at the mouth of the Ouisconsing [Wisconsin] to where it strikes the Missouri, and of the soils and rivers in its course, is desireable.

In all your intercourse with the natives, treat them in the most friendly and conciliatory manner which their own conduct will admit; allay all jealousies as to the object of your journey, satisfy them of its innocence, make them acquainted with the position, extent, character, peaceable and commercial dispositions of the U.S., of our wish to be neighborly, friendly and useful to them, and of our dispositions to a commercial intercourse with them; confer with them on the points most convenient as mutual emporiums, and the articles of most desireable interchange for them and us. If a few of their influential chiefs, within practicable distance, wish to visit us, arrange such a visit with them, and furnish them with authority to call on our officers, on their entering the U.S. to have them conveyed to this place at the public expense. If any of them should wish to have some of their young people brought up with us, and taught such arts as may be useful to them, we will receive, instruct, and take care of them. Such a mission, whether of influential chiefs or of young people, would give some security to your own party. Carry with you some matter of the kine-pox; inform those of them with whom you may be, of its efficacy as a preservative from the smallpox; and instruct and encourage them in the use of it. This may be done wherever you winter.

As it is impossible for us to foresee in what manner you will be received by those people, whether with hospitality or hostility, so is it impossible to prescribe the exact degree of perseverance with which you are to pursue your journey. We value too much the lives of citizens to offer them to probable

destruction. Your numbers will be sufficient to secure you against the unau-
thorized opposition of individuals or of small parties; but if a superior force,
authorized, or not, by a nation, should be arrayed against your further passage, and inflexibly determined to arrest it, you must decide its farther pursuit, and return. In the loss of yourselves, we should lose also the information you will have acquired. By returning safely, you may enable us to renew
the essay with better calculated means. To your own discretion therefore
must be left the degree of danger you may risk, and the point at which you
should decline, only saying we wish you to err on the side of your safety, and
to bring back your party safe even if it be with less information.

As far up the Missouri as the white settlements extend, an intercourse
will probably be found to exist between them and the Spanish posts of St.
Louis opposite Cahokia, or Ste. Genevieve opposite Kaskaskia. From still
further up the river, the traders may furnish a conveyance for letters. Beyond
that, you may perhaps be able to engage Indians to bring letters for the government to Cahokia or Kaskaskia, on promising that they shall there receive
such special compensation as you shall have stipulated with them. Avail
yourself of these means to communicate to us, at seasonable intervals, a
copy of your journal, notes and observations, of every kind, putting into
cypher whatever might do injury if betrayed.

Should you reach the Pacific ocean inform yourself of the circumstances
which may decide whether the furs of those parts may not be collected as
advantageously at the head of the Missouri (convenient as is supposed to the
waters of the Colorado and Oregon or Columbia) as at Nootka sound, or
any other point of that coast; and that trade be consequently conducted
through the Missouri and U.S. more beneficially than by the circumnaviga-
tion now practised.

On your arrival on that coast endeavor to learn if there be any port within your reach frequented by the sea vessels of any nation, and send two of
your trusty people back by sea, in such way as shall appear practicable, with
a copy of your notes: and should you be of opinion that the return of your
party by the way they went will be eminently dangerous, then ship the
whole, and return by sea, by way either of cape Horn, or the cape of good
Hope, as you shall be able. As you will be without money, clothes or provisions, you must endeavor to use the credit of the U.S. to obtain them, for
which purpose open letters of credit shall be furnished you, authorising you
to draw upon the Executive of the U.S. or any of its officers, in any part of
the world, on which draughts can be disposed of, and to apply with our rec-
ommendations to the Consuls, agents, merchants, or citizens of any nation
with which we have intercourse, assuring them, in our name, that any aids
they may furnish you, shall be honorably repaid, and on demand. Our

consuls Thomas Hewes at Batavia in Java, William Buchanan in the Isles of France and Bourbon, and John Elmslie at the Cape of good Hope will be able to supply your necessities by draughts on us.

Should you find it safe to return by the way you go, after sending two of your party round by sea, or with your whole party, if no conveyance by sea can be found, do so; making such observations on your return, as may serve to supply, correct or confirm those made on your outward journey.

On re-entering the U.S. and reaching a place of safety, discharge any of your attendants who may desire and deserve it, procuring for them immediate payment of all arrears of pay and clothing which may have incurred since their departure, and assure them that they shall be recommended to the liberality of the legislature for the grant of a soldier's portion of land each, as proposed in my message to Congress, and repair yourself with your papers to the seat of government to which I have only to add my sincere prayer for your safe return.

7. Meriwether Lewis Recounts His First Meeting with the Lemhi Shoshones, 1805

Few moments in the history of North American exploration are more dramatic than the meeting of Lewis's party with members of Cameahwait's band of Lemhi Shoshones on the continental divide between present-day Montana and Idaho. Lewis wrote a colorful account of the event and characteristically filled it with telling details of Shoshone life and the natural history of the region.

We [Lewis, George Drouillard, John Shields, and Hugh McNeal] set out very early on the Indian road which still led us through an open broken country in a westerly direction. A deep valley appeared to our left at the base of a high range of mountains which extended from S.E. to N.W. [the Lemhi Range and the Lemhi River Valley] having their sides better clad with pine timber than we had been accustomed to see. The mountains and their tops were also partially covered with snow. At the distance of five miles the road after leading us down a long descending valley for 2 miles brought us to a large creek about 10 yards wide; this we passed and on rising the hill beyond it had a view of a handsome little valley to our left of about a mile in width through which from the appearance of the timber I conjectured that a river passed. I saw near the creek some bushes of the white maple, the small shumate of the small species with the winged rib, and a species of honeysuckle much in its growth and leaf like the small honeysuckle of the Missouri only rather larger and bears a globular berry as large as a garden pea and as white as wax. This berry is formed of a thin smooth pellicle which envellopes a soft white musilagenous substance in which there are several small brown seed irregularly scattered or intermixed without any sell [cell] or perceptable membranous covering. We had proceeded about four miles through a wavy plain parallel to the valley or river bottom when at a distance of about a mile we saw two women, a man and some dogs on an eminence immediately before us. They appeared to view us with attention and two of them after a few minutes sat down as if to wait our arrival. We continued our usual pace towards them. When we had arrived within half a mile of them I directed the party to halt and leaving my pack and rifle I took a flag which I unfurled and advanced singly towards them. The women soon disappeared behind the hill. The man continued until I arrived within a hundred yards of him and then likewise absconded. Tho' I frequently repeated the word *tab-ba-bone* [a Shoshone word that may mean "people coming from the east," an expression learned from Sacagawea] sufficiently loud for him to have heard it. I now hastened to the top of the hill where they had stood but could see nothing of them. The dogs were less shy than their masters. They came about me pretty close. I therefore thought of tying a handkerchief about one of their necks with some beads and other trinkets and then let them loose to search their fugitive owners thinking by this means to convince them of our pacific disposition towards them but the dogs would not suffer me to take hold of them; they also soon disappeared. I now made signal for the men to come on. They joined me and we pursued the back track of these Indians which lead us along the same road which we had been traveling. The road was dusty and appeared to have been much traveled lately both by men and horses. These prairies are very poor. The soil is of a light yellow clay, intermixed with small smooth gravel, and produces little else but prickly pears, and bearded grass about 3 inches high. The prickly pear are of three species, that with a broad leaf common to the Missouri; that of a globular form also common to the upper part of the Missouri, and more especially after it enters the Rocky Mountains, also a third peculiar to this country. It consists of small circular thick leaves with a much greater number of thorns. These thorns are stronger and appear to be barbed. The leaves grow from the margins of each other as in the broad leafed pear of the Missouri, but are so slightly attached that when the thorn touches your moccasin it adhears and brings with it the leaf covered in every direction with many others. This is much the most troublesome plant of the three. We had not continued our route more than a mile when we were so fortunate as to meet with three female savages. The short and steep ravines which we passed concealed us

The Lewis and Clark expedition opened diplomatic relations with many western tribes. This early illustration, taken from the published journal of expedition member Sergeant Patrick Gass, records a meeting along the Missouri River in 1804.

from each other until we arrived within 30 paces. A young woman immediately took to flight, an elderly woman and a girl of about 12 years old remained. I instantly laid by my gun and advanced towards them. They appeared much alarmed but saw that we were too near for them to escape by flight. They therefore seated themselves on the ground, holding down their heads as if reconciled to die which they expected no doubt would be their fate. I took the elderly woman by the hand and raised her up, repeated the word *tab-ba-bone,* and strip up my shirt sleeve to show her my skin; to prove to her the truth of the assertion that I was a white man for my face and hands which have been constantly exposed to the sun were quite as dark as their own. They appeared instantly reconciled, and the men coming up I gave these women some beads, a few moccasin awls, some pewter looking-glasses, and a little paint. I directed Drewyer [Drouillard] to request the old woman to recall the young woman who had run off to some distance by this time fearing she might alarm the camp before we approached and might so exasperate the natives that they would perhaps attack us without enquiring who we were. The old woman did as she was requested and the fugitive soon returned almost out of breath. I bestowed an equivilant portion of trinkets on her. I now painted their tawny cheeks with some vermilion which with this nation is emblematic of peace. After they had become composed, I informed them by signs that I wished them to conduct us to their camp, that we were anxious to become acquainted with the chiefs and warriors of their nation. They readily obeyed and we set out, still pursuing the road down the river. We had marched about 2 miles when we met a party of about 60 warriors mounted on excellent horses who came in nearly full speed. When they arrived I advanced towards them with the flag, leaving my gun with the party about 50 paces behind me. The chief and two others who were a little in advance of the main body spoke to the women, and they informed them who we were and exultingly showed the presents which had been given them. These men then advanced and embraced me very affectionately in their way which is by putting their left arm over your right shoulder clasping your back, which they apply their left cheek to yours and frequently vociforate the word *ah-hi-e, ah-hi-e* that is, I am much pleased, I am much rejoiced. Both parties now advanced and we were all carressed and besmeared with their grease and paint until I was heartily tired of the national hug. I now had the pipe lit and gave them smoke; they seated themselves in a circle around us and pulled off their moccasins before they would receive or smoke the pipe. This is a custom among them as I afterwards learned indicative of a sacred obligation of sincerity in their profession of friendship given by the act of receiving and smoking the pipe of a stranger. Of which is as much as to say that they wish they may always go barefoot if they are not sincere; a pretty heavy penalty if they are to march through the plains of their country. After smoking a few pipes with them I distributed some trifles among them, with which they seemed much pleased particularly with the blue beads and vermilion. I now informed the chief that the object of our visit was a friendly one, that after we should reach his camp I would undertake to explain to him fully those objects, who we were, from whence we had come and whither we were going; that in the meantime I did not care how soon we were in motion, as the sun was very warm and no water at hand. They now put on their moccasins, and the principal chief Ca-me-ah-wait made a short speech to the warriors. I gave him the flag which I informed him was an emblem of peace among the white men and now that it had been received by him it was to be respected as the bond of union between us. I desired him to march on, which [he] did and we followed him; the dragoons [Lewis means the Indian warriors] moved on in squadron in our rear. After we had marched about a mile in this order he halted them and gave a second harange; after which six or eight of the young men rode forward to their encampment and no further regularity was observed in the order of march. I afterwards understood that the Indians we had first seen

Based on a drawing by artist Charles B. J. F. St. Memin, this engraving shows Meriwether Lewis wearing the ermine tippit or cape given to him by Shoshone headman Cameahwait.

this morning had returned and alarmed the camp. These men had come armed cap a pe [head to foot] for action expecting to meet with their enemies the Minetares of Fort de Prarie whom they call Pahkees [the Piegan Blackfeet]. They were armed with bows, arrows and shield except three whom I observed with small pieces [guns] as the North West Company furnish the natives with which they had obtained from the Rocky Mountains Indians [probably the Crow Indians] on the Yellowstone river with which they are at peace. On our arrival at their encampment on the river in a handsome level and fertile bottom at the distance of 4 miles from where we had first met them. They introduced us to a lodge made of willow brush and an old leather lodge which had been prepared for our reception by the young men which the chief had dispatched for that purpose. Here we were seated on green boughs and the skins of antelopes. One of the warriors then pulled up the grass in the center of the lodge forming a small circle of about 2 feet in diameter. The chief next produced his pipe and native tobacco and began a long ceremony of the pipe when we were requested to take off our moccasins, the chief having previously taken his off as well as all the warriors present. This we complied with. The chief then lit his pipe at the fire kindled in this little magic circle, and standing on the opposite side of the circle uttered a speech of several minutes in length at the conclusion of which he pointed the stem to the four cardinal points of the heavens first beginning at the East and ending with the North. He now presented the pipe to me as if desirous that I should smoke, but when I reached my hand to receive it, he drew it back and repeated the same ceremony three times, after which he pointed the stem first to the heavens then to the center of the magic circle, smoked himself with three whifs and held the pipe until I took as many as I thought proper; he then held it to each of the white persons and then gave it to be consumed by his warriors. This pipe was made of a dense semitransparent green stone [green serpentine] very highly polished about 2 and a half inches long and of an oval figure, the bowl being in the same direction with the stem. A small piece of burned clay is placed in the bottom of the bowl to separate the tobacco from the end of the stem and is of an irregularly rounded figure not fitting the tube perfectly close in order that the smoke may pass. Their tobacco is of the same kind of that used by the Minnetares [Hidatsa Indians], Mandans, and Ricares [Arikara Indians] of the Missouri. The Shoshones do not cultivate this plant, but obtain it from the Rocky Mountain Indians and some of the bands of their own nation who live further south. I now explained to them the objects of our journey etc. All the women and children of the camp were shortly collected about the lodge to indulge themselves in looking at us, we being the first white persons they had ever seen. After the ceremony of the pipe was over I distributed the remainder of the small articles I had brought with me among the women and children. By this time it was late in the evening and we had not tasted any food since the evening before. The chief informed me that they had nothing but berries to eat and gave us some cakes of serviceberries and choke cherries which had been dried in the sun; of these I made a hearty meal, and then walked to the river, which I found about 40 yards wide, very rapid clear and about 3 feet deep. The banks low and abrupt as those of the upper part of the Missouri, and the bed formed of loose stones and gravel. Cameahwait informed me that this stream discharged itself into another [the Salmon River] doubly as large at the distance of half a days march which came from the S.W. but he added on further inquiry that there was but little more timber below the junction of those rivers than I saw here, and that the river was confined between inacessable mountains, was very rapid and rocky insomuch that it was impossible for us to pass either by land or water down this river to the great lake where the white men lived as he had been informed. This was unwelcome information but I still hoped that this account had been exaggerated with a view to detain us among them. As to timber I could discover not any that would answer the purpose of constructing canoes or in short more than was barely necessary for fuel consisting of the narrow leafed cottonwood and willow, also the red willow, choke cherry, serviceberry and a few current bushes such as were common on the Missouri. These people [the Lemhi Shoshones] had been attacked by the Minetares of Fort de Prarie this spring and about 20 of them killed and taken prisoner. On this occasion they lost a great part of their horses and all their lodges except that which they had erected for our accommodation. They were now living in lodges of a conic figure made of willow brush. I still observe a great number of horses feeding in every direction around their camp and therefore entertain but little doubt that we shall be enabled to furnish ourselves with an adequate number to transport our stores even if we are compelled to travel by land over these mountains. On my return to my lodge an Indian called me to his bower and gave me a small morsel of the flesh of an antelope boiled, and a piece of a fresh salmon roasted, both which I ate with a very good relish. This was the first salmon I had seen and perfectly convinced me that we were on the waters of the Pacific Ocean. The course of this river is a little to the North of west as far as I can discover it; and is bounded on each side by a range of high mountains. Though those on the east side are lowest and more distant from the river.

This evening the Indians entertained us with their dancing nearly all night. At 12 O'Clock I grew sleepy and retired to rest leaving the men to amuse themselves with the Indians. I observe no essential difference between the music and manner of dancing among this nation and those of the

9. Simon Fraser Runs One of the Northwest's Most Dangerous Rivers, 1808

Simon Fraser's name and exploits are almost unknown outside the Canadian Northwest, but in the first years of the nineteenth century, the North West Company gave him one of the most demanding exploration assignments possible. Fraser ran the river that now bears his name and found that it could not be part of a fur-trade transportation system.

a. Meeting with the Atnah and Tauten Indians, May 30, 1808

We embarked at 5 A.M. Experienced a strong current. The country all along is charming, and apparently well inhabited; having seen a large number of houses. At 6 we put to shore at a large house; found a cache of fish. After taking a few salmon and leaving the value we secured the rest for the owners. Observed some vestiges of horses at this place. A little below we put ashore again, and left a bale of salmon in cache. This caused some delay. Passed several rapids in the afternoon. This country, which is interspersed with meadows and hills, dales and high rocks, has upon the whole a romantic but pleasant appearance.

Continuing our course expeditiously, on a sudden we perceived some of the natives on the left shore seemingly in great confusion. We crossed to the right and landed at a large house. Our Indians [Fraser's guides] then called out to the strangers on the opposite shore, informing them that we were white people going to the sea.

A woman of the Atnah nation who happened to be within hearing on our side of the water, came running towards us, speaking as loud as possible, but our interpreter could not understand her—yet she still continued speaking, and endeavoured to supply the deficiency by signs. In this manner she continued, at one time addressing the people on the other side, at another directing her discourse to us; in the meantime we crossed the river. But we were still on the water when some couriers were despatched on horseback with the news of our arrival to the next Indians; and we only found a man and a woman with three children of the Atnah nation at the campment; these were alarmed at our strange appearance.

We found a young boy, whose mother was of the Tauten nation, who understood a little of the Carrier language; by this means we learned that, in consequence of the couriers just now sent off, many of the natives would make their appearance in that day; and that it would be dangerous for us to proceed before our intentions were publicly known. This information, added to a desire of procuring guides, induced me to remain the rest of the day.

In the afternoon, some Tautens and Atnahs arrived on horse back. They seemed peaceably inclined, and appeared happy to see us, and observed that having heard by their neighbors that white people were to visit their country this season, they had remained near the route on purpose to receive us.

According to the accounts we received here, the river below was but a succession of falls and cascades, which we should find impossible to pass, not only through the badness of the channel, but also through the badness of the surrounding country, which was rugged and mountainous. Their opinion, therefore, was that we should discontinue our voyage and remain with them. I remarked that our determination of going on was fixed. They, then, informed us that at the next camp, the great Chief of the Atnah had a slave who had been to the sea, who perhaps we might procure as guide.

These Indians had heard of fire-arms, but had never seen any. Seeing our fire-arms, they desired us to explain the manner in which they were used. In compliance we fired several shots, the report of which astonished them to that degree as to make them drop off their legs. Upon recovering from their surprise, we made them examine the effect; seeing the marks on the trees, they appeared uneasy, and observed that the Indians in that quarter were good and peaceable people, and would never make use of their arms to annoy white people. Yet, they remarked, that we ought to be on our guard, and act with great caution when we approached villages; for should we surprise the natives they would be apt to mistake us for enemies, and through fear attack us with their arrows. During the above mentioned experiment in firing, we lost our swivel [a small cannon]. It had a flaw before, and firing at this time, perhaps with an overcharge, it broke into pieces, and wounded our gunner. This accident alarmed the Indians, but having convinced them that the injury was of no great consequence, they were reconciled.

The Atnah language has no affinity to any other that I know, and it was by the means of two different interpreters that we were enabled to understand it. The men of this tribe are of a diminutive size but of an active appearance. They dress in skins prepared in the hair; their weapons are bows and arrows neatly finished. The country round consists of plains, well stocked with animals. Some of our men who were out a hunting saw plenty of deer.

b. The Rapids of the Fraser River

This morning all hands were employed the same as yesterday. We had to pass over huge rocks, in which we were assisted by the Indians. Soon after we met Mr. Stuart and the man. They reported that the navigation was absolutely impracticable. That evening they had slept on the top of a mountain in sight of our smoke.

As for the road by land we scarcely could make our way in some parts even with our guns. I have been for a long period among the Rocky Mountains, but have never seen any thing equal to this country, for I cannot find words to describe our situation at times. We had to pass where no human being should venture. Yet in those places there is a regular footpath impressed, or rather indented, by frequent traveling upon the very rocks. And besides this, steps which are formed like a ladder, or shrouds of a ship, by poles hanging to one another and crossed at certain distances with twigs and withes [tree boughs], suspended from the top to the foot of precipices, and fastened at both ends to stones and trees, furnished a safe and convenient passage to the natives—but we, who had not the advantages of their experience, were often in imminent danger, when obliged to follow their example.

10. David Thompson Watches Salmon Spawn on the Upper Columbia, 1808

> David Thompson's reputation rested on his uncanny abilities as an explorer and cartographer, but he was also a prose stylist of considerable skill. This brief description of salmon on the upper Columbia reveals Thompson as a writer with a keen sense of the natural world.

We there builded log houses, and strongly stockaded them on three sides, the other side resting on the steep bank of the river. The logs of the house, and the stockades, bastions, etc. were of a peculiar kind of a heavy resinous fir [larch], with a rough black bark. It was clean grown to about twenty feet, when it threw off a head of long rude branches, with a long narrow leaf for a fir, which was annually shed, and became from green to a red colour. The stockades were all ball-proof, as well as the logs of the houses.

At the latter end of autumn, and through the winter, there are plenty of red deer and the antelope, with a few mountain sheep. The goats with their long silky hair were difficult to hunt, from their feeding on the highest parts of the hills, and the natives relate that they are wicked, kicking down stones on them. But during the summer and early part of the autumn very few deer were killed; we had very hard times and were obliged to eat several horses; we found the meat of the tame horse better than the wild horse; the fat was not so oily.

At length the salmon made their appearance, and for about three weeks we lived on them; at first they were in tolerable condition, although they had come upwards of twelve hundred miles from the sea, and several weighed twenty-five pounds. But as the spawning went on upon a gravel bank a short distance above us, they became poor and not eatable; we preferred horse meat.

As the place where they spawned had shoal swift clear water on it, we often looked at them. The female with her head cleared away the gravel, and made a hole to deposit her spawn in, of perhaps an inch or more in depth by a foot in length; which done, the male then passed over it several times, when both covered the hole well up with gravel. The Indians affirm, and there is every reason to believe them, that not a single salmon of the myriads that come up the river ever returns to the sea; their stomachs have nothing in them, probably from no food in fresh water; the shores of the river, after the spawning season, were covered with them, in a lean dying state, yet even in this state many of the Indians eat them.

11. Thomas Hart Benton Keeps the Dream of the Passage to India Alive, 1849

With a flowery language now gone from American political rhetoric, Benton reveals not only American dreams of wealth and power but also the continuing attraction of the passage idea.

The history of commerce up the Missouri, into the Rockies, and down the trail to Santa Fe is often told as a series of romantic and colorful adventures. The mountain man and the Santa Fe trader have become stock characters in a "central casting" version of the American West. The documents in this chapter take us to a more complicated and surely more interesting West.

1. Thomas James Describes His Life as a Fur Trapper, 1809–1810

Born in Maryland in 1782, Thomas James moved with his pioneer family to southern Illinois around 1803. In 1806 he and his father took up land at Florissant, an old settlement north of St. Louis. Three years later, the younger James joined a large-scale trading expedition organized by Manuel Lisa and the Missouri Fur Company. The expedition's travels eventually brought James up the Missouri and into the Three Forks country of present-day southwestern Montana. Like many other fur traders, James did not stay in the mountains. Until his death in 1847, he was a merchant, politician, and militia officer.

The three selections reprinted here are from James's memoir, *Three Years Among the Indians and Mexicans,* first published in 1846. His comments in the second excerpt on the numbers of buffalo are especially important because they indicate a decline even before massive killings by white hunters.

a. Pushing Up the Missouri

We started from St. Louis in the month of June, 1809, and ascended the Missouri by rowing, pushing with poles, cordeling, or pulling with ropes, warping, and sailing. My crew were light-hearted, jovial men, with no care or anxiety for the future and little fear of any danger. In the morning we regularly started by daybreak and stopped, generally, late at night. The partners, or *bourgeoises,* as the French called them, were in the forward barge, with a strong crew of hardy and skilfull voyageurs, and there Lisa and some of his colleagues lorded it over the poor fellows most arrogantly, and made them work as if their lives depended on their getting forward with the greatest possible speed. They peremptorily required all the boats to stop in company for the night, and our barge being large and heavily loaded, the crew frequently had great difficulty in overtaking them in the evening. We occasionally had races with some of the forward barges, in which my crew of Americans proved themselves equal in a short race to their more experienced French competitors.

We thus continued, with nothing of interest occurring, till we passed the Platte. Six weeks of hard labor on our part had been spent when our allotted provisions gave out and we were compelled to live on boiled corn, without salt. At the same time all the other boats were well supplied and the gentlemen proprietors in the leading barge were faring in the most sumptuous and luxurious manner. The French hands were much better treated on all occasions than the Americans. The former were employed for a long period at stated wages and were accustomed to such service and such men as those in command of them, while we were private adventurers for our own benefit, as well as that of the Company, who regarded us with suspicion and distrust. Many Americans on the passage up the river, disgusted with the treatment they received, fell off in small companies and went back. At Cote Sans Dessein, opposite the mouth of the Osage [River], most of them returned. On reaching the Mandan country we numbered about ten Americans, having started from St. Louis with about one hundred and seventy-five and an equal number of French.

b. River Scenery

The scenery of the Upper Missouri is so familiar to the world as to render any particular description of it unnecessary. As you ascend the river the woods diminish in number and extent. Beyond Council Bluffs, about 700 miles above the mouth, they entirely disappear, except on the river bottoms, which are heavily timbered. The prairies are covered with a short, thick grass, about three or four inches high. At this time the game was very abundant. We saw elk and buffaloes in vast numbers, and killed many of them. Prairie dogs and wolves were also very numerous. The Indians have thinned off the game since that time, so much that their own subsistence is frequently very scanty and they are often in danger of starvation. Their range for hunting now extends far down into the Comanche country and Texas, and the buffaloes, their only game of importance, are fast disappearing. When these valuable animals are all gone, when they are extinct on the west, as they are on the east side of the Mississippi, then will the Indian race, the aboriginals of that vast region, be near their own extinction and oblivion. They cannot survive without the game and with it will disappear.

The western declivity of the Mississippi Valley from the mountains to the Father of Waters is nearly all one great plain, with occasional rocky elevations. We saw hills at the foot of which were large heaps of pumice stone, which had the appearance of having been crumbled off from above by the action of fire. The scenery of Illinois or Missouri is a fair example of that of the whole country west to the mountains. The prairies here, however, are vaster and more desolate. One extensive plain is usually presented to the eye of the traveller, and stretches to the horizon, without a hill, mound, or shrub to arrest the sight.

c. In the Three Forks Country

We arrived at the Three Forks of the Missouri on the third day of April, 1810, ten months after leaving St. Louis and two months and one day after quitting my cabin above the Gros Ventre village. We had now reached our place of business, trapping for beaver, and prepared to set to work. [John] Dougherty, [William] Brown, [William] Weir, and myself agreed to trap in company on the Missouri between the Forks and the Falls [present-day Great Falls, Montana], which lie several hundred miles down the river to the north from the Forks. We made two canoes by hollowing out the trunks of two trees, and on the third or fourth day after our arrival at the Forks we were ready to start on an expedition down the river.

The rest of the Americans with a few French, in all eighteen in number, determined to go up the Jefferson River for trapping, and the rest of the company under Colonel [Pierre] Menard remained to complete the fort and trading house at the Forks between the Jefferson and Madison rivers. On parting from Cheek [a fellow American trapper] he said in a melancholy tone: "James, you are going down the Missouri, and it is the general opinion that you will be killed. The Blackfeet are at the Falls, encamped, I hear, and we fear you will never come back. But I am afraid for myself as well as you. I know not the cause, but I have felt fear ever since I came to the Forks, and I never was afraid of anything before. You may come out safe, and I may be killed. Then you will say, there was Cheek afraid to go with us down the river for fear of death, and now he has found his grave by going up the river. I may be dead when you return."

His words made little impression on me at the time, but his tragical end a few days afterwards recalled them to my mind and stamped them on my memory forever. I endeavoured to persuade him to join our party, while he was equally urgent for me to join his, saying that if we went in one company our force would afford more protection from Indians than in small parties, while I contended that the fewer our numbers the better would be our chance of concealment and escape from any war parties that might be traversing the country. We parted, never to meet again, taking opposite directions and both of us going into the midst of dangers. My company of four started down the river and caught some beaver on the first day. On the second we passed a very high spur of the mountain on our right. The mountains in sight on our left were not so high as those to the east of us. On the third day we issued from very high and desolate mountains on both sides of us, whose tops are covered with snow throughout the year, and came upon a scene of beauty and magnificence combined, unequalled by any other view of nature that I ever beheld. It really realized all my conceptions of the Garden of Eden. In the west the peaks and pinnacles of the Rocky Mountains shone resplendent in the sun. The snow on their tops sent back a beautiful reflection of the rays of the morning sun. From the sides of the dividing ridge [the continental divide] between the waters of the Missouri and the Columbia there sloped gradually down to the bank of the river we were on, a plain, then covered with every variety of wild animals peculiar to this region, while on the east another plain arose by a very gradual ascent and extended as far as the eye could reach. These and the mountain sides were dark with buffalo, elk, deer, moose, wild goats, and wild sheep; some grazing, some lying down under the trees, and all enjoying a perfect millennium of peace and quiet. On the margin the swans, geese, and pelicans cropped the grass or floated on the surface of the water. The cottonwood trees seemed to have been planted by the hand of man on the bank of the river to shade our way, and the pines and cedars waved their tall, majestic heads along the base and on the sides of the mountains.

The whole landscape was that of the most splendid English park. The stillness, beauty, and loveliness of this scene struck us all with indescribable emotions. We rested on the oars and enjoyed the whole view in silent astonishment and admiration. Nature seemed to have rested here, after creating the wild mountains and chasms among which we had voyaged for two days. Dougherty, as if inspired by the scene with the spirit of poetry and song, broke forth in one of Burns' noblest lyrics, which found a deep echo in our hearts. We floated on till evening through this most delightful country, when we stopped and prepared supper on the bank of the river. We set our traps and before going to rest for the night we examined them and found a beaver in every one, being twenty-three in all. In the morning we were nearly as successful as before, and were cheered with thoughts of making a speedy fortune.

stir into action. William H. Ashley and his partner Andrew Henry led the way, organizing a series of trading and exploring ventures up the Missouri and into the Rockies. When Ashley's push up the Missouri was thwarted in 1823 by Arikara Indian resistance, Ashley sent his men westward overland to seek new trapping grounds.

One of those trapper-explorers was Daniel T. Potts (1794–*c.* 1830). Born in Pennsylvania, Potts was both literate and inquisitive. Five of Potts's letters to his brother Robert, covering the period 1824–1828, survive. In his letters Potts recorded some of the most important exploring journeys taken by American traders. In the first selection below—a classic in the literature of fur-trade exploration— he details the trek he and other Ashley men made in 1822–1826 into the Green River country of present-day Wyoming and then south to the Great Salt Lake. In the second selection Potts offers what is probably the first written description of Yellowstone Lake and the surrounding country.

a. Letter to His Brother Robert, July 16, 1826

[This letter was published in the Philadelphia *Gazette and Daily Advertiser,* November 14, 1826]

After I left Philadelphia I was taken with a severe spell of rheumatism which continued with me for about two months. I arrived in Illinois on the 1st of July in the same year [1821], where I remained until March following, when I took my departure for Missouri, from thence immediately entered on an expedition of Henry and Ashley, bound for the Rocky Mountain and Columbia River. In this enterprise I consider it unnecessary to give you all the particulars appertaining to my travels. I left St. Louis on April 3d, 1822, under command of Andrew Henry with a boat and one hundred men and arrived at Council Bluffs on May 1st; from thence we ascended the river to Cedar Fort [near present-day Chamberlain, South Dakota], about five hundred miles. Here our provisions being exhausted, and no prospect of game near at hand, I concluded to make the best of my way back in company with eight others, and unfortunately was separated from them. By being too accesaary [nearby] in this misfortune, I was left in the prairie without arms or any means of making fire, and half starved to death. Now taking into consideration my situation, about three hundred and fifty miles from my frontier post, this would make the most cruel heart sympathize for me. The same day I met with three Indians, whom I hailed, and on my advancing they prepared for action by presenting their arms, though I approached them without hesitation, and gave them my hand. They conducted me to their village, where I was treated with the greatest humanity imaginable. There I remained four days, during which time they had many religious ceremonies too tedious to insert, after which I met with some traders who conducted me as far down as the [blank in text] village—this being two hundred miles from the post. I departed alone as before, with only about a fourth pound of suet, and in six days reached the post, where I met General Ashley, on a second expedition, with whom I entered a second time, and arrived at the mouth of the Yellowstone about the middle of October. This is one of the most beautiful situations I ever saw; from this I immediately embarked for the mouth of the Musselshell [River], in company with twenty-one others and shortly after our arrival, eight returned to the former place. Here the game being very scarce, the prospect was very discouraging, though after a short time the buffaloes flocked in in great abundance; likewise the mountain goats; the like I have never seen since. Twenty-six of the latter were slain in the compass of 100 yards square, in the space of two hours. During the winter the buffaloes came into our camp. The winter set in early, and the ice on the river froze to the immense thickness of four feet, and the snow of an ordinary depth. The river did not discharge itself until the 4th of April; on the 5th we were visited by a party of Indians, and on the 6th we embarked in canoes for the river Judith.

In about one day's travel we discovered where a party of Indians had wintered who were our enemies, but fortunately had not discovered us. On the 11th [of April] I was severely wounded through both knees by an accidental discharge of a rifle; whereby I was obliged to be conducted to our establishment at the mouth of the Yellowstone; here I remained until September. We were favored by the arrival of Major Henry from the Arikaras who had departed from this place with a small brigade for the relief of General Ashley, who was defeated by that nation, with the loss of sixteen killed and fourteen wounded, out of forty men. After Major Henry joined them and the troops from Council Bluffs, under the command of Colonel Leavenworth, they gave them battle; the loss of our enemy was from sixty to seventy. The number of wounded not known, as they evacuated their village in the night. On our part there was only two wounded, but on his return he was fired upon by night by a party of Mandans wherein two was killed and as many wounded. Only two of our guns were fired which dispatched an

Indian and they retreated. Shortly after his arrival we embarked for the Bighorn [River] on the Yellowstone in the Crow Indian country, where I made a small hunt for beaver. From this place we crossed the first range of Rocky Mountains into a large and beautiful valley adorned with many flowers and interspersed with many useful herbs. At the upper end of the valley on the Bighorn is the most beautiful scene of nature I have ever seen. It is a large boiling spring [located near present-day Thermopolis, Wyoming] at the foot of a small burnt mountain about two rods in diameter and depth not ascertained, discharging sufficient water for an overshot mill, and spreading itself to a considerable width forming a great number of basins of various shapes and sizes, of incrustation of sediment, running in this manner for the space of 200 feet, there falling over a precipice of about 30 feet perpendicular into the head of the Bighorn or confluence of Wind River. From thence across the second range of mountains [the Owl Creek Mountains] to Wind River valley. In crossing this mountain I unfortunately froze my feet and was unable to travel from the loss of two toes. Here I am obliged to remark [on] the humanity of the natives (the Indians) towards me, who conducted me to their village, into the lodge of their chief, who regularly twice a day divested himself of all his clothing except his breech clout, and dressed my wounds until I left them. Wind River is a beautiful transparent stream, with hard gravel bottom about 70 or 80 yards wide, rising in the main range of the Rocky Mountains, running East North East, finally north through a picturesque small mountain bearing the name of the stream: after it discharges through this mountain it loses its name. The valleys near the head of this river and its tributary streams are tolerably timbered with cottonwood, willow, etc. The grass and herbage are good and plenty, of all varieties common to this country. In this valley the snow rarely falls more than three or four inches deep and never remains more than three or four days, although it is surrounded by stupendous mountains. Those on the southwest and north are covered with eternal snow. The mildness of this winter in this valley may readily be imputed to the immense number of hot springs which rise near the head of this river. I visited but one of those which rise to the south of the river in a level plain of prairie, and occupies about two acres; this is not so hot as many others but I suppose to be boiling as the outer verge was nearly scalding hot. There is also an oil spring in this valley, which discharges 60 to 70 gallons of pure oil per day. The oil has very much the appearance, taste and smell of British oil. From this valley we proceeded by southwest direction over a tolerable route to the heads of the Sweetwater, a small stream which takes an eastern course and falls into the north fork of the Great Platte, 70 or 80 miles below. This stream rises and runs on the highest ground in all this country. The winters are extremely [cold], and even the summers are disagreeably cold.

Louis Nicolas, "Otter—Beaver—Cat Fish—Sea Tiger," *Codex Canadensis, c.* 1700. The "cat fish" appears to be a seal, and the "sea tiger" a sea lion.

Atlantic from that of the Pacific. At or near this place heads the Siskadee [the Green River] of California. Stinking Fork [Shoshone River], Yellowstone south fork of Missouri and Henrys Fork all those head at one angular point. That of the Yellowstone has a large fresh lake near its head on the very top of the mountain which is about one hundred by forty miles in diameter and as clear as crystal. On the south borders of this lake [the West Thumb area of present-day Yellowstone National Park] is a number of hot and boiling springs and some of water and others of most beautiful fine clay and resembles that of a mush pot and throws its particles to the immense height of from twenty to thirty feet in height. The clay is white, and of a pink color and the water appears fathomless as it appears to be entirely hollow underneath. There is also a number of places where pure sulphur is sent forth in abundance. One of our men visited one of those whilst taking his recreation. There at an instant the earth began a tremendious trembling and he with difficulty made his escape when an explosion took place resembling that of thunder. During our stay in that quarter I heard it every day. From this place by a circuituous route to the northwest we returned. Two others and myself pushed on in the advance for the purpose of accumulating a few more beaver and in the act of passing through a narrow confine [pass] in the mountain we were met plumb in face by a large party of Blackfeet Indians who not knowing our number fled into the mountain in confusion and we to a small grove of willows. Here we made every preparation for battle after which finding our enemy as much alarmed as ourselves we mounted our horses which were heavily loaded; we took the back retreat. The Indians raised a tremendious yell, showered down from the mountain top, and almost cut off our retreat. We here put the whip to our horses and they pursued us at close quarters until we reached the plains where we left them behind. On this trip one man was closely fired on by a party of Blackfeet; several others were closely pursued. On this trip I have lost one horse by accident and the last spring two by the Utaws [Ute Indians] who killed them for the purpose of eating, one of which was a favorite buffalo horse. This loss cannot be computed at less than four hundred and fifty dollars, by this you may conclude keeps my nose close to the grindstone.

4. Jedediah Strong Smith Describes His Journey Overland to California, 1826–1827

Although some fur-trade explorers, among them Daniel T. Potts, have slipped from public memory, Jedediah Strong Smith remains identifiable to many Americans. Born in 1799, Smith was both well educated and remarkably inquisitive. As he explained in the opening lines of his California journal, "In taking charge of our Southwestern expedition I followed the bent of my strong inclination to visit this unexplored country and unfold those hidden resources of wealth and bring to light those wonders which I readily imagined a country so extensive might contain." Smith confessed that he wanted "to be the first to view a country on which the eyes of a white man had never gazed and to follow the course of rivers that run through a new land." In 1822 Smith traveled to St. Louis and soon became one of William H. Ashley's most able lieutenants. In 1823–1824 Smith and his party conducted a remarkable reconnaissance in what is now Wyoming, a journey that included the rediscovery of South Pass.

The selections reprinted here recount Smith's journey to California in 1826–1827. This venture marked the first American overland enterprise to California. In the first excerpt Smith describes his meeting (late August 1826) with Conmarrowap's Ute band, camped near present-day Tucker, Utah. After a harrowing crossing of the Mojave Desert, Smith reached Mission San Gabriel in late November 1826. He continued his exploring ventures until May 1831, when he was killed by Comanches along the Santa Fe Trail.

---

a. The Meeting with Conmarrowap, August 1826

On a creek in the vicinity found some beaver sign and nearby some Indians of the Ute nation. Understanding by them that the principal chief [Conmarrowap] with his band was not far off I sent an Indian for him. I was anxious to see him and if possible persuade him to make a treaty with the Snake [Shoshone] Indians for they had been constantly at war. I likewise wished to procure some information as to the country to the south. In two days the Indian returned. But the chief could not be persuaded to come. He was afraid to leave his band on account of the Snakes [Shoshones] who he was apprehensive might take the opportunity of his absence to make an attack. He sent word that if beaver hunting was my object I had better pass his village as there were a good many beaver a short distance beyond where he then was. This I concluded to do and after three days travel from the lake [Utah Lake] I arrived at his village on the 23rd of August. The country through which we travelled was quite rough and mountainous. I found at that place about 35 lodges, some of skins and some of brush. Each family has 4 or 5 horses. These Indians are constantly moving about like the Snakes and at this time live almost entirely on serviceberries which are now ripe. I remained at this place two days and concluded a treaty with these Indians by which the Americans are allowed to hunt and trap in and pass through their country unmolested and the chief after mature deliberation declared he would go thus far toward making peace with the Snakes that hostilities should cease. I then told him that the Snakes had consented to an armistice until a meeting could be had between the two nations which on my return from my fall hunt I engaged to forward by every means in my power. I found these Indians more honest than any I had ever been with in the country. They appear to have very little disposition to steal and ask for nothing unless it may be a little meat. As stealing and begging are the most degrading features in the Indian character and as their prevalence is almost universal so to be exempt from them is no ordinary merit. The Utes are cleanly, quiet, and active and make a nearer approach to civilized life than any other Indians I have seen in the interior. Their leggings and shirts which are made of the skins of the deer, mountain sheep, or antelope are quite clean. As they sometimes visit the buffalo country they have robes. Their arms are like those of the Mountain Snakes, elk and sheep horn bows. Having some communication with the Spanish villages of Taos and Santa Fe, they have more guns than the Snakes.

b.   The Mission San Gabriel

The country through which we passed was strikingly contrasted with the rocky and sandy deserts through which we had so long been traveling. There we had passed many high mountains, rocky and barren, many plains whose sands drank up the waters of the river and springs where our need was the greatest. There sometimes a solitary antelope bounded by to vex our hunger and the stunted useless sedge grew as in mockery of the surrounding sterility. There for many days we had traveled weary hungry and thirsty drinking from springs that increased our thirst and looking in vain for a boundary of the interminable waste of sands. But now the scene was changed and whether it was its own real beauty or the contrast with what we had seen it certainly seemed to us enchantment. Our path was through a fertile and well watered valley and the herds of cattle and the bands of wild horses as they sniffed the wind and rushed wildly across our way reminded me of the plains of the buffalo east of the mountains that seemed to me as a home or of the cattle of the more distant prairies of Missouri and Illinois.

Even in the idea that we were approaching the abode of comparative civilization there was a pleasure not however entirely unmixed with dread for we knew not how we might be received. As we advanced the white brant and mallard were seen in great numbers, it being now their season. And we passed a farm on a creek where a number of Indians were at work. They gazed and gazed again considering us no doubt as strange objects in which they were not much in error. When it is considered that they were not accustomed to see white men walking with horses packed as mine were with furs, traps, saddlebags, guns, and blankets and every thing so different from any thing they had ever seen and add to this our ragged and miserable appearance I should not have been surprised if they had run off at first sight for I have often been treated in that manner by savages. Arrived at the farm houses I was kindly received by an elderly man, an Indian who spoke Spanish and immediately asked me if I would have a bullock killed. I answered that I would and away rode two young Indians in a moment, it being the custom in this country as I have since learned to keep a horse or horses constantly tied at the door saddled and bridled and of course ready to mount at a moments warning. In a short time the Indians returned bringing a cow as fast as she could gallop. She was held between the two horsemen by ropes thrown over her horns and having the other end fast to the pomel of the Spanish saddle one riding before and the other behind. She was forced along without the power of resistance. They were anxious that I should shoot the cow which I did. Novel as the scenery of this country was to me, it seemed that we ourselves were a still greater wonder to our semi-civilized friends. As I afterwards learned, they wondered how Indians could be so white having no idea that civilized people lived in the direction from which we came. It was also a great wonder to them that we had guns and other articles and more than all that there should be with us one of the people of reason [gente de razón], this being the name by which they were learned to distinguish Spaniards from Indians and which they readily applied to one of my men who spoke Spanish.

The farm house consisted of two buildings each about 100 feet long, 20 feet wide, and 12 feet high, placed so as to form two sides of a square. The walls are of unburnt [adobe] brick about 2 feet thick and at intervals of 15 feet; loop holes are left for the admission of light. The roofs are thatched. It should be premised that I had at this time but a vague idea of the peculiarities of the country in which my fortune had placed me. I therefore was in the dark as to the manner in which I should conduct myself and determined to be guided by circumstances as they should transpire. In pursuance of this plan when the old overseer asked me if I was not going to write the Father [Fr. José Bernardo Sanchez, head of the Franciscan mission at San Gabriel], I told him I was and immediately set down and wrote a few lines briefly stating where I was from and the reason of my being there. An Indian mounting one of the horses that are always in readiness took my note and was off in an instant. In about an hour the answer was returned by a man who the overseer told me was the commandant but in fact [was] a corporal. He asked me how I did and congratulated me that I had escaped the Gentiles [the Indians of the Mojave Desert] and got into a Christian country and offering me some cigars made with paper according to the common custom of the country when I would take one he insisted that I should take the bunch. He then presented me the note from the Father written in Latin and as I could not read his Latin nor he my English it seemed that we were not likely to become general correspondents. I however ascertained that he wished me to ride to the Mission so giving Mr. Rogers [Harrison G. Rogers, Smith's clerk and second-in-command] instructions how to proceed in my absence, I took my interpreter and in company with the corporal and a soldier moved on at the gate [gait] that appears quite common in this country, a gallop passing large fields laid out on both sides of the road and fenced with posts set in the ground with rails tied to them by means of strong pieces of raw hide, there being also thousands of cattle skulls in rows on each side of the road conveying the idea that we were approaching an immense slaughter yard. Arrived in view of a building [Mission San Gabriel] of ancient and castle-like appearance and not knowing why I was brought there or who I was to see, the current of my thoughts ran rapidly through my mind as to deprive me of the power of coming to any conclusion so that when we passed in front of the building and the corporal after pointing to an old man sitting in the portico and observing that there was the Father immediately rode off, I was left quite embarrassed hardly knowing how to introduce myself. Observing this I presume the Father took me by the hand and quite familiarly asked me to walk in, making at the same time many enquiries. Soon some bread and cheese were brought in and some rum of which I drank to please the Father but much against my own taste. I then related to him as well as in my power the course of my being in that country but it was to him a thing so entirely new and my interpreter perhaps not giving a correct translation of my words he was not able to comprehend the subject and told me there was an American [Joseph Chapman, the first American settler in Los Angeles] residing in the vicinity for whom he would send as he spoke good Spanish and on his arrival we might have a good understanding. In the meantime he told me to make myself as contented as possible and consider myself at home. He ordered a steward to show me to a room about 20 feet square in which there was a bed. Taking possession of it I was left alone to reflect on my singular situation for about two hours when the bell ringing for supper a boy came and invited me in. The old Father invited me to pass up next to him. We were seated on a long bench with a back to it, one of these occupying each side of the table. On the opposite side of the table sat a Spanish gentleman and a Father from the neighboring village of the Angels and the steward of the mission. At my side sat my interpreter. As soon as we were seated the Father said Benediction and each one in the most hurried manner asked the blessing of heaven—and even while the last words were pronouncing the Fathers were reaching for the different dishes. About a dozen Indian boys were in attendance who passing the different dishes to the Fathers they helping themselves and passing them to the next. Our knives and forks according to the common custom of the country were rolled up in a napkin and laid by the side of the plates. The supper consisted principally of meats and an abundance of wine. Before the cloth was removed, cigars were passed around. I may be excused for being particular in this table scene when it is recollected that it was a long time since I had the pleasure of sitting at a table and never before in such company.

5. Warren Angus Ferris Recalls His Adventures as a Mountain Man, 1830–1835

Born into a prosperous Buffalo, New York, family in 1810, Warren Angus Ferris trained to be a land surveyor before drifting to St. Louis in 1829. Faced with hard times and no prospect of employment, he joined the Western Department of the American Fur Company in 1830. Ferris spent the next five and a half years in the mountains—a time of intense competition between the American Fur Company and its rivals.

Ferris traded and traveled throughout the Rockies, made careful notes on what he saw, and eventually drafted an important map of the fur country. Like his contemporaries, Washington Irving and Frederick Ruxton, Ferris was not above portraying fur traders as the wild rovers of the West. In the first selection Ferris writes with an eye to what his eastern audience expected. This excerpt captures the image of freedom and adventure that eastern audiences believed lay at the heart of the western fur trade. But Ferris lived enough of the trapping life to know the realities. And despite what he says here, Ferris probably knew that most fur traders were eager to leave the

and alarm, and all the other adjuncts that belong to so vagrant a condition, in a harsh, barren, untamed, and fearful region of desert, plain, and mountain. Yet so attached to it do they become, that few ever leave it, and they deem themselves, nay are, with all these bars against them, far happier than the in-dwellers of towns and cities, with all the gay and giddy whirl of fashion's mad delusions in their train.

b. Mountain Man Skills

It may seem to the reader a trifling matter to note the track of footmen, the report of firearms, the appearance of strange horsemen, and curling vapor of a far off fire, but these are the far from trivial incidents in a region of the country where the most important events are indiced by such signs only. Every man carries here emphatically his life in his hand, and it is only by the most watchful precaution, grounded upon and guided by the observation of every unnatural appearance however slight, that he can hope to preserve it. The footmark may indicate the vicinity of a war party hovering to destroy; the report of firearms may betray the dangerous neighborhood of a numerous, well armed, and wily enemy; strange horsemen may be but the outriding scouts of a predatory band at hand and in force to attack; the rising smoke may indeed curl up from a camp of friends or an accidental fire, but it more probably signals the gathering forces of an enemy recruiting their scattered bands for the work of plunder and massacre. Thus every strange appearance becomes an important indication which the ripest wisdom and experience are needful to interpret; and the most studious care and profound sagacity are requisite to make the most advantage from. It is only in this manner that the hunter's life is rendered even comparatively secure, and it is thus that the most trivial occurance assumes a character of the gravest moment, freighted as it may be with the most alarming and perilous consequences.

c. The Grand Cavalcade

We departed southeastward [from a camp near present-day Anaconda, Montana] for the Jefferson River on the morning of the fifteenth [of September, 1831], accompanied by all the Indians; and picturesque enough was the order and appearance of our march. Fancy to yourself, reader, three thousand horses of every variety of size and color, with trappings almost as varied as their appearance, either packed or ridden by a thousand souls from squalling infancy to decrepit age, their persons fantastically ornamented with scarlet coats, blankets of all colors, buffalo robes painted with hideous little figures, resembling grasshoppers quite as much as men for which they were intended, and sheep skin dresses garnished with porcupine quills, beads, hawk bells, and human hair. Imagine this motley collection of human figures, crowned with long black locks gently waving in the wind, their faces painted with vermilion, and yellow ochre. Listen to the rattle of numberless lodge poles trailed by packhorses, to the various noises of children screaming, women scolding, and dogs howling. Observe occasional frightened horses running away and scattering their lading over the prairie. See here and there groups of Indian boys dashing about at full speed, sporting over the plain, or quietly listening to traditionary tales of battles and surprises, recounted by their elder companions. Yonder see a hundred horsemen pursuing a herd of antelopes, which sport and wind before them conscious of superior fleetness,—there as many others racing towards a distant direction crowds of hungry dogs chasing and worrying timid rabbits, and other small animals. Imagine these scenes, with all their bustle, vociferation and confusion, lighted by the flashes of hundreds of gleaming gun barrels, upon which the rays of a fervent sun are playing, a beautiful level prairie, with dark blue snow-capped mountains in the distance for locale, and you will have a faint idea of the character and aspect of our march.

6. Josiah Gregg Writes the Classic Description of the Santa Fe Trail, 1844

While other merchants and adventurers pioneered the trade route between Santa Fe and the Missouri towns of Franklin, Independence, and St. Louis, Missouri-born Josiah Gregg (1806–1850) wrote the most comprehensive and engaging account of the trail and its peoples. Educated first as a surveyor and later as a lawyer and physician, Gregg found his real vocation as a Santa Fe trader. When doctors prescribed a western trip as a tonic for frail health, Gregg joined a Santa Fe caravan. From 1831 until 1840 he was a regular on the trail, taking four trips to Santa Fe. Out of that experience came *Commerce of the Prairies* (1844), one of the most important and readable books on the American West.

Far more than a simple history of commerce on the trail, Gregg's book is a virtual encyclopedia of southern plains and southwestern life. The selections reprinted here describe the departure of the wagon caravan from Council Grove in present-day eastern Kansas and the arrival in Santa Fe.

a. Under Way from Council Grove

Owing to the delays of organizing and other preparations, we did not leave the Council Grove camp until May 27th [1831]. Although the usual hour of starting with the prairie caravans is after an early breakfast, yet, on this occasion, we were hindered till the afternoon. The familiar note of preparation, "Catch up! Catch up!" was now sounded from the captain's camp, and re-echoed from every division and scattered group along the valley. On such occasions, a scene of confusion ensues, which must be seen to be appreciated. The woods and dales resound with the gleeful yells of the light-hearted wagoners, who, weary of inaction, and filled with joy at the prospect of getting under way, become clamorous in the extreme. Scarcely does the jockey on the race-course ply his whip more promptly at that magic word "Go," than do these emulous wagoners fly to harnessing their mules at the spirit-stirring sound of "Catch up." Each teamster vies with his fellows who shall be soonest ready; and it is a matter of boastful pride to be the first to cry out—"All's set!"

The uproarious bustle which follows—the hallooing of those in pursuit of animals—the exclamations which the unruly brutes call forth from their wrathful drivers; together with the clatter of bells—the rattle of yokes and harness—the jingle of chains—all conspire to produce a clamorous confusion, which would be altogether incomprehensible without the assistance of the eyes; while these alone would hardly suffice to unravel the labyrinthian manoeuvers and hurly-burly of this precipitate breaking up. It is sometimes amusing to observe the athletic wagoner hurrying an animal to its post—to see him heave upon the halter of a stubborn mule, while the brute as obstinately sets back, determined not to move a peg till his own say. "Wait till your hurry's over!" I have more than once seen a driver hitch a harnessed animal to the halter, and by that process haul "his mulishness" forward, while each of his four projected feet would leave a furrow behind; until at last the perplexed master would wrathfully exclaim, "A mule will be a mule any way you fix it!"

The Santa Fe Trail

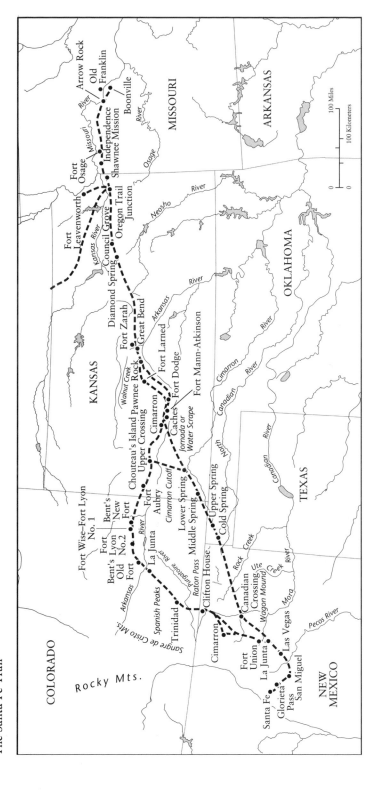

COLORADO

Rocky Mts.

Fort Wise–Fort Lyon
No. 1

Bent's
New
Fort

Fort
Lyon
No.2

Bent's
Old Fort

La Junta

Fort
Aubry

KANSAS

Chouteau's Island Pawnee Rock
Upper Crossing

Cimarron

Caches
Fort Dodge
Jornada or
Water Scrape

Fort Mann-Atkinson

Cimarron Cutoff
Lower Spring
Middle Spring
Upper Spring
Cold Spring

Diamond Spring
Fort Zarah
Great Bend

Fort Larned

Council Grove
Oregon Trail
Junction

Fort
Leavenworth

Fort
Osage

Independence
Shawnee Mission

Boonville

Arrow Rock
Old
Franklin

MISSOURI

ARKANSAS

OKLAHOMA

TEXAS

NEW
MEXICO

Santa Fe
Glorieta
Pass
San Miguel

Las Vegas

Fort
Union
La Junta

Cimarron

Wagon Mound
Canadian
Crossing

Clifton House

Trinidad

Spanish Peaks

Sangre de Cristo Mts.

Raton Pass

Arkansas River

Purgatoire River

Neosho

Walnut Creek

Arkansas
River

River

Cimarron
River

North
Canadian
River

Canadian
River

Rock
Creek

Ute
Creek

Mora
River

Pecos River

Missouri
River

Kansas River

Osage
River

River

100 Miles

100 Kilometers

0

0

"All's set!" is finally heard from some teamster—"All's set," is directly responded from every quarter. "Stretch out!" immediately vociferates the captain. Then, the "heps!" of drivers—the cracking of whips—the trampling of feet—the occasional creak of wheels—the rumbling of wagons—form a new scene of exquisite confusion, which I shall not attempt further to describe. "Fall in!" is heard from headquarters, and the wagons are forthwith strung out upon the long inclined plain, which stretches to the heights beyond Council Grove.

b. Reaching Santa Fe

A few miles before reaching the [capital] city, the road again emerges into an open plain. Ascending a table ridge, we spied [Gregg had gone ahead of the main caravan] in an extended valley to the northwest, occasional groups of trees, skirted with verdant corn and wheat fields, with here and there a square block-like protuberance in the midst. A little further, and just ahead of us to the north, irregular clusters of the same opened to our view. "Oh, we are approaching the suburbs!" thought I, on perceiving the cornfields, and what I supposed to be brick kilns scattered in every direction. These and other observations of the same nature becoming audible, a friend at my elbow said, "It is true those are heaps of unburnt bricks, nevertheless they are *houses*—this is the city of Santa Fe."

Five or six days after our arrival, the caravan at last hove in sight, and wagon after wagon was seen pouring down the last declivity at about a mile's distance from the city. To judge from the clamorous rejoicings of the men, and the state of agreeable excitement which the muleteers seemed to be laboring under, the spectacle must have been as new to them as it had been to me. It was truly a scene for the artist's pencil to revel in. Even the animals seemed to participate in the humor of their riders, who grew more and more merry and obstreperous as they descended towards the city. I doubt, in short, whether the first sight of the walls of Jerusalem were beheld by the crusaders with much more tumultuous and soul-enrapturing joy.

The arrival produced a great deal of bustle and excitement among the natives. *"Los Americanos!"*—*"Los carros!"*—*"La entrada de la caravana!"* were to be heard in every direction; and crowds of women and boys flocked around to see the new-comers; while crowds of *leperos* [vagabonds] hung about as usual to see what they could pilfer. The wagoners were by no means free from excitement on this occasion. Informed of the "ordeal" they had to pass, they had spent the previous morning in "rubbing up" and now they were prepared, with clean faces, sleek combed hair, and their choicest

Taken from Josiah Gregg's *Commerce of the Prairies* (1844), this engraving depicts the arrival of a trading caravan in Santa Fe.

ARRIVAL OF THE CARAVAN AT SANTA FE.

Sunday suit, to meet the "fair eyes" of glistening black that were sure to stare at them as they passed. There was yet another preparation to be made in order to show off to advantage. Each wagoner must tie a brand new "cracker" to the lash of his whip; for, on driving through the streets and the *plaza pública,* every one strives to outvie his comrades in the dexterity with which he flourishes this favorite badge of authority.

Our wagons were soon discharged in the ware-room of the custom house; and a few days' leisure being now at our disposal, we had time to take that recreation which a fatiguing journey of ten weeks had rendered so necessary. The wagoners, and many of the traders, particularly the novices, flocked to the numerous fandangoes, which are regularly kept up after the arrival of a caravan. But the merchants generally were anxiously and actively engaged in their affairs—striving who should first get his goods out of the custom house, and obtain a chance at the "hard chink" [Spanish coins] of the numerous country dealers, who annually resort to the capital on these occasions.

7. Susan Shelby Magoffin Portrays Life at Bent's Fort, 1846

When eighteen-year-old Susan Shelby (1827–1855) married Santa Fe trader Samuel Magoffin in 1846, she took a giant step away from the life of privilege she had enjoyed as a member of Kentucky's most prestigious family. In June 1846, with the Mexican War just months old, the Magoffins joined a trade caravan bound for Santa Fe by way of Bent's Fort.

Susan Magoffin kept a diary, which she filled with the daily events of travel as well as the more dramatic news of the war. The selection reprinted here describes life at Bent's Fort, the key trading establishment on the southern plains. The fort, built in 1833 by Charles and William Bent and their partner Ceran St. Vrain, was located on the north bank of the Arkansas River near present-day La Junta, Colorado. Magoffin spares nothing in this entry, including a description of her own painful miscarriage at the very time that her Indian neighbor gave birth to a healthy child.

And now for something of a description. Well, the outside [of the fort] exactly fills my idea of an ancient castle. It is built of adobes, unburnt brick, and Mexican style so far. The walls are very high and very thick with rounding corners. There is but one entrance, this is to the east rather.

Inside is a large space some ninety or an hundred feet square, all around this and the next wall are rooms, some twenty-five in number. They have dirt floors—which are sprinkled with water several times during the day to prevent dust. Standing in the center of some of them is a large wooden post as a firmer prop to the ceiling which is made of logs. Some of these rooms are occupied by boarders as bed chambers. One is a dining room—another a kitchen—a little store, a blacksmith's shop, a barber's and an ice house, which receives perhaps more customers than any other.

On the south side is an enclosure for stock in dangerous times and often at night. On one side of the top wall are rooms built in the same manner as below. We are occupying one of these, but of that anon.

They have a well inside, and fine water it is—especially with ice. At present they have quite a number of boarders. The traders and soldiers chiefly, with a few loafers from the States, come out because they can't live at home.

There is no place on earth where man lives and gambling in some form or other is not carried on. Here in the fort, and who could have supposed such a thing, they have a *regularly established billiard room!* They have a regular race track. And I hear the cackling of chickens at such a rate some times I shall not be surprised to hear of a cock-pit.

Now for our room; it is quite roomy. Like the others it has a dirt floor, which I keep sprinkling constantly during the day; we have two windows one looking out on the plain, the other on the patio or yard. We have our own furniture, such as bed, chairs, wash basin, table furniture, and we eat in our own room. It is keeping house regularly, but I beg leave not to be allowed *that* privilege much longer.

They have one large room as a parlor; there are no chairs but a cushion next [to] the wall on two sides, so the company set all round in a circle. There is no other furniture than a table on which stands a bucket of water, free to all. Any water that may be left in the cup after drinking is unceremoniously tossed onto the floor.

When we came last evening, while they were fixing our room, I sat in the parlor with *las señoritas,* the wife of Mr. George Bent, and some others. One of them sat and combed her hair all the while notwithstanding the presence of Mr. Leitensdorfer [Dr. Eugene Leitensdorfer], whose lady (a Mexican) was present. After combing she paid her devoirs to a crock of oil or grease of some kind, and it is not exaggeration to say it almost *dripped* from her hair to the floor. If I had not seen her at it, I never would have believed it grease, but that she had been washing her head.

Tuesday 28th [of July, 1846]. The doctor [Dr. Philippe Auguste Masure] has just left and I shall endeavour to write a little before dinner. I've been busy all morning. Wrote a long letter to Mama, which Capt. Moore [Captain Benjamin D. Moore, U.S. Army] says I can send by the government express. The army affords me one convenience in this. Though I cannot hear from home, it is a gratification to know that I can send letters to those who will take pleasure in reading them.

Dr. Masure brought me medicine, and advises *mi alma* [Susan's affectionate phrase for her husband Samuel] to travel me through Europe. The advice is rather better to take than the medicine, anything though to restore my health. I never should have consented to take the trip on the plains had it not been with that view and a hope that it would prove beneficial; but so far my hopes have been blasted, for I am rather going down hill than up, and it is so bad to be sick and under a physician all the time. But cease my rebellious heart! How prone human nature is to grumble and to think his lot harder than any one of his fellow creatures, many of whom are an hundred times more diseased and poor in earthly assistance and still they endure all, and would endure more.

Wednesday 29th. The same routine today as yesterday, several gentlemen, among the traders and officers called and paid their respects to the "Madam." My health, though not good, is drank by them all, and some times a complimentary toast is ingeniously slipped in. The fort is not such a bad place after all. There are some good people in and about it as well as in other places. I am not very much displeased with Col. Kearny [Stephen Watts Kearny, commander of American forces in the conquest of New Mexico and California] for sending us here, but he has arrived himself this afternoon and gives the command to leave in three days. The idea of getting onto those rough, jolting roads, and they say this is rather worse, if anything, than the one we have passed, is truly sickening.

I have concluded that the plains are not very beneficial to my health so far; for I am thinner by a good many pounds than when I came out. The dear knows what is the cause!

Thursday July 30th. Well this is my nineteenth birthday! And what? Why I feel rather strange, not surprised at its coming, nor to think that I am growing rather older, for that is the way of the human family, but this is it, I am sick! Strange sensations in my head, my back, and hips. I am obliged to lie down most of the time, and when I get up to hold my hand over my eyes.

There is the greatest possible noise in the patio. The shoeing of horses, neighing, and braying of mules, the crying of children, the scolding and fighting of men, are all enough to turn my head. And to add to the scene, like some of our neighbors we have our own private troubles. The servants are all quarreling and fighting among themselves, running to us to settle their difficulties; they are gambling off their clothes till some of them are next to nudity, and though each of them are in debt to *mi alma*, for advancement of their wages, they are coming to him to get them out of their scrapes.

Friday morning 31st of July. My pains commenced and continued till 12 o'clock at night, when after much agony and severest of pains, which were relieved a little at times by medicine given by Dr. Masure, *all was over.* [In the early morning hours of August 1, Susan suffered a miscarriage.] I sunk into a kind of lethargy, in *mi alma's* arms. Since that time I have been in bed till yesterday a little while, and part of today.

My situation was very different from that of an Indian woman in the room below me. She gave birth to a fine healthy baby, about the same time, *and in half an hour after she went to the river and bathed herself and it,* and this she has continued each day since. Never could I have believed such a thing, if I had not been here, and *mi alma's* own eyes had not seen her coming from the river. And some gentleman here tells him, he has seen them immediately after the birth of a child go to the water and *break the ice* to bathe themselves!

It is truly astonishing to see what customs will do. No doubt many ladies in civilized life are ruined by too careful treatments during child-birth, for this custom of the heathen is not known to be disadvantageous, but it is a "heathenish custom."

August. 1846. Thursday 6. The mysteries of a new world have been shown to me since last Thursday! In a few short months I should have been a happy mother and made the heart of a father glad, but the ruling hand of a mighty Providence has interposed and by an abortion [miscarriage] deprived us of the hope, the fond hope of mortals! But with the affliction He does not leave us comfortless!

In the meantime things have been going on prosperously without [outside], so I have been daily informed by my attendants. The troops *en mass* left about 10 o'clock Sunday morning, and made rather a grand show, at least in numbers. Till their departure the court yard, the patio, was thronged. I was not able to look out, but the massive sound filled my ear the while was quite sufficient criterion to judge by. Although it was the Sabbath, necessity compelled them to be busily employed. The clang of the blacksmith's hammer was constant. The trumpet sounded oft and loud; swords rattled in their sheaths, with the tinkling spur served as an echo. Ever and anon some military command was heard issuing, and doubtless promptly answered.

The fort is quite desolate. Most who are here now of the soldiers are sick. Two have died, and have been buried in the sand hills, the common fate of man.

SUGGESTIONS FOR FURTHER READING

Brown, Jennifer S. H. *Strangers in the Blood: Fur Trade Company Families in Indian Country*. Vancouver: University of British Columbia Press, 1980.

Brown, William E. *The Santa Fe Trail: National Park Service 1963 Historic Sites Survey*. St. Louis: Patrice Press, 1988.

Chalfant, William Y. *Dangerous Passage: The Santa Fe Trail and the Mexican War*. Norman: University of Oklahoma Press, 1994.

Franzwa, Gregory M. *The Santa Fe Trail Revisited*. St. Louis: Patrice Press, 1989.

Ray, Arthur J. *Indians in the Fur Trade, 1660–1870*. Toronto: University of Toronto Press, 1974.

Rich, E. E. *The Fur Trade and the Northwest to 1857*. Toronto: McClelland and Stewart, 1967.

Van Kirk, Sylvia. *Many Tender Ties: Women in Fur Trade Society, 1670–1870*. Norman: University of Oklahoma Press, 1980.

Wishart, David J. *The Fur Trade of the American West, 1807–1840*. Lincoln: University of Nebraska Press, 1979.

CHAPTER 7

―――――――――――――――

Gardens, Deserts, and Gold Camps

―――――――――――――――

Revealing America to a wider world never meant replacing old myths and tired illusions with new facts and fresh realities. Rather, what happened was more like an endless contest spanning several centuries, an ongoing struggle between different images and dreams. Some of those images and expectations accurately described the physical realities of North America, while others charted a reality more imaginary than material.

This competition, pitting one geography against another, was especially intense with regard to the American West. Each generation of outsiders constructed a West suited to its immediate needs and larger preoccupations. These efforts at image making were more than idle exercises in geographic fantasy. Notions about the West as a garden, desert, or gold field had profound consequences for the lives of thousands of Americans, natives and newcomers alike. American and Canadian policies on everything from Indian affairs and homesteading to railroads and irrigation were determined in large part by eastern images of western realities.

One of the best ways by which to understand this contest between different images and rival geographies is to study the records left behind by two seemingly dissimilar groups—government explorers and California gold seekers. Both groups of adventurers were on missions of more than personal importance. These travelers, bound for many destinations, represented the ambitions of large-scale economic and political institutions. Capitalist enterprise and high finance rode with every forty-niner caravan; imperial aspirations were implicit (and often explicit) in the instructions carried by every official expedition. The reports, evaluations, letters, and newspaper accounts that came from these journeys both reflected and promoted rival images of the West.

When Thomas Jefferson compiled his "Official Account of Louisiana" in 1803, he gave eloquent expression to the dream of the West as the garden of the world. While the president admitted that the precise boundaries of Louisiana were both "extensive" and "obscure," he waxed confident about the nature of this vast country so recently added to the United States. It was "one immense prairie," a garden sure to sustain generations of Americans living in republican virtue and simplicity. In his enthusiasm for this grassland Eden, Jefferson went so far as to imply that hard work—a central value in the republican ideology on which the United States had been founded—might be less essential in the West. The western garden, he wrote, would "yield an abundance of all the necessaries of life, and almost spontaneously; very little labor being required in the cultivation of the earth." Throughout the nineteenth century Jefferson's optimistic garden geography shaped individual lives and destinies as well as government policies.

Jefferson was not alone in his passionate attachment to the fertile lands beyond the Missouri. Historical geographers John L. Allen and Martyn J. Bowden have surveyed the literature about the West available to Jefferson and found that the most pervasive image was the garden. Words like *lush, fertile,* and *beautiful* were far more common than terms like *sterile* and *barren.* Directed to find gardens, explorers like the American Meriwether Lewis (1774–1809) and the Canadian Henry Youle Hind (1823–1908) eagerly reported their grassland discoveries. Writing to his mother in 1805, Lewis portrayed the Missouri River country of present-day Nebraska and the Dakotas as "one of the fairest portions of the globe." It was a phrase railroad and land promoters of the 1870s and 1880s would have gladly quoted to prospective settlers. From the vantage point of Canada and the British Empire in the 1850s, Hind accepted the idea of a desert somewhere in the West but insisted that it was small and mostly confined to territory claimed by the United States! Prairie Canada—today's Manitoba, Saskatchewan, and southern Alberta—was to Hind the real American garden.

Neither Lewis nor Hind thought about gardens as natural wilderness places. Gardens, whether at Jefferson's Monticello or in the far West, were structured and manicured places, products of human imagination, planning, and engineering. When Lieutenant Charles Wilkes (1798–1877), commander of the U.S. Exploring Expedition to the Pacific Ocean, visited Fort Vancouver in late May 1841, he found a community with a complex economy and a remarkably diverse population. Located along the Columbia River near present-day Portland, Oregon, the fort was the Hudson's Bay Company's principal establishment in the Pacific Northwest. But this was no mere trading post. Dr. John McLoughlin, the fort's chief factor, directed a large work force that prepared furs, raised and harvested grain, milked cows, baked bread, and planted extensive gardens. Fort Vancouver came close to matching Thomas Jefferson's image of the well-ordered rural society.

Even the growing influence of the industrial revolution, with its celebration of machine technology, could not replace the enduring image of the garden. In fact, many industrial engineers and builders incorporated images of the garden and nature in the designs of machines and factories. Eight decades after Lewis described the Missouri River Valley in glowing terms, Nebraska historian and town promoter William W. Cox fashioned a landscape shaped to fit the dreams of farmers and mechanics, of country women and their in-town sisters.

But not every explorer and traveler bound for the Great Plains, the Rockies, and beyond embraced the garden vision. A handful of observers, mostly army officers from the newly established (1838) Corps of Topographical Engineers, directly challenged the garden wisdom by describing the West as a desert. Conditioned by an eastern environment of forests, abundant rainfall, and temperate climate, these explorers found the western landscape—especially the lands west of the 100th meridian—strangely unsettling. Meriwether Lewis hinted at the reasons for this feeling when he told his mother that "the want of timber" was "a very serious one." While Lewis believed that the absence of trees did not mean that the plains lacked fertile soil, others were not so sure. Indeed, many explorers from the wooded and green East noted the region's deficiency—few trees, no navigable rivers, unpredictable weather, and a land often more brown than green. Sergeant John Ordway, for example, a member of the Lewis and Clark expedition, boldly challenged the garden image. Writing perhaps the earliest English-language description of the West as desert, Ordway looked at what is today eastern Montana and declared that "this country may with propriety be called the Deserts of North America for I do not conceive any part of it can ever be settled as it is deficient of or in water except this river, and of timber and too steep to be tilled." Zebulon Montgomery Pike (1779–1813), Stephen H. Long (1784–1864), Edwin James (1797–1861), John C. Frémont (1813–1890), and other explorers used the word *desert* not only to describe vast expanses of sandy waste but to convey the cultural meanings and prospects of a country quite unlike that east of the Mississippi.

While influential mid-nineteenth-century explorers agreed that a large part of the American West could be termed a desert, considerable debate revolved around the political significance of what became known as the Great American Desert. Was this desert an unchanging feature of the landscape, something unalterable and perhaps even valuable for its seemingly barren nature? Pike, James, and Long, three of the earliest proponents of the desert image, saw the barren lands as a useful barrier, a deterrent against too rapid expansion across the continent. It was, James wrote, "an unfit residence for any but a nomad population." Like some political thinkers of the time, these explorers feared that the unity of the American republic might be shattered by uncontrolled expansion. Just as Jefferson thought that the West could preserve the nation by being a farmer's paradise, some explorers hoped that the West's desolateness would keep the republic small and compact. In short, to be culturally and politically useful, the West had to remain the great desert.

Other observers of the Great Plains desert were not persuaded that the plains and the Rockies would forever stand as "waste" lands. When army explorer John C. Frémont traveled the Oregon Trail through the Platte River Valley in 1842, he praised the northern Great Plains as a fertile country with boundless promise. A year later, Frémont named and analyzed the Great Basin, a term that describes most of present-day Utah and parts of adjacent Oregon, California, and Nevada. Frémont was a careful and thorough explorer, and in the language of modern physical geography, he was beginning to regionalize the ideas of desert and garden. Whether he knew it or not, Frémont used desert and garden language both to describe terrain and to assess its economic potential. One judgment was scientific; the other, profoundly conditioned by cultural values. Frémont's "Great Interior Basin" was a world apart, a place that the explorer was sure would make outsiders think "Asiatic thoughts." Within that world Frémont found both native peoples who seemed to represent the past and lands that promised future economic development. Frémont understood that the Great Basin differed starkly from such places as Ohio and Nebraska. At the same time, he was not about to write it off as a land shielded from the expansionist energies of the American nation.

In the nineteenth-century debate over garden-versus-desert ideas, no traveler and scientist played a more spirited part than John Wesley Powell (1834–1902), explorer of the Colorado River, director of the United States Geographical and Geological Survey of the Rocky Mountain Region, and member of the federal Public Lands Commission. Powell had firsthand experience with the arid West. His pathbreaking *Report on the Lands of the Arid Region of the United States* (1878) directly challenged conventional wisdom about extending the garden image beyond the Great Plains. Powell's experience as an explorer had taught him that the intermontane region from the Rockies to the Sierra-Cascade mountain system demanded a new cultural vocabulary and a different public-lands policy. Even before submitting his *Report,* Powell asserted that "all of the region of country west of the 100th or 99th meridian except a little of California, Oregon, and Washington Territory, is arid, and no part of that country can be cultivated, with the exceptions I have mentioned; no part of it can be redeemed for agriculture, except by irrigation." Powell did not propose, however, that the arid West be forever the empty West. Unlike Pike, Long, and James, he believed that enlightened federal policies and modern scientific engineering could transform the West. Powell considered the Homestead Act's 160-acre land grant insufficient for ranching and too large for irrigated farming. To replace it, he proposed legislation that would create four-square-mile "pasture farms" and much smaller irrigation units. Powell's favorite word was *redeem,* by which he referred to rescuing the West from inappropriate uses and making the region productive. Despite his astute analysis of aridity, Powell still believed in the West as an engineered garden. This belief testified to the durability of Jefferson's western vocabulary.

The argument about gardens and deserts took a dramatic turn at the end of the 1840s with the American conquest of what is now New Mexico, Arizona, and California. The discovery of gold (1848) in California, moreover, brought further attention to a West that seemed more yellow in color than green. The flood of news from the California gold fields returned the debate about western lands to an earlier time when Spanish adventurers searched for Cíbola and Quivira. Now California promised a get-rich-quick El Dorado. Americans suffering through the financial difficulties of the 1840s found the promise of a golden West irresistible. One newspaper reported that "at present the people [in California] are running over the country and picking it [gold] out of the earth here and there, just as a thousand hogs let loose in a forest would root up the ground-nuts."

But as the gold seekers would soon learn, digging for treasure in what they viewed as a garden of gold was hard work with no guarantee of success. Men and women toiling in mining camps and on claims got both more and less than they bargained for—more work and usually less gold. For all its disappointments and failed dreams, however, the California gold rush changed many Americans' thinking about the West. For some, talk of deserts and gardens was now beside the point. Who could care about planting and harvesting in the garden of the world when capitalist dreams were coming true in California? The rush to California, what one observer called "the great frenzy," revealed not only the mining life but the passion for wealth and power.

A. The Garden

1. Meriwether Lewis Tells His Mother About the Great Plains, 1805

On the eve of departing from Fort Mandan for territories not yet traveled by Europeans, Lewis wrote to his mother. He characterized the lands that he had already seen in optimistic garden language of which Jefferson would have approved. At the same time, Lewis recognized that even the limited range of the Great Plains he had seen was a country quite different from his native Virginia.

This immense river [the Missouri River] so far as we have yet ascended, waters one of the fairest portions of the globe, nor do I believe that there is in the universe a similar extent of country, equally fertile, well watered, and intersected by such a number of navigable streams. The country as high up this river as the mouth of the river Platte [present-day Omaha, Nebraska], a distance of 630 miles is generally well timbered; at some little distance above this river the open or prairie country commences. With respect [to] this open country I have been agreeably disappointed. From previous information I had been led to believe that it was barren, sterile and sandy; but on the contrary I found it fertile in the extreme, the soil being from one to 20 feet in depth, consisting of a fine black loam, intermixed with a sufficient quantity of sand only to induce a luxuriant growth of grass and other vegetable productions, particularly such as are not liable to be much injured, or wholly destroyed by the ravages of fire. It is also generally level yet well watered; in short there can exist no other objection to it except that of the want of timber, which is truly a very serious one. This want of timber is by no means attributable to a deficiency in the soil to produce it, but owes its origin to the ravages of the fires, which the natives kindle in these plains at all seasons of the year. The country on both sides of the river, except some of its bottom lands, for an immense distance is one continued open plain, in which no timber is to be seen, except a few detached and scattered copses, and clumps of trees, which from their moist situations, or the steep declivities of hills are sheltered from the effects of fire. The general aspect of the country is level so far as the perception of the spectator will enable him to determine, but from the rapidity of the Missouri, it must be considerably elevated as it passes to the Northwest; it is broken only on the borders of the watercourses.

2. Lieutenant Charles Wilkes Finds the Garden on the Columbia River, 1841

In this excerpt from his *Narrative of the United States Exploring Expedition* (1845), Wilkes reports on a tour he made of Fort Vancouver and its outlying farms.

The scenery before reaching the lower mouth of the Willamette, is diversified with high and low land, which, together with three lofty snowy peaks, afford many fine views. The country begins to open here, and is much better adapted to agriculture than that lower down. On the approach to Vancouver, we passed one of the dairies, and some rich meadow-land, on which were grazing herds of fine cattle. We afterwards saw some flocks of sheep of the best English and Spanish breeds.

We came in at the back part of the village, which consists of about fifty comfortable log houses, placed in regular order on each side of the road. They are inhabited by the Company's servants, and were swarming with children, whites, half-breeds, and pure Indians. The fort stands at some distance beyond the village, and to the eye appears like an upright wall of pickets, twenty-five feet high: this encloses the houses, shops, and magazines [storehouses] of the Company. The enclosure contains about four acres, which appear to be under full cultivation. Beyond the fort, large granaries were to be seen. At one end is Dr. McLoughlin's house, built after the model of the French Canadian, of one story, weather-boarded and painted white. It has a piazza and small flower-beds, with grape and other vines, in front. Between the steps are two old cannons on sea-carriages, with a few shot, to speak defiance to the natives, who no doubt look upon them as very formidable weapons of destruction. I mention these, as they are the only warlike instruments to my knowledge that are within the pickets of Vancouver, which differs from all the other forts in having no bastions, galleries, or loop-holes. Nearby are the rooms for the clerks and visitors, with the blacksmiths' and coopers' shops. In the center stands the Roman Catholic chapel and nearby the flag-staff; beyond these again are the stores, magazines of powder, warerooms, and offices.

The Company's establishment at Vancouver is upon an extensive scale, and is worthy of the vast interest of which it is the center. The residents mess [dine] at several tables: one for the chief factor and his clerks; one for their wives (it being against the regulations of the Company for their officers and wives to take their meals together); another for the missionaries; and another for the sick and the Catholic missionaries. All is arranged in the best order, and I should think with great economy. Every thing may be had within the fort: they have an extensive apothecary shop, a bakery, blacksmiths' and coopers' shops, trade-offices for buying, others for selling, others again for keeping accounts and transacting business; shops for retail, where English manufactured articles may be purchased at as low a price, if not cheaper, than in the United States, consisting of cotton and woollen goods, ready-made clothing, ship-chandlery, earthen and iron ware, and fancy articles; in short, every thing, and of every kind and description, including all sorts of groceries, at an advance of eighty percent on the London prime cost.

The farm at Vancouver is about nine miles square. On this they have two dairies, and milk upwards of one hundred cows. There are also two other dairies, situated on Wapauto Island on the Willamette River, where they have one hundred and fifty cows, whose milk is employed, under the direction of imported dairymen, in making butter and cheese for the Russian settlements.

They have likewise a grist and saw mill, both well constructed, about six miles above Vancouver, on the Columbia River.

One afternoon we rode with Mr. Douglas [James Douglas, Fort Vancouver's accountant and second-in-command] to visit the dairy-farm, which lies to the west of Vancouver, on the Callepuya. This was one of the most beautiful rides I had yet taken, through fine prairies, adorned with large oaks, ash, and pines. The large herds of cattle feeding and reposing under the trees, gave an air of civilization to the scene, that is the only thing wanting in the other parts of the territory.

This dairy is removed every year, which is found advantageous to the ground, and affords the cattle better pasturage. The stock on the Vancouver farm is about three thousand head of cattle, two thousand five hundred sheep, and about three hundred brood [breeding] mares.

At the dairy, we were regaled with most excellent milk; and found the whole establishment well managed by a Canadian and his wife. They churn in barrel-machines, of which there are several. All the cattle look extremely well, and are rapidly increasing in numbers. The cows give milk at the age of eighteen months. Those of the California breed give a very small quantity of milk; but when crossed with those from the United States and England, do very well. I saw two or three very fine bulls, that had been imported from England. The sheep have lambs twice a year: those of the California breed yield a very inferior kind of wool, which is inclined to be hairy near the hide, and is much matted. This breed has been crossed with the Leicester, Bakewell, and other breeds, which has much improved it. The fleeces of the mixed breed are very heavy, weighing generally eight pounds, and some as much as twelve. Merinos have been tried, but they are not found to thrive.

I also visited the grist-mill, which is situated on a small stream, but owing to the height of the river, which threw a quantity of backwater on the wheel, it was not in action. The mill has one run of stones, and is a well-built edifice. Annexed to it is the house of the miller, who is also the watchmaker of the neighborhood. The mill is amply sufficient for all the wants of the Company, and of the surrounding country. The saw-mill is two miles beyond the grist-mill. A similar mistake has been made in choosing its position, for the mill is placed so low that for a part of the season when they have most water, they are unable to use it. There are in it several runs of saws, and it is remarkably well built. In few buildings, indeed, can such materials be seen as are here used. The quality of timber cut into boards, is inferior to what we should deem merchantable in the United States, and is little better than our hemlock. The boards are shipped to the Sandwich

[Hawaiian] Islands, and we here found the brig *Wave* taking on a cargo of lumber. These boards sell at Oahu for eighty dollars per thousand. I could not ascertain their cost here. About twenty men (Canadians and Sandwich Islanders) are employed at the mill.

3.   Henry Youle Hind Moves the Garden to Prairie Canada, 1857–1858

Half a century after Lewis wrote his evaluation of the grassland garden, geologist Henry Youle Hind produced a remarkably similar account of what are today Canada's prairie provinces. Hind and other Canadian explorers believed that there was a "fertile belt" of land stretching from the Lake of the Woods to the eastern slope of the Rockies.

It is impossible to examine a correct map of the North American continent without being impressed with the remarkable influence which the Great American Desert must exercise upon the future of the United States and British North America. The general character of this desert south of the 49th parallel [the border between the United States and Canada] is described elsewhere, and the important fact has been noticed, that any railroad constructed within the limits of the United States must pass, for a distance of twelve hundred miles west of the Mississippi, through uncultivable land, or in other words, a comparative desert. Along the 32nd parallel the breadth of this desert is least, and the detached areas of fertile soil greatest in quantity, but the aggregate number of square miles of cultivable lands amounts only to 2300 in a distance of 1210 miles. The northern limit of the Great American Desert is an imaginary line drawn from the Touchwood Hills to the Moose Woods on the South Branch, then south of Battle River as far as longitude 112 degrees, when turning south it sweeps along the flanks of the Rocky Mountains. North of this limit of the Great American Desert there is a broad strip of fertile country, rich in water, woods, and pasturage, drained by the North Saskatchewan and some of its affluents, and being a continuation of the fertile prairies of Red River, the eastern watershed of the Assinniboine and Red Deer River, with the outlying patches called the Touchwood Hills, File Hill, etc.

IT IS A PHYSICAL REALITY OF THE HIGHEST IMPORTANCE TO THE INTERESTS OF BRITISH NORTH AMERICA THAT THIS CONTINUOUS BELT CAN BE SETTLED AND

CULTIVATED FROM A FEW MILES WEST OF THE LAKE OF THE WOODS TO THE PASSES OF THE ROCKY MOUNTAINS, AND ANY LINE OF COMMUNICATION, WHETHER BY WAGON ROAD OR RAILROAD, PASSING THROUGH IT, WILL EVENTUALLY ENJOY THE GREAT ADVANTAGE OF BEING FED BY AN AGRICULTURAL POPULATION FROM ONE EXTREMITY TO THE OTHER.

No other part of the American continent possesses an approach even to this singularly favorable disposition of soil and climate, which last feature, notwithstanding its rigor during the winter season, confers, on account of its humidity, inestimable value on British North America south of the 54th parallel.

The natural resources lying within the limits of the Fertile Belt, or on its eastern borders, are themselves of great value as local elements of future wealth and prosperity; but in view of a communication across the continent they acquire paramount importance.

Timber available for fuel and building purposes; lignite coal, though not equal to true coal, nevertheless suitable for many of the different objects to which true coal is applied; iron ore widely distributed, of great purity and in considerable abundance; salt in quantity sufficient for a dense population. All these crude elements of wealth lie within the limits or on the borders of a region of great fertility, and drained by a river of the first class, navigable by steamer during several months of the year for five hundred miles of its course, and by batteaux [flat-bottomed boats] for nearly double that distance.

The position which the colony occupying the basin of Lake Winnipeg [Hind means present-day southern Manitoba] may assume at the close of the next decade, few will be prepared to define. Bounded on the west by British Columbia, whose gold wealth will ensure her a marvellously rapid progress, and on the east by the powerful, energetic, and loyal colony of Canada [present-day Ontario and Quebec] which now, in conjunction with the sister provinces, contains a population exceeding by ONE MILLION that of the thirteen United States during the revolutionary war, is it likely that British enterprise and patriotism will permit the intervening country to remain a wilderness, or pass into the hands of a foreign government?

4. The Garden Meets the Machine in Nebraska, 1888

When William W. Cox wrote his *History of Seward County* at the end of the 1880s, he did more than record the early days of an eastern Nebraska county. Drawing on decades of garden imagery, Cox portrayed Seward County as a rural paradise. Like so many other western promoters, moreover, he believed that his home on the plains stood at the very center of the garden of the world. At the same time, Cox put technology in his Nebraska garden. And that garden was increasingly located not in the countryside but in the city of Seward, the county seat. As he had explained earlier, farms and workshops belonged side by side. Thus Cox's Seward County was at once pastoral and industrial, a garden engineered for republican virtue and capitalist productivity.

Beautiful city! She that has been celebrated in poetry and song as the "sleeping beauty of the Blue valley" has awakened to a new life. She has awakened from her restful sleep refreshed and strengthened, and today she sits a "very queen" upon this commanding hill, overlooking vast stretches of scenery most magnificent, with the meandering river gently gliding by her feet and stretching from away in the northward to the southward, marked by its long line of timber in graceful curves, loops, and bows, singing in its ripples a sweet song of her power to turn the wheels of mills and factories as she wends her way toward the sunny south; Plum Creek, coming from the northeast, adding a charm as it winds among the beautiful farms and meadows, with its clusters of timber and varied landscapes; and from the northwest comes that grand stream, with name immortal, Lincoln Creek, through "verdant fields," a "very paradise."

Here she sits rejoicing in the richness and splendor of the surroundings. These lands, rich in verdure, rich in all things necessary to make happy homes, orchards, meadows, and fruitful fields, rich in the "cattle upon a thousand hills," rich in hogs and horses, rich in its pure, sweet water and running streams, rich in railways and all the means of an extended commerce, rich in factories and workshops, rich in merchant princes, rich in churches with their spires pointing to the *only* better land, rich in schools and all opportunities for mental culture and advancement, and "last, but not least," rich in strong arms, and brave hearts, ready and willing to pursue in the pathway of progress and achievement.

In the blazing light of the electric torch we may count tonight near three thousand souls within the city [the city of Seward], and quite a number in its immediate environs, which will soon become a part of the city. Forty substantial brick business houses grace our streets, many of which would be a credit to the largest cities. Three great lines of railway reaching in six directions, and making accessible to us the whole business of the world—the silks and teas of the Orient, the fruits of the Occident, the gold, silver, and rich gems of the mountains, the products of the great plains, the factories of New England, and all the vast and varied interests of our great country. Three miles of telegraph bearing to us on lightening's wings words of hope and cheer from all lands. A telephone through which we may talk to one another and to a hundred cities beside. An electric light to brighten our pathway. Well may we exclaim in the language of the old prophet, "Our light is come and the glory of God is risen upon us."

Our Morris keyless lock factory, one of the most extensive manufacturing institutions in the West, and the most national in its character of any factory in Nebraska, in fact we may say the field of its operations is the world. Its trade will soon reach into all lands, even to the islands of the sea. It is a matter of pride that the inventor of the lock is a citizen of Seward. Our oat meal mill, with its capacity of a hundred barrels of meal per day and using a thousand bushels of oats per day, freighting in and out from six to eight hundred car loads of grain and products per year. Our canning establishment, with its enormous capacity for using vegetables and storing them up for winter food for tens of thousands, and giving a grand market for the produce of farms and gardens, and giving out labor for hundreds of men, women, and children. A machine shop and foundry of large capacity, a creamery, four banks, with a multitude of mercantile establishments in all the various lines of trade, with one of the best hotels in the West, "The Windsor," and several smaller ones, and numerous boarding houses, six restaurants, and nearly a hundred workshops, large and small, including factories, etc. We mention blacksmiths, wagon makers, wire fence, tailoring, dress makers, millinery, cigars, broom makers, tinners, barbers, carpenters, newspapers, butchers, photographers, etc. With one of the best graded schools in our state, with a fine structure for the high school, seven departments, and four primary buildings, and employing twelve teachers. With eight church edifices, with large congregations of worshipers and flourishing Sabbath-schools. A magnificent Odd Fellows hall, a good opera house, three weekly newspapers, an excellent flouring mill, many splendid residences and beautiful yards, splendid streets and handsome parks, all amply supplied with trees and shrubs lending their enchantment and refreshing shade.

During the year just closed the growth in population and improvement has been wonderful. Her waste places have been made glad by the accession of a splendid new railroad, of three great new factories, of a host of new buildings, several almost princely dwellings, one grand church, a great host of new people, and best of all a perfect restoration of confidence, and closing the old year with the electric torch—a grand triumph. We close this sketch of this beautiful city, our home, feeling the inspiration of our hope, always buoyant, now doubly sure that the possibilities of Seward are grand.

Railroad company promotion posters like this one promised "Millions of Acres" in the West, the garden of the world.

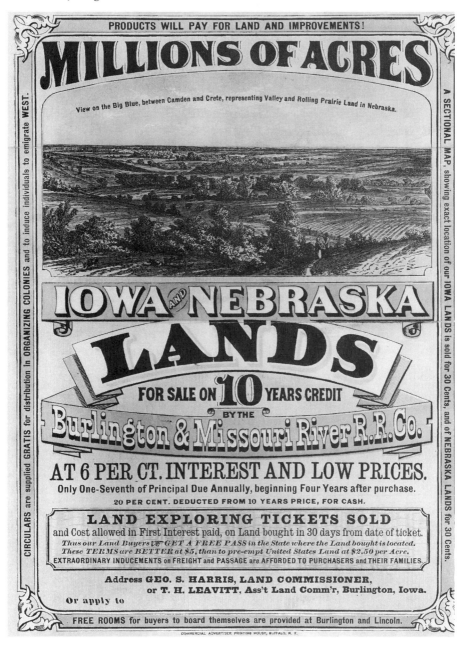

B. The Desert

1. Zebulon Montgomery Pike Finds the Desert in Colorado, 1806–1807

Sent by his commanding officer, General James Wilkinson, to reconnoiter Spanish territories, Pike soon became lost and was captured by Spanish forces near present-day Alamosa, Colorado. His description of the southern Great Plains is one of the earliest commentaries in English on the desert image.

Numerous have been the hypotheses formed by various naturalists, to account for the vast tract of untimbered country that lies between the waters of the Missouri, Mississippi, and the western ocean. Although not flattering myself to be able to elucidate *that,* which numbers of highly scientific characters, have acknowledged to be beyond their depth of research; still, I would not think I had done my country justice, did I not give birth to what few lights my examination of those internal deserts has enabled me to acquire. In that vast country [Pike means the southern Great Plains, today's western Kansas, eastern Colorado, and New Mexico] of which we speak, we find the soil generally dry and sandy, with gravel, and discover that the moment we approach a stream, the land becomes more humid with small timber; I therefore conclude, that this country was never timbered, as from the earliest age, the aridity of the soil having so few water courses running through it, and they being principally dry in summer, has never afforded moisture sufficient to support the growth of timber. In all timbered land, the annual discharge of the leaves, with the continual decay of old trees and branches, creates a manure and moisture, which is preserved from the heat of the sun not being permitted to direct his rays perpendicularly, but only to shed them obliquely through the foliage. But here a barren soil, parched and dried up for eight months in the year, presents neither moisture nor nutrition sufficient, to nourish the timber. These vast plains of the western hemisphere, may become in time equally celebrated as the sandy deserts of Africa; for I saw in my route, in various places, tracts of many leagues, where the wind had thrown up the sand, in all the fanciful forms of the ocean's rolling wave, and on which not a speck of vegetable matter existed.

But from these immense prairies may arise one great advantage to the United States, *viz:* The restriction of our population to some certain limits, and thereby a continuation of our union. Our citizens being so prone to rambling and extending themselves, on the frontiers, will, through necessity, be constrained to limit their extent on the west, to the borders of the Missouri and Mississippi, while they leave the prairies incapable of cultivation to the wandering and uncivilized aborigines of the country.

2. Edwin James Portrays the Great Plains as a Desert, 1819–1820

Recruited as a geologist for Major Stephen H. Long's western expedition (1819–1820), Edwin James had worked as a physician in Albany, New York, before joining Long's party. The Long expedition was charged with exploring the territory between the Mississippi River and the Rockies, with special emphasis on the lands of the Arkansas and Red rivers. The expedition account, entitled *An Account of an Expedition from Pittsburgh to the Rocky Mountains* (1823), prepared by James, presents the classic statement of the Great American Desert.

In regard to this extensive section of the country [the southern Great Plains], we do not hesitate in giving the opinion, that it is almost wholly unfit for cultivation, and of course unhabitable by a people depending upon agriculture for their subsistence. Although tracts of fertile land, considerably extensive, are occasionally to be met with, yet the scarcity of wood and water, almost uniformily prevalent, will prove an insuperable obstacle in the way of settling the country. This objection rests not only against the immediate section under consideration, but applies with equal propriety to a much larger portion of the country. Agreeably to the best intelligence that can be had, concerning the country both northward and southward of the section, and especially to the inferences deducible from the account given by Lewis and Clark, of the country situated between the Missouri and the Rocky Mountains, above the river Platte, the vast region commencing near the sources of the Sabine, Trinity, Brazos, and Colorado, and extending northwardly to the forty-ninth degree of north latitude in that direction, is throughout, of a similar character. The whole of this region seems peculiarly adapted as a range for buffaloes, wild goats, and other wild game, incalculable multitudes of which, find ample pasturage and subsistence upon it.

This region, however, viewed as a frontier, may prove of infinite importance to the United States, inasmuch as it is calculated to serve as a barrier to prevent too great an extension of our population westward, and secure us against the machinations or incursions of an enemy, that might otherwise be disposed to annoy us in that quarter.

3. John Charles Frémont Describes the Great Basin, 1843

John C. Frémont was the most famous, most widely read U.S. government explorer in the nineteenth century. Lionized in the press as "The Pathfinder," Frémont and his wife, Jessie Benton Frémont, prepared official reports that blended science and colorful language. In the first excerpt, Frémont describes the Great Basin as he saw it on September 6, 1843, when he and his party descended the western slopes of the Wasatch Range, in present-day Utah. In the second selection, Frémont offers a detailed analysis of the boundaries of the Great Basin.

a. Journal Entry for September 6, 1843

Leaving the encampment early, we again directed our course for the peninsular butte across a low scrubby plain, crossing in a way a slough-like creek with miry banks, and wooded with thickets of thorn which were loaded with berries. This time we reached the butte [Little Mountain, near Plain City, Utah] without any difficulty, and ascending to the summit, immediately at our feet beheld the object of our anxious search—the waters of the Inland Sea [the Great Salt Lake], stretching in still and solitary grandeur far beyond the limit of our vision. It was one of the great points of the exploration; and as we looked eagerly over the lake in the first emotions of excited pleasure, I am doubtful if the followers of Balboa felt more enthusiasm when, from the heights of the Andes, they saw for the first time the great Western ocean. It was certainly a magnificent object, and a noble *terminus* to this part of our expedition; and to travellers so long shut up among mountain ranges, a sudden view over the expanse of silent waters had in it something sublime. Several large islands raised their high rocky heads out of the waves; but whether or not they were timbered, was still left to our imagination, as the distance was too great to determine if the dark hues upon them were woodland or naked rock. During the day the clouds had been gathering black over the mountains to the westward, and, while we were looking, a storm burst down with sudden fury upon the lake, and entirely hid the islands from our view. So far as we could see, along the shores there was not a solitary tree, and but little appearance of grass; and on Weber's fork, a few miles below our last encampment, the timber was gathered in groves, and then disappeared entirely. As this appeared to be the nearest point to the lake where a suitable camp could be found, we directed our course to one of the groves, where we found a handsome encampment, with good grass and an abundance of rushes.

b. A Description of the Boundaries of the Great Basin

Differing so much from the Atlantic side of our continent, in coast, mountains, and rivers, the Pacific side differs from it in another most rare and singular feature—that of the Great interior Basin, of which I have so often spoken, and the whole form and character of which I was so anxious to ascertain. Its existence is vouched for by such of the American traders and hunters as have some knowledge of that region; the structure of the Sierra Nevada range of mountains requires it to be there; and my own observations confirm it. Mr. Joseph Walker [Joseph Rutherford Walker, a noted mountain man and guide], who is so well acquainted in those parts, informed me that, from the Great Salt Lake west, there was a succession of lakes and rivers which have no outlet to the sea, nor any connection with the Columbia, or with the Colorado or the Gulf of California. He described some of these lakes as being large, with numerous streams, and even considerable rivers, falling into them. In fact, all concur in the general report of these interior rivers and lakes; and, for want of understanding the force and power of evaporation, which so soon establishes an equilibrium between the loss and supply of waters, the fable of whirlpools and subterraneous outlets has gained belief, as the only imaginable way of carrying off the waters which have no visible discharge. The structure of the country would require this formation of interior lakes for the waters which would collect between the Rocky Mountains and the Sierra Nevada, not being able to cross this formidable barrier, nor to get to the Columbia or the Colorado, must naturally collect into reservoirs, each of which would have its little system of streams

Charles Preuss and John C. Frémont, *Map of an Exploring Expedition to the Rocky Mountains in the Year 1842 and to Oregon and North California in the Years 1843–1844.* A landmark in the cartographic history of the American West, this map describes Frémont's recognition of the Great Basin.

and rivers to supply it. This would be the natural effect; and what I saw went to confirm it. The Great Salt Lake is a formation of this kind, and quite a large one; and having many streams, and one considerable river [Bear River], four or five hundred miles long, falling into it. This lake and river I saw and examined myself; and also saw the Wasatch and Bear River mountains which enclose the waters of the lake on the east, and constitute, in that quarter, the rim of the Great Basin. Afterwards, along the eastern base of the Sierra Nevada, where we travelled for forty-two days, I saw the line of lakes and rivers which lie at the foot of that Sierra; and which Sierra is the western rim of the Basin. In going down Lewis's Fork [the Snake River] and the main Columbia, I crossed only inferior streams coming in from the left, such as could draw their water from a short distance only; and I often saw the mountains at their heads, white with snow; which, all accounts said, divided the waters of the desert from those of the Columbia, and which could be no other than the range of mountains which form the rim of the Basin on its northern side. And in returning from California along the Spanish Trail, as far as the head of the Santa Clara fork of the Rio Virgin, I crossed only small streams making their way south to the Colorado, or lost in the sand—as the Mohave; while to the left, lofty mountains, their summits white with snow, were often visible, and which must have turned water to the north as well as to the south, and thus constituted, on this part, the southern rim of the Basin. At the head of the Santa Clara fork, and in the Vegas de Santa Clara, we crossed the ridge which parted the two systems of waters. We entered the Basin at that point, and have travelled in it ever since, having its southeastern rim (the Wasatch Mountains) on the right, and crossing the streams which flow down into it. The existence of the Basin is therefore an established fact in my mind; its extent and contents are yet to be better ascertained. It cannot be less than four or five hundred miles each way, and must lie principally in the Alta California; the demarcation latitude of 42 degrees, probably cutting a segment from the north part of the rim. Of its interior, but little is known. It is called a *desert,* and, from what I saw of it, sterility may be its prominent characteristic; but where there is so much water, there must be some oasis. The great river, and the great lake, reported, may not be equal to the report; but where there is so much snow, there must be streams; and where there is no outlet, there must be lakes to hold the accumulated waters, or sands to swallow them up. In this eastern part of the Basin, containing Sevier, Utah, and the Great Salt Lakes, and the rivers and creeks falling into them, we know there is good soil and good grass, adapted to civilized settlements. In the western part, on Salmon Trout River, and some other streams, the same remark may be made.

The contents of this Great Basin are yet to be examined. That it is peopled, we know; but miserably and sparsely. From all that I heard and saw, I should say that humanity here appeared in its lowest form, and in its elementary state. Dispersed in single families; without fire arms; eating seeds and insects; digging roots, (and hence their name)—such is the condition of the greater part. Others are a degree higher, and live in communities upon some lake or river that supplies fish, and from which they repulse the miserable Digger. The rabbit is the largest animal known in this desert; its flesh affords a little meat; and their bag-like covering is made of its skins. The wild sage is their only wood, and here it is of extraordinary size—sometimes a foot in diameter, and six or eight feet high. It serves for fuel, for building material, for shelter to the rabbits, and for some sort of covering for the feet and legs in cold weather. Such are the accounts of the inhabitants and productions of the Great Basin; and which, though imperfect, must have some foundation, and excite our desire to know the whole.

The whole idea of such a desert, and such a people, is a novelty in our country, and excites Asiatic, not American ideas. Interior basins, with their own systems of lakes and rivers, and often sterile, are common enough in Asia; people still in the elementary state of families, living in deserts, with no other occupation than the mere animal search for food, may still be seen in that ancient quarter of the globe; but in America such things are new and strange, unknown and unsuspected, and discredited when related. But I flatter myself that what is discovered, though not enough to satisfy curiosity, is sufficient to excite it, and that subsequent explorations will complete what has been commenced.

4. John Wesley Powell Defines the Limits of the Desert, 1878

In this selection Powell argues that farming in the West is possible only with carefully engineered irrigation systems and cooperative enterprise. Powell believed that most western lands were best suited to large-scale grazing and ranching, not agriculture.

The Arid Region is the great Rocky Mountain Region of the United States, and it embraces something more than four-tenths of the whole country, excluding Alaska. In all this region the mean annual rainfall is insufficient for agriculture, but in certain seasons some localities, now here, now there, receive more than their average supply. Under such conditions crops will mature without irrigation. As such seasons are more or less infrequent even in the most favored localities, and as the agriculturalist cannot determine in advance when such seasons may occur, the opportunities afforded by excessive rainfall cannot be improved.

In Utah Territory agriculture is dependent upon irrigation. To this statement there are some small exceptions. In the more elevated regions there are tracts of meadow land from which small crops of hay can be taken: such lands being at higher altitudes need less moisture, and at the same time receive a greater amount of rainfall because of the altitude; but these meadows have been, often are, and in future will be, still more improved by irrigation. Again, on the belt of country lying between Great Salt Lake and the Wasatch Mountains the local rainfall is much greater than the general rainfall of the region. The water evaporated from the lake is carried by the westerly winds to the adjacent mountains on the east and again condensed, and the rainfall thus produced extends somewhat beyond the area occupied by the mountains, so that the foot hills and contiguous bench lands receive a modicum of this special supply. In some seasons this additional supply is enough to water the lands for remunerative agriculture, but the crops grown will usually be very small, and they will be subject to seasons of extreme drought when all agriculture will result in failure. Most of these lands can be irrigated, and doubtless will be, from a consideration of the facts already stated, namely, that crops will thereby be greatly increased and immunity from drought secured. Perhaps other small tracts, on account of their subsoils, can be profitably cultivated in favorable seasons, but all of these exceptions are small, and the fact remains that agriculture is there dependent on irrigation. Only a small part of the territory, however, can be redeemed, as high, rugged mountains and elevated plateaus occupy much of its area, and these regions are so elevated that summer frosts forbid their occupation by the farmer. Thus thermic conditions limit agriculture to the lowlands, and here another limit is found in the supply of water. Some of the large streams run in deep gorges so far below the general surface of the country that they cannot be used; for example, the Colorado River runs through the southeastern portion of the Territory and carries a great volume of water, but no portion of it can be utilized within the Territory from the fact that its channel is so much below the adjacent lands. The Bear River, in the northern part of the Territory, runs in a somewhat narrow valley, so that only a portion of its waters can be utilized. Generally the smaller streams can be wholly employed for agriculture, but the lands which might thus be reclaimed are of greater extent than the amount which the streams can serve; hence in all such regions the extent of irrigable land is dependent upon the volume of water carried by the streams.

This statement of the facts relating to the irrigable lands of Utah will serve to give a clearer conception of the extent and condition of the irrigable lands throughout the Arid Region. Such as can be redeemed are scattered along the water courses, and are in general the lowest lands of the several districts to which they belong. In some of the states and territories the percentage of irrigable land is less than in Utah, the others greater, and it is probable that the percentage in the entire region is somewhat greater than in the territory which we have considered.

A stranger entering this Arid Region is apt to conclude that the soils are sterile, because of their chemical composition, but experience demonstrates the fact that all soils are suitable for agricultural purposes when properly supplied with water. It is true that some of the soils are overcharged with alkaline materials, but these can in time be "washed out." Altogether the fact suggests that far too much attention has heretofore been paid to the chemical composition of soils and too little to those physical conditions which moisture and air are supplied to the roots of the growing plants.

Small streams can be taken out and distributed by individual enterprise, but cooperative labor or aggregated capital must be employed in taking out the larger streams.

In Utah Territory cooperative labor, under ecclesiastical organization, has been very successful. Outside of Utah there are but few instances where it has been tried; but at Greeley, in the State of Colorado, this system has been eminently successful.

C. The California Gold Camps

1. A Federal Bureaucrat Prepares for the Journey to California, 1849

Few prospective gold seekers were better placed to obtain reliable information about California than J. Goldsborough Bruff (1804–1889). A draftsman at the Bureau of Topographical Engineers, he had access to the most recent news from the gold fields. Bruff was an organizer and captain of the Washington City and California Mining Association, one of the many traveling parties bound for gold-rush country. In the first excerpt, Bruff describes some of the early planning for the California journey. In the second selection, he writes to a friend, Colonel Peter Force, giving further details about the proposed trip.

a. Planning the Washington City and California Mining Association

[undated fragment in the Bruff papers]

Having made duplicate drawings of all of Frémont's Reports, maps, plates, etc. for the two houses of Congress—it revived the Spirit of adventure so long dormant and I was anxious to travel over, and see what my friend had so graphically and scientifically realized: more particularly when a golden reward appeared to be awaiting us at the nether end of the route. At first, I had mentioned it to a few friends whom I thought might desire to try it also: they told others, and we were nearly resolved on forming a company of 12 or 15, for the occasion, when some citizens called a meeting to be held at Apollo Hall—(between 12 and 13 Sts), to consider about forming an emigrating party. I went, was unanimously called to the Chair, organized by election of a Secretary, and adjourned to meet at my residence a few days later. Regular weekly meetings ensued, the organization was perfected; members signed the Articles, committee on supplies etc. appointed, and the men regularly drilled as light infantry—A Committee was sent to Pittsburgh, to contract for manufacture of the 14 company wagons, as many large tents, and the purchase provisions and stores of all kinds: whilst another committee proceeded far ahead—to procure mules—some 70 being needed. The company, mostly young men, was 66 strong, neatly uniformed in grey frock and pants, and felt hats—armed with rifles, muskets, and a few large fowling pieces, all necessary accoutrements, canteens etc., gum [rubber] suits, blanket, pair of revolvers in belt, large Bowie knives, and belt hatchet—and lots of ammunition. Of stores, we had a supply of all necessary mechanical tools and appliances: a traveling forge, obtained here from the government—and were well-prepared for any emergency that might happen.

b. Bruff Writes to His Friend, Colonel Peter Force, Washington, D.C., January 30, 1849

The Washington City Mining Company may be said to have been formed. At least 24 energetic, honorable men have determined to go, and in the mode, and under the rules I have advised. It will be much augmented, no doubt to 50, but of the same character material, as the nucleus.

We go via the plains and South Pass of the Rocky Mountains, with wagons, provisions, and implements and tools. Each man efficiently armed and equipped. On arrival at the [Sierra] Nevada mountains, we propose selecting an eligible site for mining, trading, water, health, etc., and there construct a log stockade, both for protection and comfort. Common stock and equal dividends throughout. Shares for the general outfit of wagons, animals, tools, provisions, etc., not yet fully ascertained, but supposed to be about $300. Shareholders may supply an active substitute, with their own mutual understanding about the profits.

A correct and precise journal will be kept en route, for which I shall furnish sketches and meteorological observations. This, when published, will not only be interesting, but a perfect guide in every respect to all future travellers on that route. We go as a body of energetic gentlemen, to enrich ourselves, if possible, by every honorable means. I, perhaps, will be worse off, pecuniarily, than any other one of the party; a speculation I am engaged in may yield me, by 1st April, sufficient, and it may not. My family (whom I love as much as any husband and father can) I shall be compelled to leave on credit, awaiting probably eight months, ere I will be enabled to send a remittance to them. In a few days I shall commence packing up my valuable collection [coins and minerals] and such articles as the family will not need: these I must store somewhere. This will afford me the opportunity of giving you many maps. The association will continue in active operation from 10 to 18 months.

Acquainted with nearly all the officers of the U.S. Army, I cannot be very unfortunate in California, and if gold shall have vanished, my abilities will guarentee a handsome salary.

I take with me all the maps and works on the country, mineralogical works, tests, etc. So you see that our principles are of the best character to insure security, comfort, and success.

2. A. M. Williams Tells His Father About Life in the Gold Fields, 1850

A young gold seeker from Missouri, A. M. Williams was part of an overland caravan that left Independence in April 1850. Letters sent to his father were reprinted in several local newspapers, a common way to spread news about the gold rush. Williams's letter of November 10 first appeared in the Missouri *Gazette* and then was reprinted in the St. Joseph *Adventure* on February 21, 1851. Despite the grim picture Williams painted in this letter, he also told his father that California was "the garden spot of the United States."

A miner's life, I think, is the hardest in the world. On arriving in the country, he gathers all the information he can, as to the best place to settle, buys his tools and provisions for a week or two, and hires a wagon to take them and his clothing to the mines, going himself afoot from 50 to 100 miles. When he gets in the neighborhood of the place, he will meet a great many with their washers, picks, shovels, clothing and camp equipage on their backs, just leaving the place, and hunting other diggings. He goes on into the neighborhood of the place, or as near as he can with the wagon, when he must pack his things the balance of the way (some 4 or 5 miles) over almost perpendicular mountains, on his back, making some three or four trips to do it; finally he gets all his trumpery landed under some trees, as near the diggings as he can that is not occupied by some other person. He next sets about hunting some place to dig in the bends of the river, (called bars) and if not lucky enough to hit some place where the gold has been deposited under ground, (and about which, from the appearance of the ground, he can make no calculations,) he may dig all day, and at night he may have one, two, or three dollars—digging, prying away the large rocks, that have been rolling off for centuries from the sides of the mountains, into the streams—while the sun pours down in rays with a power he never before felt—surrounded all the time by strangers who care nothing for him, nor he for them—night comes on, and he goes to his tree, cooks his supper, spreads his blanket on the ground, and goes to sleep; gets up in the morning out of the dust, cooks his breakfast, and goes to work as before, not stopping except to get his dinner, which consists of bread and pickled pork, and occasionally potatoes, which cost him 20 cents per pound, or onions, which cost 90 cents per pound, comes in at night with probably some luck, may be better, may be worse. He works on that way for three or four days, finding his hole won't pay he hunts another place, throws off three or four or five feet of the top rock and dirt, and tries his new hole, finds out it won't do—hunts a third, and so on, every time he moves; moving his rocker and frame to rock it on, to the sides of the river as near his claim as he can, carrying the dirt to it in buckets, over the holes that others have dug, and the rock and dirt they have thrown up, he finds out, (unless lucky) that none of his holes will pay, and seeing no other spot, but what has been dug up, or prospected, (which is digging a hole in the ground to see whether there is any gold underneath or not) he probably hears of some other place, some 10 or 15 miles off where the miners are doing remarkably well, and it comes so straight from those he has been acquainted with, and who has a partner that has just come from there. He sells off as much of his plunder as he can at half price, puts a mule's load on his back, leaving the balance to take care of itself, and starts off over the mountains, hills and rocks, without road, chart or compass, and finally after much toil and labor gets in the neighborhood of the new diggings, and meets twenty or thirty men loaded like himself, finds out that they are from the very place he is hunting; asks how the miners are doing, and is told that a few are doing very well, but the great majority are not more than clearing expenses, asks them where they are going, they will tell him of some extraordinary place, or probably they are going to the very place he left. Such is gold hunting in California. But he goes on to his new diggings, hunts another tree to shield him from the sun, deposits his load and recruits [rests] his wasted store of plunder at a high price, and goes to work as before, with probably the same success—takes the diarrhea (as nearly every one does) gets well in three or four weeks, or well enough to do half work, goes to work, and takes it again, or dies and is buried somewhere close by, by some one who don't know his name, for no one knows the name of another in California, although well acquainted.

His friends at home hear nothing from him, until absence and silence force them to believe that their child, or father, or husband, has been buried far from home, where the tear of affection can never be shed over his grave, or the spot told on which he lies.

If a miner, however, happens to have the good luck to hit on a rich spot, he may make a handsome sum in a few weeks,—in which case he writes back to his friends at home, probably adding a little to the amount he has dug, from what he expects to dig; which flies through the neighborhood or is published in the papers, and starts out the next season 50 or 100 more, to be disappointed as thousands here now are, and whose voices are not heard at home. The reason that they will not write back is that they are in hopes that their luck may change, and that they may have something pleasant to tell. You may think that this is giving too dark a coloring on the black side, but it is what I have found to be true.

3. A New England Woman Describes Running a Mining-Camp Boarding House, 1849

First printed in the Portland (Maine) *Advertizer* and reprinted in the October 6, 1849, issue of the Missouri *Republican,* this letter reveals both the economic advantages and the social dislocation that women experienced in the gold rush.

We have now been keeping house three weeks. I have ten boarders, two of which we board for the rent. We have one hundred and eighty-nine dollars per week for the whole. We think we can make seventy-five of it clear of all expenses, but I assure you I have to work mighty hard—I have to do all my cooking by a very small fire place, no oven, bake all my pies and bread in a dutch oven, have one small room about 14 feet square, and a little back room we use for a store room about as large as a piece of chalk. Then we have an open chamber over the whole, divided off by a cloth. The gentlemen occupy the one end, Mrs. H—— and daughter, your father and myself, the other. We have a curtain hung between our beds, but we do not take pains to draw it, as it is no use to be particular here.

The gentleman of whom we hire the house has been at housekeeping; he loaned us some few things (for furniture), but I assure you we do not go into luxuries. We sleep on a cot without any bedding or pillow except our extra clothing under our heads.

Tell Betty they have to pay twenty-five dollars for making a dress. If there was anything pleasant here I should like to have you all come immediately. But there has been no rain for three months, nor won't be for so long to come; not a green thing to be seen except a few stunted trees, and so cold we have to keep a fire to be comfortable. When you are eating corn and beans think of your poor mother, who does not get any fruit or vegetables excepting potatoes, and those eight dollars a bushel, and as soon as we are worth ten thousand dollars I shall come home; if I do not find some pleasanter place than this. Mrs. H—— took some ironing to do, and what time I had I helped, and made seven dollars in as many hours. I have not been in the street since I began to keep house; I don't care to go into a house until I get ready to go home; not that I am homesick, but it is nothing but gold, gold—no social feelings—and I want to get my part and go where my eyes can rest upon some green things.

4. Gold Rush City, 1849

The gold rush quickly became an international event as miners from France, Chile, China, and many other parts of the world flooded into California. As this report, first published in the New York *Herald* and then reprinted in the St. Joseph *Adventure* on November 9, 1849, makes clear, San Francisco had become a global city filled with hustlers and entrepreneurs.

A "bee hive" is the best comparison for the town of San Francisco. To define who is "king bee" would puzzle a smarter fellow than ever emanated from the "Philadelphia bar." What is strange medley is the composition of the population located here—by far the largest portion are the citizens of the "old States," but every part of Europe is represented, as well as Africa and Asia—all classes and conditions. I meet every day men who, at home, were esteemed wealthy, and many that I know have been—those who have led the fashions, gave morning concerts at gilded salons, and first Dilettanti at the opera, active merchants, etc.—now bustling about in all eagerness of trade, leaving behind them the enjoyments of the social circle, family, friends and comfortable quarters to carry on business in a shanty or canvas house, enduring all sorts of privations, and in many instances, forced to do their own "pulling and hauling"; then there are hosts in speculators in real estate, brokers in gold dust, "black legs," [swindlers] and broken down gentlemen—all bent upon one sole subject—"gold." "But where the honey is there you will find the bees."—and, by the way, judging from the number of gambling establishments about town, and the high rates they pay for room hire, they are the ones who will pocket all the loose gold.

5. Mining Rearranges the California Landscape, 1860

Scenes of individual miners panning for gold soon gave way to large-scale engineering projects that rerouted rivers and washed away whole hillsides. Such changes were detailed by an anonymous author in the April 1860 issue of *Harper's New Monthly Magazine*. As this excerpt reveals, gold camps had become part of industrial America.

Within a few miles of Auburn [California], a considerable mining town of Placer County, we visited a well known bend in the middle fork of the American River called Murderer's Bar, where one of the earliest attempts was made to turn the course of a large river with a view of exploring the bottom for gold. Every bend or shallow place in the numerous mountain streams of the gold region has been thus attacked, the waters diverted from their course and made to pass through artificial channels, leaving the old course dry for mining operations. Works such as that of Murderer's Bar, in

El Dorado County, are carried on by large companies, who have among them carpenters, surveyors, engineers, and stout hands. Sometimes the water is taken into a strongly-built flume from above and conducted in a long box through the old bed of the river, by this avoiding the necessity of a canal. The bed of the river thus laid dry, the company enter it and search in every crevice and pocket for the golden deposits which should have naturally accumulated by the action of the river against the bases of the adjacent hills. These enterprises often yield immense riches, every depression in the bed rock holding its quota of brightly-burnished gold. The operations are frequently so extensive as to occupy several successive seasons before the whole can be explored. At others, the premature approach of the rainy season, and the consequent freshets, carry away the whole works in a night; but on renewing them the following year, the crevices and holes are often found to have collected an amount of gold almost equal to the original deposits brought down by the floods from the numerous diggings above. Frequently the place has been injudiciously chosen and after months of hard labor the river proves entirely bare of gold. The river operations at Murderer's Bar are the property of a company of some seventy-five men, one of whom informed us that they employed nearly two hundred more during the dry season. As fresh deposits of gold are made each year, the place may be considered a perpetual investment. It is estimated that only one in three of these river enterprises proves remunerative.

SUGGESTIONS FOR FURTHER READING

Caughey, John W. *Gold Is the Cornerstone.* Berkeley: University of California Press, 1948.

Cline, Gloria Griffen. *Exploring the Great Basin.* Norman: University of Oklahoma Press, 1963.

Dick, Everett. *Conquering the Great American Desert.* Lincoln: Nebraska State Historical Society, 1975.

Emmons, David. *Garden in the Grasslands: Boomer Literature of the Central Great Plains.* Lincoln: University of Nebraska Press, 1971.

Goetzmann, William. *New Lands, New Men: America and the Second Great Age of Discovery.* New York: Viking Press, 1986.

Kolodny, Annette. *The Land Before Her: Fantasy and Experience of the American Frontiers, 1630–1860.* Chapel Hill: University of North Carolina Press, 1984.

Paul, Rodman W. *Mining Frontiers of the Far West, 1848–1880.* New York: Holt, Rinehart and Winston, 1963.

Smith, Henry Nash. *Virgin Land: The American West as Symbol and Myth.* Cambridge, Massachusetts: Harvard University Press, 1950.

Stegner, Wallace. *Beyond the Hundredth Meridian: John Wesley Powell and the Second Opening of the West.* Boston: Houghton Mifflin Co., 1954.

Van Orman, Richard. *The Explorers: Nineteenth Century Expeditions in Africa and the American West.* Albuquerque: University of New Mexico Press, 1984.

CHAPTER 8

Overland by Trail and Rail

In late June 1846, mountain man and trail guide Jim Clyman was heading back east along the Oregon Trail when he met several companies of overland emigrants. Their naive optimism about the far West and the journey ahead both amazed and worried Clyman. "It is remarkable," the veteran trapper later wrote, "how anxious these people are to hear from the Pacific country." What puzzled Clyman was that "so many of all kinds and classes of People should sell out comfortable homes in Missouri and Elsewhare, pack up and start across such an emmence Barren waste to settle in some place of which they have at most so uncertain information." Clyman's only explanation was his laconic comment, "This is the character of my countrymen." Some days later, after having spent more time with the covered-wagon folk, Clyman expressed his admiration for "these honest looking, open harted people." Young Francis Parkman, fresh from Boston by way of Harvard College, was not nearly so charitable. He found the overlanders "totally devoid of any sense of delicacy or propriety." In notes that became the basis for his book *The Oregon Trail* (1849), Parkman suggested that if more well-bred New Englanders were in charge of the wagon trains, the journey would be safer and better organized. Repelled by "this strange migration" and not grasping its larger meanings, Parkman and his Beacon Hill traveling companion Quincy Adams Shaw hurried out of Independence, Missouri, in search of literary Indians and picturesque scenery.

Clyman and Parkman were witnesses to what some historians believe is one of the most symbolic of all American journeys: the mid-nineteenth-century overland emigrations to Oregon, California, and Utah. From 1840 to 1866—the dates usually given for the migration—a quarter of a million Americans left home for the western country. Whether these overlanders struck out alone or traveled with large, well-organized companies, they were all drawn to the West by a powerful set of promises. Land, gold, religious freedom, and renewed health were just some of the rewards that emigrants saw beckoning on the western horizon. Mormon exiles, California gold seekers, and Oregon settlers were at the center of the emigration, but the movement began well before 1840 and lasted past the 1860s.

This chapter takes a broad view of the overland experience, reaching back to missionary journeys to Oregon in the 1830s and concluding with travels on the transcontinental railroad. Here are many voices—a young missionary pregnant with her first child, a teenage girl who survived the horrors of Donner Lake, an English journalist with a tabloid mentality, a distinguished American poet, and the future author of *The Strange Case of Dr. Jekyll and Mr. Hyde.*

While the drama of what historian Dale Morgan called "human nature on the loose" escaped Francis Parkman, many emigrants had some inkling that their journey was more than a simple jaunt to the Pacific. Merrill J. Mattes's comprehensive bibliography *Platte River Road Narratives, 1812–1866* records more than 2000 overland accounts, some just bare lists of mileage and camping places but others richly detailed, often personal reflections on the way West. Whatever the length and quality of the narratives, they all had a common purpose—to preserve the memory of an important journey and to ponder its significance. In ways that few emigrant overlanders would have predicted, the narratives set down thoughts not so much about the desired place as about the journey itself. The great event memorialized in the journals (and in many pioneer societies founded later) was not arrival in the promised land but the experience of getting there.

These vivid memories of unforgettable journeys reveal four aspects of the American experience. As with the first European explorers, overland emigrants took mental journeys long before leaving home. These at-home travels were part desire and fantasy, part thoughtful consideration about the way ahead. Overlanders imagined not only the nature of the destination but the shape of the journey's terrain. Mary Richardson Walker, zealous to win Indian souls for the Christian God, imagined the Oregon Trail as a sacred highway leading to a holy Eden. George and Tamsen Donner contemplated a journey that would take them to a fertile and healthy country. The railway overlanders went through a similar process, conditioned by guidebook literature and the tradition of the European Grand Tour. Part tourist, part social critic, railroad voyagers like Samuel Bowles, William F. Rae, and Walt Whitman made the journey to experience the trip itself. For them, the journey was the desired goal. Just like the emigrant overlanders, these rail explorers could not escape assumptions made before boarding the train. These adventurers fashioned images of romance and wonder and then projected them on the western landscape. Other contemporary travelers had done the same thing in India, Africa, and South America. Assumptions conditioned impressions, whether the observer went in search of a rising national empire or the grandest meanings of the American dream.

Space—the sheer stretch of western space—most often challenged and sometimes confounded overlanders. Whether they viewed space from a wagon seat or through a passenger car window, its expanse squinted eyes, pulled the mind, and left otherwise articulate writers almost wordless or far too wordy. Walt Whitman, crossing the Great Plains to Colorado in the fall of 1879, knew what happened when vocabularies made for eastern forests collided with the sweep of the Great Plains. "One wants new words in writing about these plains, and all the inland American West—the terms *far, large, vast,* etc. are insufficient." Whitman instinctively understood that those writing about their overland experiences were grappling with a classic American problem—how to make sense of open space. Each writer in this chapter found a solution of one sort or another. Charles Stanton tamed the unruly western landscape with the language of descriptive geology; Tamsen Donner domesticated space by the vocabulary of friendship; Robert Louis Stevenson fled from space, finding security inside a passenger car.

The overland narratives remind us about community. Although travelers bound for the Pacific sometimes celebrated individual accomplishment, they almost always journeyed in company with others. As one emigrant put it, "Our journey has not been as solitary as we feared." Gold seekers and land-hungry settlers often created large-scale traveling companies with elected officers and elaborate rules. Indeed, despite the prevailing American ideology of individualism, the overlanders came out of close-knit communities and wanted to travel within such familiar settings. Railway cars like the ones that took Samuel Bowles and William Rae west in 1869 were communities on the move. Overlanders also took note of new communities. Places like Fort Laramie and Fort Bridger were important service centers, meeting the needs of travelers along the trail. Railroads created their own set of trackside towns—settlements that seemed signs of either American progress or social stagnation, depending on the observer's angle of vision.

The earliest European efforts at revealing America placed native peoples at the center of the story, either as partners or as enemies. Steeped in such accounts, mid-nineteeenth-century wagon-train overlanders (often armed to the teeth) sometimes engaged in bloody fantasies about Indian attacks. But as John D. Unruh, Jr., explains in *The Plains Across: The Overland Emigrants and the Trans-Mississippi West, 1840–1860,* native attacks occurred less frequently than emigrant violence directed against Indians. (Unruh counts some 426 recorded Indian deaths at overlanders' hands; the best estimate of emigrants' deaths, by contrast, is that 362 travelers died as a result of Indian attacks between 1840 and 1860.) Yet even as fears of native violence lingered, white overlanders, whether would-be settlers, gold seekers, or tourists, no longer put native peoples at the heart of their narratives. Now the story plot was more about a world where Indians were outsiders, mere reminders of an almost vanished past. When Samuel Bowles saw some American soldiers lined up at a railroad station, he recalled that the "Indian question" remained unanswered. But Bowles had no doubt about the answer and its meaning for both the Indians and the soldiers: The future lay with the energy of the railroad and the force of the troopers.

1. Mary Richardson Walker Records an Early Missionary Journey to Oregon, 1838

Along with her husband, Elkanah, and several other Protestant missionaries, Mary Richardson Walker (1811–1897) was part of an overland party bound for the mission established by Marcus and Narcissa Whitman on the Walla Walla River in present-day southeastern Washington. An inveterate diary keeper—her journals span fifty-seven years—Walker left an overland account that covers the journey from Missouri to the Whitman mission. The entries reprinted here follow the missionary party from present-day western Nebraska to the Whitman mission.

Some of Walker's most memorable entries recount her misadventures at the fur-traders' rendezvous on the Wind River north of present-day Riverton, Wyoming. Despite her misgivings, Mary Walker proved a sturdy and capable overlander.

Sunday, June 10. Platte River. Today they were designing to cross the Platte but the rain prevents. So we have for the first time an opportunity to lay by on the Sabbath. I am not sufficiently well to enjoy it as much as I should. Yet I am glad to rest. I have reflected much on the goodness and mercy of God. My health at present is rather feeble [she was in the first trimester of a pregnancy] and I find it difficult to keep up a usual degree of cheerfulness. If I were to yield to inclination I should cry half my time without knowing what for. My circumstances are rather trying. So much danger attends me on every hand; a long journey yet before me, going I know not whither. Without mother or sister to attend me, can I survive it all? I feel that God is able to carry me through all, if He sees good. But I cannot escape suffering. Hope I shall have grace to bear it patiently. Thus far I have been enabled to keep my temper on all occasions, though my feelings have been tried exceedingly by some of the company.

Friday, June 15. Last night camped at the Sweet water [Sweetwater River] at the foot of Rock Independence [in present-day central Wyoming], so called because the Fur Company once celebrated Independence here. This morning, there being no dew, went in company with Mr. and Mrs. Gray [William and Mary Gray] to the top of the rock. It is I should judge more than 100 feet high and half a mile in circumference, eliptical in form. The rock is a coarse granite in which the quartz predominates. It appears as if it had been scraped hardly by something. I forgot to say that near it we passed a salt pond half a mile one way, and a mile the other, at the edge of which were concretions resembling stone. We forded the Sweetwater, and soon passed the place [known today as Devil's Gate] where the Rock Mountain is cleft to its base and the Sweetwater passes. The rock on either hand perpendicular is perhaps 200 feet high. Rock Independence forms the entrance some say to the Rocky Mountains, others say not. We have traveled today about 15 miles over a level prairie or plain, encircled by naked mountains of solid granite. The scenery has been beautiful, and magnificent; and with me the pleasure of beholding it has relieved in great measure the weariness of the way.

Monday, June 18. Made only one camp. Not so much fatigued as sometimes. Weather quite warm and pleasant. Our tent close to the bank of the Sweetwater which is a remarkably pleasant stream; not turbid like most we have seen. Most of the country we have traveled since leaving Fort William [present-day Fort Laramie, Wyoming] has been a sandy desert, bearing little but sedge and wormwood, flowers and grease wood. Most of the way plenty of fuel though lately we have often had nothing but sedge. The minerals are interesting. But I have to ride over most of them without picking them up. If I could only mount and dismount without help how glad I would be. Not at all discouraged by the way. Ride in company with Dr. and Mrs. Gray most of the time. Mr. Walker [her husband Elkanah] gets along without quarreling, a strange thing for which I cannot be sufficiently thankful. If he has as much difficulty as most of the company, I think I should be homesick enough.

Monday, June 25. Rendezvous. Spent most of the day talking and dividing things with Mrs. Smith [wife of Rev. A. B. Smith].

Thursday, July 5. Last night disturbed by drunkards. Rose early and washed. A large company arrived under the command of Capt. Bridger [Jim Bridger]. A band of them came to salute us. One man carried the scalp of the

Blackfoot. The music consisted of tin horns accompanied by the inarticulate sound of the voice. They halloed, danced, fired and acted as strangely as they could.

Friday, July 6. The same place. Some of the squaws [wives of the traders] came to get some dresses cut. We were again saluted by a company on foot. The same music, scalp, etc. Their faces were painted. White men acted like Indians. It is said that many of the white men in the mountains try to act as much like Indians as they can and would be glad if they really were so. Several squaws were here who united in the dance. They were warmly clad, the weather excessively hot. For several nights the noise in the camp has continued most of the night. Some of the captains and, I suppose, many or most of the men are drunk nearly all the time.

Monday, July 16. In the forenoon rode ten miles. Encamped on Big Sandy [the Big Sandy River in southwestern Wyoming]. Got my horse in the mire; not hurt any. Felt well; picked gooseberries at noon. In the afternoon rode 35 miles without stopping. Pretty well tired out, all of us. Stood it pretty well myself. But come to get off my horse almost fainted. Laid as still as I could till after tea; then felt revived. Washed my dishes, made my bed, rested well. In the morning spent an hour washing, rubbing and dressing. But 45 miles to ride in one day is hard.

Thursday, July 19. Noon. Have passed most of the way through woods of pine and fir. Saw yellow violets, and strawberries in blossom, and a great variety of new plants, the poison hemlock, a plant resembling Angelica, and good to eat. Have been in camp one hour; and husband just arriving. Am very glad to see him alive; but am sorry he has lost his coat. Have suffered more from fear than anything else. Was so excited in descending one hill that when I reached the foot I almost fainted. Have felt that God only could make us go safely. Perhaps were my eyes opened I might behold angels standing by the way not as they stood to stay the wicked prophet but stationed there to guard my feet from falling. Dread the afternoon ride. Afternoon. Had a pleasant ride. Not so very bad places to pass.

Saturday, July 28. Fort Hall [located north of present-day Pocatello, Idaho]. Pretty much sick all day; had to let my work all go. Wrote part of a letter to our folks.

Thursday, August 16. Last night encamped opposite Boisie [modern Boise, Idaho]. Had milk and butter for supper. Found that what we had expected was only 40 was nearer to a hundred miles. Animals pretty well worn out. Today had salmon, boiled pudding, turnip sauce for dinner. One cow at the fort [Fort Boise] gave 24 quarts of milk a day. Have pumpkins too. Weather hot.

Wednesday, August 29. Waiilatpu. Left baggage behind to hasten on. Rode my pony through the woods, then took Mr. Walker's and then cantered on. Arrived at Dr. Whitman's about 2 P.M. Found Mr. and Mrs. Spaulding [Henry and Eliza Spaulding] there. Mr. Gray and wife gone to Walla Walla. We were feasted at first on mellons, pumpkin pies, and milk. Captain Sutor [John Augustus Sutter, then on his way to California] was with us. Just as we were sitting down to eat mellons the house became thronged with Indians. So we were obliged to suspend eating and shake hands with some 30, 40 or 50 of them. Toward night we partook of a fine dinner of vegetables, salt salmon, bread, butter, cream, etc. So our long and toilsome journey has at length come to a close.

2.   The Letters of the Donner Party, 1846–1847

In the American imagination no overlanders have captured more attention over the years than the Donner party. Most of the fascination comes from knowing the tragic fate of the Donners and their friends during the winter of 1846–1847. But the surviving records of the Donner emigrants tell us more than just one story, no matter how terrible that tale. Letters written by George Donner (1784–1847), his wife Tamsen (1801–1847), James Frazier Reed (1800–1874), Virginia E. B. Reed (1833–1921), and Charles T. Stanton (1811–1847) reveal the daily life of the emigration. Details about routes, camp sites, food, and personal relationships abound. More than simply describing the common routines of overlander life, these letters also reveal times of uncommon suffering and courage.

a.   George Donner et al. Advertisement, Springfield, Illinois, March 18, 1846

George Donner was a prosperous farmer from the country around Springfield, Illinois, when he and several others placed the following notice in a local newspaper.

WESTWARD, HO! FOR OREGON AND CALIFORNIA! Who wants to go to California without costing them anything? As many as eight young men, of good character, who can drive an ox team, will be accommodated by gentlemen who will leave this vicinity about the first of April. Come, boys! You can have as much land as you want without costing you any thing. The government of California gives large tracts of land to persons who have to move there. The first suitable persons who apply, will be engaged. The emigrants who intend moving to Oregon or California this spring, from the adjoining counties, would do well to be in this place about the first of next month. Are there not a number from Decatur, Macon county, going?

b. Tamsen Donner to Eliza Poor, Independence, Missouri, May 11, 1846

Tamsen Donner, George's third wife, was born in Massachusetts and had taught school before marrying into the Donner family.

My dear sister,

I commenced writing to you some months ago but the letter was laid aside to be finished the next day and was never touched. A nice sheet of pink letter paper was taken out and has got so much soiled that it cannot be written upon and now in the midst of preparation for starting across the mountains I am seated on the grass in the midst of the tent to say a few words to my dearest only sister. One would suppose that I loved her but little or I should have not neglected her so long, but I have heard from you by Mr. Greenleaf and every month have intended to write. My three daughters are round me, one [Frances] at my side trying to sew, Georgeanna [Georgia] fixing herself up in an old india rubber cap, and Eliza Poor knocking on my paper asking me ever so many questions. They often talk to me of Aunty Poor. I can give you no idea of the hurry of this place at this time. It is supposed there be 7000 wagons start from this place, this season. We go to California, to the bay of Francisco. It is a four months trip. We have three wagons furnished with food and clothing etc. drawn by three yoke of oxen each. We take cows along and milk them and have some butter though not as much as we would like. I am willing to go and have no doubt it will be an advantage to our children and to us. I came here last evening and start tomorrow on the long journey. William's family was well when I left Springfield a month ago. He will write to you soon as he finds another home. He says he has received no answer to his last two letters, is about to start to Wisconsin as he considers Illinois unhealthy.

William T. Ranney, *The Old Scout's Tale* (1853) captures the role that many former mountain men played as guides for overland emigrants.

c. Charles T. Stanton to Sidney Stanton, "Emigrants' Trail," June 12, 1846

Stanton was a bachelor traveler who joined the Donner party looking for adventure and a fresh start in California. He escaped the snows at Donner Lake, only to die in an effort to rescue those still trapped.

For the past few days we have got along finely, having travelled at the rate of from 20 to 25 miles a day. We are now encamped upon the Great Platte, 500 miles from Independence, and 300 from Fort Laramie.

My last was dated June 2, soon after crossing the Blue River, where we were detained by high water several days.

After travelling one or two days, we encamped upon the Little Blue [on the present-day Kansas-Nebraska border] which abounds in fish, and my skill as a fisherman was here put to the test; but I succeeded in catching the finest cat you ever saw, which we had the next morning for breakfast. I have eaten of the salmon, the Mackinaw trout and the celebrated white fish, but I think I never ate anything better than the fine fish caught from the waters of the Blue.

We journeyed for several days up this delightful stream, and every night found romantic camping ground. The scenery was most beautiful—the eye wandered over fair prospects of hill and dale. A strong north wind prevailed for two or three days; all the men wore their overcoats to keep warm, and the women wrapped themselves up in shawls, or walked on foot, to do the same.

In our encampment we had several Oregon families, constituting twenty wagons. Some little disturbance arising, they concluded to withdraw from our party and go on their own hook, forming a company of their own, mustering a force of some twenty fighting men.

They went on ahead, and for several days encamped within one or two miles of us. In their party there were many young ladies—in ours, mostly young men. Friendships and attachments had been formed which were hard to break; for, ever since, our company is nearly deserted, by the young men every day riding out on horseback, pretending to hunt, but instead of pursuing the bounding deer or fleet antelope, they are generally found among the fair Oregon girls! Thus they go, every day, making love by the roadside, in the midst of the wildest and most beautiful scenery, now admiring the meanderings of some delightful stream, or course of some noble river!

This little party, one day before they reached the Platte, were surprised by a band of 20 or 30 Pawnees, drawn up in battle array, coming down full sweep to attack them; but they were no sooner seen than the men formed in order of battle to meet them. The cunning Pawnees, seeing this little band drawn out, and fearing their deadly rifle, immediately turned their war party into a visit—shaking hands, hugging men, and attempting to embrace the women. After receiving some presents, they went away apparently as well pleased as if they had taken all of their scalps.

Every one was anxious to reach the Platte. It was in every body's mouth "when shall we get to the Platte?" We had now travelled four days up the Blue, and one day's march would take us to that great river. This day's march, therefore, was resumed with alacrity. We had to cross a high elevated plain, the dividing ridge between the waters of the Kansas and the Platte. About eleven A.M. we could perceive, as we crossed the highest elevation, that the land gradually descended both ways, and far in the distance could see the little mounds or hillocks, which formed the ridge of bluffs of the noble river. Here we stopped "to noon," after which we journeyed on, a part on horseback, going ahead (myself among the number) to catch the first view of the river. It was about two P.M., when, in ascending a high point of land [around present-day Hastings, Nebraska], we saw, spread out before us, the valley of the noble Platte. We all hallooed with pleasure and surprise.

The valley of the Platte! there is none other like it. The bluffs are from ten to fifteen miles apart, the river, of over a mile in width, flowing through the center. The bluffs suddenly fall down from 50 to 100 feet, when there is a gradual slope to the water's edge. There is not a single stick of timber to be seen on either side of the river—it is one interminable prairie as far as the eye can extend; yet there is a relief found in the numerous islands of the river being generally covered with wood. We encamped for the first time, on the 9th [of June], on the Platte, and for three days have been travelling up its beautiful valley.

About noon today we met some fur traders going down with boats, loaded with buffalo and other skins. By them I shall send this letter to you. They are staying in our encampment tonight. Tomorrow morning they will leave for the East, and we, on our long journey, for the West.

d. Tamsen Donner to a Friend in Springfield, Illinois, "Near the Junction of the North and South Platte," June 16, 1846

We are now on the Platte [near present-day North Platte, Nebraska], 200 miles from Fort Laramie. Our journey, so far, has been pleasant. The roads have been good, and food plentiful. The water for a part of the way has been indifferent—but at no time have our cattle suffered for it. Wood is now very scarce, but *"Buffalo chips"* are excellent—they kindle quick and retain heat surprisingly. We had this evening buffalo steaks broiled upon them that had the same flavor they would have had upon hickory coals.

We feel no fear of Indians. Our cattle graze quietly around our encampment unmolested. Two or three men will go hunting twenty miles from camp;—and last night two of our men lay out in the wilderness rather than ride their horses after a hard chase. Indeed if I do not experience something far worse than I have yet done, I shall say the trouble is all in getting started.

Our wagons have not needed much repair, but I cannot yet tell in what respects they may be improved. Certain it is they cannot be too strong. Our preparation for the journey, in some respects, might have been bettered. Bread has been the principal article of food in our camp. We laid in 150 lbs. of flour and 75 lbs. of meat for each individual, and I fear bread will be scarce. Meat is abundant. Rice and beans are good articles on the road—corn meal, too, is very acceptable. Linsey [a strong fabric blended from wool and cotton] dresses are the most suitable for children. Indeed if I had one it would be comfortable. There is so cool a breeze at all times in the prairie that the sun does not feel so hot as one would suppose.

We are now 450 miles from Independence. Our route at first was rough and through a timbered country which appeared to be fertile. After striking the prairie we found a first rate road, and the only difficulty we had has been crossing creeks. In that, however, there has been no danger. I never could have believed we could have travelled so far with so little difficulty. The prairie between the Blue and Platte rivers is beautiful beyond description. Never have I seen so varied a country—so suitable for cultivation. Every thing was new and pleasing. The Indians frequently come to see us, and the chiefs of a tribe breakfasted at our tent this morning. All are so friendly that I cannot help feeling sympathy and friendship for them. But on one sheet, what can I say?

Since we have been on the Platte we have had the river on one side, and the ever varying mounds on the other—and have travelled through the bottom lands from one to ten miles wide with little or no timber. The soil is sandy, and last year, on account of the dry season, the emigrants found grass here scarce. Our cattle are in good order, and where proper care has been taken none has been lost. Our milch cows have been of great service—indeed, they have been of more advantage than our meat. We have plenty of butter and milk.

We are commanded by Capt. Russel [William Henry Russell]—an amiable man. George Donner is himself yet. He crows in the morning, and shouts out "Chain up, boys!—chain up!" with as much authority as though he was "something in particular." John Denton [a hired man working for the Donners] is still with us—we find him a useful man in camp. Hiram Miller and Noah James are in good health and doing well. We have of the best of people in our company, and some, too, that are not so good.

Buffalo show themselves frequently. We have found the wild tulip, the primrose, the lupine, the ear-drop, the larkspur, and creeping hollyhock, and a beautiful flower resembling the bloom of the beech tree, but in bunches large as a small sugar-loaf, and of every variety of shade, to red and green. I botanize and read some, but cook a "heap" more.

e. Virginia E. B. Reed to Mary C. Keyes, Independence Rock, July 12, 1846

The stepdaughter of James Frazier Reed, one of the Donner party leaders, Virginia Reed was thirteen years old at the time she wrote this letter. Spelling and sentence structure have been modernized.

My Dear Cousin,

I take this opportunity to write to you to let you know that I am well at present and hope that you are well. We have all had good health. We came to the Blue [River]. The water was so high we had to stay there four days. In the meantime gramma [Sarah Keyes] died. She became speechless the day before she died. We buried her very decent. We made a neat coffin and buried her under a tree. We had a headstone and had her name cut on it and the date and year very nice, and at the head of the grave was a tree. We cut some letters on it. The young men sodded it all over and put flowers on it. We miss her very much. Every time we come into the wagon we look at the bed for her. We have come through several tribes of Indians, the Crow Indians, the Sioux, the Shawnees. At the Crow village paw [James Frazier Reed] counted 250 Indians. We didn't see no Indians from the time we left the Crow village till we come to Fort Laramie. The Crow [here Reed means the Sioux] are going to war with the Crows. We have to pass through their fighting ground. The Sioux Indians are the prettiest dressed Indians there is. Paw goes buffalo hunting most every day and kills 2 or 3 buffalo every day. Paw shot an elk. Some of our companions saw a grizzly bear. We have the thermometer 102 degrees—average for the last six days. We celebrated the Fourth of July on plat [Platte River] at Beaver Creek. Several of the gentlemen in Springfield gave paw a bottle of liquor and said it shouldn't be opened until the Fourth of July and paw was to look to the east and drink it and they was to look to the west and drink it at 12 o'clock. Paw treated the company and we all had some lemonade. Maw and Paw is well and sends their best love to you all. I send my best love to you all. We have heard from Uncle Cad several times. He went to California and now is gone to Oregon. He is well. I am going to send this letter by a man [Wales B. Bonney] coming from Oregon himself. He is going to take his family to Oregon. We are all doing well and in high spirits so I must close your letter. You are forever my affectionate cousin.

At the end of July, the Donner Party reached Fort Bridger, located in present-day southwestern Wyoming. There they expected to meet Lansford W. Hastings—lecturer, promoter, traveler, and author of the *Emigrants' Guide to Oregon and California* (1845). Hastings was not at Fort Bridger, but others present readily passed on his ideas about a "cutoff" short route across the mountains to California. While experienced frontiersmen like Jim Clyman had cautioned against such shortcuts, the Donners accepted the Hastings route, thus putting themselves directly in harm's way.

Gold seeker J. Goldsborough Bruff sketched this view from Independence Rock in present-day Wyoming in 1849.

A VIEW from the SUMMIT of INDEPENDENCE ROCK.

Hastings' Cut-Off had been used successfully by other emigrants. It was bad timing and terrible weather in the Sierras that doomed the Donners.

---

f. James Frazier Reed to James or Gersham Keyes, Fort Bridger, July 31, 1846

James Frazier Reed was an energetic Illinois businessman whose enterprises in manufacturing and railroad contracting had fallen on hard times. His friendship with George Donner brought him into the overland party.

We have arrived here safe with the loss of two yoke of my best oxen. They were poisoned by drinking water in a little creek called Dry Sandy, situated between the Green Spring in the Pass of the Mountains, and Little Sandy. The water was standing in puddles. Jacob Donner also lost two yoke, and George Donner a yoke and a half, all supposed from the same cause. I have replenished my stock by purchasing from Messrs. Vasquez [Louis Vásquez] and Bridger [Jim Bridger], two very excellent and accommodating gentlemen who are the proprietors of this trading post. The new road, or Hastings' Cut-off, leaves the Fort Hall road here, and is said to be a saving of 350 or 400 miles in going to California, and a better route. There is, however, or thought to be, one stretch of 40 miles without water; but Hastings and his party, are out ahead examining for water, or a route to avoid this stretch. I think that they cannot avoid it, for it crosses an arm of the Eutaw Lake, now dry. Mr. Bridger, and other gentlemen here, who have trapped that country, say that the lake has receded from the tract of country in question. There is plenty of grass which we can cut and put into the wagons, for our cattle while crossing it.

g. Charles T. Stanton to Sidney Stanton, Bear River, August 3, 1846

We take a new route to California, never travelled before this season; consequently our route is over a new and interesting region. We are now in the Bear River valley, in the midst of the Bear [Uinta] Mountains, the summits of which are covered with snow. As I am now writing, we are cheered by a warm summer's sun, while but a few miles off, the snow covered mountains are glittering in its beams.

h.   Virginia E. B. Reed to Mary C. Keyes, Napa Valley, California, May 16, 1847

Written after the rescue of the Donner survivors, this letter also contains comments written in by Virginia's stepfather, James Frazier Reed. Most historians are confident that Virginia penned the core of the letter. The text has been edited and modernized.

I take this opportunity to write to you to let you know that we are all well at present and hope this letter may find you all well. My dear cousin, I am going to write to you about our troubles in getting to California. We had good luck til we came to Big Sandy. There we lost our best yoke of oxen. We came to Bridger's Fort and we lost another one. We sold some of our provision and bought a yoke of cows and oxen. The people at Bridger's Fort pursuaded us to take Hastings' Cutoff over the salt plain. They said it saved 3 hundred miles. We went that road and we had to go through a long drive of 40 miles without water or grass. Hastings said it was 40 miles but I think it was 80 miles. We travelled a day and night and at noon pa went on to see if he could find water. He had not been gone long till some of the oxen gave out and we had to leave the wagons and take the oxen on to water. Walter Herron and Bailos [Baylis Williams] stayed with us and the others went on with the cattle to water. Pa was coming back to us with water and met the men. They was about 10 miles from water. Pa said they would get to water that night, and the next day bring the cattle back for the wagons and bring some water. Pa got to us about daylight next morning. The man that was with us took the horse and went on to water. We waited there thinking they would come. We waited till night and we thought we would start and walk to Mr. Donner's wagons that night, 10 miles distant. We took what little water we had and some bread and started. Pa carried Thomas [Thomas Reed, age 3] and all the rest of us walk. We got to Donner and they were all asleep so we laid down on the ground. We spread one shawl down. We laid down on it and spread another over us and then put the dogs on top. It was the coldest night you ever saw. The wind blew very hard and if it hadn't been for the dogs we would have frozen. As soon as it was day we went to Mrs. Donner. She said we could not walk to the water and if we stayed we could ride in their wagons to the spring. So pa went on to the water to see why they did not bring the cattle. When he got there, there was but one ox and cow there. [The emigrants did not know that Indians had driven off the stock.] None of the rest got to water. Mr. Donner come out that night with his cattle and brought his wagons and all of us in. We stayed there [the springs at the base of present-day Pilot Peak, Nevada] a week [September 9–15] and hunted our cattle and could not find them, so some of the company took their oxen and went out and brought in one wagon and cached the other two and a great many things. All but what we could put in our wagon we had to divide with the company to get them to carry them. We got three yoke with our oxen and cow. So we went on that way a while and we got out of provisions and pa had to go on to California for provisions. [Virginia Reed did not reveal that her stepfather had killed John Snyder in a bloody fight and was expelled from the party.] We could not get along that way. In 2 or 3 days after pa left we had to cache our wagon and take Mr. Graves' [Franklin W. Graves] wagon and cache some more of our things. Well we went on that way a while and then we had to get Mr. Eddies [William H. Eddy] wagon. We went on that way a while and then we had to cache all of our clothes except a change or 2 and put them in Mr. Brins [Patrick Breen] wagon, and Thomas and James [James Reed, age 5] rode the other 2 horses and the rest of us had to walk. We went on that way a while and we come to another long drive of 40 miles. We went with Mr. Donner. We had to walk all the time. We was travelling up the Truckee River. We met a man [Charles T. Stanton] and 2 Indians that we had sent on for provisions to Captain Sutter's Fort. They had met pa not far from Sutter's Fort. He looked very bad. He had not ate but 3 times in 7 days and the last three days without anything. His horse was not able to carry him. They gave him a horse and he went on. So we cached some more of our things all but what we could pack on one mule and we started. Martha [Martha Reed, age 8] and James rode behind the two Indians. It was raining then in the valleys and snowing on the mountains. So we went on that way 3 or 4 days till we come to the big mountain [the Sierra Nevada mountains] or the California Mountain. The snow then was about 3 feet deep. There was some wagons there. They said they had attempted to cross and could not. Well, we thought we would try it so we started and they started again with their wagons. The snow was then up to the mules side. The farther we went up the deeper the snow got so the wagons could not go on. So they packed their oxen and started with us carrying a child a piece and driving the oxen in snow up to their waist. The mule Martha and the Indian was on was the best one so they went and broke the road and that Indian was the pilot. So we went on that way 2 miles and the mules kept falling down on the snow head foremost and the Indian said he could not find the road. We stopped and let the Indian and man [Stanton] go on to hunt the road. They went on and found the road to the top of the mountain and come back and said they thought we could get over if it did not snow anymore. Well, the women were all so tired carrying their children that they could not go over that night so we made a fire and got something to eat and ma spread down a buffalo robe and we all laid down on it and spread something over us and ma sat up by the fire. And it snowed one foot on top of the bed so we got up in the morning and the snow was so deep we could not go over and we had to go back to the cabin [a shelter built by overlanders two years before] and built more cabins and stay there [at present-day Donner Lake] all winter without pa. We had not the first thing to eat. Ma made arrangements [a trading deal with other members of the party] for some cattle, giving 2 for 1 in California. We seldom thought of bread for we had not had any since [words missing] and the cattle was so poor they couldn't hardly get up when they laid down. We stopped there the 4th of November and stayed till March and what we had to eat I can't hardly tell you. And we had that man [Stanton] and Indians to feed too. Well, they [Stanton and his companions] started over afoot and had to come back. So they made snow shoes and started again and it come on to storm and they had to come back. It would snow 10 days before it would stop. They waited till it stopped and started again. I was going with them and I took sick and could not go. There was 15 [the snow shoe party left Donner Lake on December 16] started and there was 7 got through, 5 women and 2 men. It come a storm and they lost the road and got out of provisions and the ones that got through had to eat them that died. Not long after they started we got out of provisions and had to put Martha at one cabin, James at another, Thomas at another. Ma, Eliza [Eliza Williams, the Reed family cook], Milt Elliott [teamster for the Reeds] and I dried up what little meat we had and started to see if we could get across and had to leave the children. O Mary, you may think that hard to leave them with strangers and did not know whether we would see them again or not. We could not hardly get away from them but we told them we would bring them bread and then they was willing to stay. We went and was out 5 days in the mountains. Eliza gave out and had to go back. We went on a day longer. We had to lay by a day and make snow shoes and we went on a while and could not find the road. And we had to turn back. I could go on very well while I thought we were getting along but as soon as we had to turn back I could hardly get along but we got to the cabins that night [January 8, 1847]. I froze one of my feet very bad and that same night there was the worst storm we had that winter and if we had not come back that night we would never got back. We had nothing to eat but ox hides. O Mary I would cry and wish I had what you all wasted. Eliza had to go to Mr. Graves cabin and we stayed at Mr. Breen. They had meat all the time. We had to kill little Cash the dog and eat him. We ate his head and feet and hide and everything about him. O my dear cousin you don't know what trouble is yet. A many a time we had on the last thing cooking and did not know where the next would come from. But there was always some way provided. There was 15 in the cabin we was in and half of us had to lay abed all the time. There was 10 starved to death while we were there. We was hardly able to walk. We lived on little Cash a week and after Mr. Breen would cook his meat and boil the bones two or three times we would take the bones and boil them 3 or 4 times at a time. Ma went down to the other cabin and got half a hide. Carried it in snow up to her waist. It snowed and [word missing] would cover the cabin all over so we could not get out for 2 or 3 days at a time. We would have to cut pieces of the logs inside to make fire with. I could hardly eat the hides and had not eat anything 3 days. Pa started out to us with provisions and then came a storm and he could not go. [James F. Reed added the following: On the first of November and came into the great California Mountain, about 80 miles and in one of the severest storms known for years past, raining in the valley and a hurricane of snow in the mountains, it came so deep that the horses and mules swamped so they could not go on.] He [Reed] cached his provision and went back on the other side of the bay to get a company of men and the San Joaquin River got so high he could not cross. Well, they made up a company at Sutters Fort and sent out. We had not ate anything for 3 days and we had only a half a hide and we was out on the top of the cabin and we seen them [the rescue party] coming.

O my dear cousin you don't know how glad I was. We run and met them. One of them we knew. We had traveled with them on the road. They stayed there 3 days to recruit [rest] a little so we could go. There was 20 started. All of us started and went a piece and Martha and Thomas gave out and so the men had to take them back. Ma and Eliza, James and I come on and O Mary that was the hardest thing yet to come on and leave them there. One of the party said he was a Mason and pledged his life that if we did not meet Pa in time he would come and help his children. Did not know but what they would starve to death. Martha said, well ma, if you never see me again do the best you can. The men said they could hardly stand it. It made them all cry but they said it was better for all of us to go on for if we was to go back we would eat that much more from them. They gave them a little meat and flour and took them back and we come on. Ma agreed to leave Thomas and Martha from the promise of Mr. Glover, if we should not meet pa, which we did in a few days. We went over great high mountain as steep as stair steps in snow up to our knees. Little James walked the whole way over all the mountain in snow up to his waist. He said every step he took he was getting nigher to Pa and something to eat. Wolverines took the provision the men had cached and we had but very little to eat. When we had traveled 5 days travel we met pa with 13 men going to the cabins. O Mary you do not know how glad we was to see him. We had not seen him for 5 months. We thought we would never see him again. He heard we was coming and he made some seed cakes the night before at his camp to give us and the other children with us. He said he would see Martha and Thomas the next day. He went in 2 days what took us 5 days. When pa went to the cabins some of the company was eating from them that died but Thomas and Martha had not to eat any. Pa and the men started with 12 people. Hiram O. Miller carried Thomas and Pa carried Martha and they were caught in a snow storm which lasted two days and nights. And they had to stop two days. It stormed so they could not go and the wolverines took their provision and they were 4 days without anything. Pa and Hiram and all the men started [with] one of the Donner boys. Pa carrying Martha, Hiram carrying Thomas and the snow was up to their waist and it a snowing so they could hardly see the way. They wrapped the children up and never took them out for 4 days and they had nothing to eat in all that time. Thomas asked for something to eat once. Those that they brought from the cabins, some of them was not able to come and some would not come. There was 3 died and the rest eat them. They was 10 days without any thing to eat but the dead. Pa brought Tom and Paddy [Martha Reed] on to where we was. None of the men Pa had with him was able to go back for some people still at the cabins. Their feet was froze very bad so there was another company went and brought them all in. They are all in from the mountains now but four men went out after them and was caught in a storm and had to come back there. Was another company gone there, was half got through that was stopped there sent to their relief. There was but two families [the Reeds and the Breens] that all of them got through. We was one. O Mary I have not wrote you half of the trouble we have had but I have wrote you enough to let you know what trouble is. But thank the Good God [we were] the only family that did not eat human flesh. We have left everything but I don't care for that we have got through with our lives but don't let this letter dishearten anybody. Never take no cutoffs and hurry along as fast as you can.

3. Horace Greeley Sketches Colorado's New Society, 1859

Horace Greeley (1811–1872) was mid-nineteenth-century America's most influential and widely read newspaper editor and an important force in national politics and reform movements. Although he did not say "Go west, young man"—a line properly attributed to John

Soule—Greeley believed that taking up homesteads in the West would solve many social and economic problems. In the summer of 1859, Greeley made a western tour, visiting Kansas and Colorado before heading to California. First published as a series of letters in the *New York Tribune,* his book *An Overland Journey from New York to San Francisco in the Summer of 1859* (1860) revealed a West rapidly becoming urbanized and ethnically diverse. The selection reprinted here records his comments on the many kinds of characters drawn to the Colorado gold fields and the raw town of Denver.

I know it is not quite correct to speak of Colorado as "Western," seeing that it is in fact the center of North America and very close to its backbone. Still, as the terms "Eastern" and "Western" are conventional and relative, I take the responsibility of grouping certain characters I have noted on the plains and in or about the mountains as "Western," begging that most respectable region which lies east of the buffalo range—also that portion which lies west of Colorado—to excuse the liberty.

The first circumstance that strikes a stranger traversing this wild country is the vagrant instincts and habits of the great majority of its denizens—perhaps I should say, of the American people generally, as exhibited here. Among any ten whom you successively meet, there will be natives of New England, New York, Pennsylvania, Virginia or Georgia, Ohio or Indiana, Kentucky or Missouri, France, Germany, and perhaps Ireland. But, worse than this; you cannot enter a circle of a dozen persons of whom at least three will not have spent some years in California, two or three have made claims and built cabins in Kansas or Nebraska, and at least one spent a year or so in Texas. Boston, New York, Philadelphia, New Orleans, St. Louis, Cincinnati, have all contributed their quota toward peopling the new gold region. The next man you meet driving an ox team, and white as a miller with dust, is probably an ex-banker or doctor, a broken merchant or manufacturer from the old states, who has scraped together the candle-ends charitably or contemptuously allowed him by his creditors on settlement, and risked them on a last desperate cast of the dice by coming thither. Ex-editors, ex-printers, ex-clerks, ex–steamboat men, are here in abundance—all on the keen hunt for the gold which only a few will secure. One of the stations at which we slept on our way up—a rough tent with a cheering hope (since blasted) of a log house in the near future—was kept by an ex-lawyer of Cincinnati and his wife, an ex-actress from our New York Bowery—she being cook. Omnibus drivers from Broadway repeatedly handled the ribbons; ex–border ruffians from civilized Kansas—some of them of unblessed memory—were encountered on our way, at intervals none too long. All these, blended with veteran mountain men, Indians of all grades from the tamest to the wildest, halfbreeds, French trappers and voyageurs (who have generally two or three Indian wives apiece) and an occasional Negro, compose a medley such as hardly another region can parallel. Honolulu, or some other port of the South Sea Islands, could probably match it most nearly.

4. William Fraser Rae Tells His English Readers About the Wild West, 1871

The American republic long held a special fascination for English writers and travelers. By the 1830s, the United States, and especially the American frontier, was on the "grand tour" required as part of a proper English education. Those who could not afford the journey found dozens of books claiming to reveal the truth about people who spoke English but were surely not English! Charles Dickens, Harriet Martineau, and Frances Trollope all made American journeys and wrote at length about their experiences. So did English journalist William Fraser Rae.

Rae left England in August 1869 on a tour that took him from New York City to San Francisco, with a side trip to Salt Lake City. The title of his book, *Westward by Rail: The New Route to the East,* recalls the power and fascination of the Northwest Passage idea. Rae's work was typical of the travel literature at the time, a compilation of quick sketches designed to entertain a distant audience. Rae served up an American West suited to any Wild West show featuring desolate landscapes, tales of Indian menace and emigrant suffering, and even a hair-raising train ride down the mountains.

For 200 miles to the west of Elko [Nevada] the scenery continued to be monotonous, consisting of wide barren plains bordered by mountain slopes. The Humboldt river, with its banks fringed with shrubs and plants, and the land for some distance on either side affording grazing grounds for herds of cattle, alone gave a slight variety to the scene. Now and then a prairie wolf slunk aside as the passing train startled it from its lair. More than one rude monument was pointed out to me as indicating the spot where a foul murder had been perpetrated or a bloody combat had been waged. It was in this locality that the Indians made a savage onslaught on those engaged in constructing the line, murdering, scalping, and plundering several white men. Some Indians were among the passengers on this train. I was told that they are carried gratis. In return they sometimes help to heap wood on the tender at the appointed stopping places. They were Shoshones, and were said to be very peaceable.

An American train resembles a steamer in this, that all the passengers are thrown together in a way which is impossible when they are cooped up in compartments as on an English railway. Every carriage communicates in such a way that it is possible at any moment to enjoy a welcome change by walking from end to end of the train. In my car there were several Californians on their way home after a visit to their native places in the Eastern States. One of them had several bottles of choice old Bourbon whisky with him, and he was persistent in asking his acquaintances to "take a drink." The whisky bottle was produced as early as six in the morning and was passed from hand to hand at short intervals till the hour came for going to bed. The number of drinks must not be taken as a criterion of the extent of drunkenness. A sip of liquor constitutes a drink. It is the form rather than the effect which seems to give pleasure. The Westerners and Californians hold that, not to drink at all is the mark of a milksop, while to drink too much demonstrates a fool.

Reno is the last halting place of importance during the Westward journey through the State of Nevada. It is within a few miles of Virginia City, the headquarters of the miners who work the numerous silver and gold mines in this district. Here, as with other similar places, a large number of passengers left the train and a new set entered it. The amount of the local passenger traffic was far in excess of my expectations. Indeed, the proportion of through passengers is very small when compared with the number journeying from one intermediate station to another. Near Boca, which is 127 miles distant from Sacramento, the line crosses the boundary which separates the state of Nevada from the state of California. The Californians rejoiced when the train entered their state, and spoke with pleasure about soon basking in the sunshine which has made the Pacific slope a modern Garden of Eden. The ascent now becomes very steep, and two engines are employed to drag the train. At short intervals there are strong wooden sheds of about a thousand feet long, erected to guard the line against destruction from what we call avalanches, and what here are called "snow slides." Indeed, these sheds are very much like tunnels. They have been constructed at a vast expense, and in a solid manner. It has yet to be seen how far they will serve their purpose. They have the drawback of interrupting the view of some of the most

The Great American Panorama, based on a painting by Joseph H. Becker, celebrated the transcontinental railroad. It also reveals the central role of Chinese laborers in building the railway.

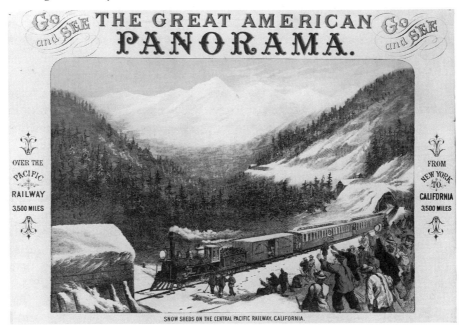

romantic scenery on the line. The glimpses one gets are just sufficient to tantalise and not prolonged enough to satisfy. The view of Donner Lake is the most charming of them all. This lake is picturesquely situated in the gorge of the Sierras. It was once the theater of a terrible tragedy. [Here Rae offers a quick review of the Donner disaster, emphasizing cannibalism.] Such a story furnishes confirmation of the saying that truth outstrips fiction. It is more puzzling and revolting than any which the modern writer of sensational novels has yet produced for the gratification of depraved tastes.

Summit Station, though the highest point on this line, is not so high as Sherman Station on the Union Pacific. It is 7,042 feet above the level of the sea. This represents not the altitude of the Sierra Nevada range, but only the elevation of this mountain pass. Above the station the peaks of the mountains tower cloudwards. The scene is one of unprecedented grandeur. Owing to the delay caused by an accident, the speed of the train had been increased.

The engine driver had been running extra risks in order, as the Americans phrase it, to "make time" so as to arrive "on time." The descent was thus made with exceptional rapidity. From Summit Station to Sacramento the distance is 105 miles. Between these places the descent from a height nearly half as great as that of Mont Blanc to fifty-six feet above sea level has to be made. The velocity with which the train rushed down this incline, and the suddenness with which it wheeled round the curves, produced a sensation which cannot be reproduced in words. The line is carried along the edge of declivities stretching downwards for two or three thousand feet, and in some parts on a narrow ledge which had been excavated from the mountain side by men swung from the upper parts in baskets. The speed under these circumstances seemed terrific. The axle-boxes smoked with the friction, and the odor of burning wood pervaded the cars. The wheels were nearly red hot. In the darkness of the night they resembled discs of flame. Glad though all were to reach Sacramento, not a few were specially thankful to have reached it with whole limbs and unbruised bodies.

5. Robert Louis Stevenson Finds the Plains a "Huge Sameness," 1879

In the summer of 1879, Robert Louis Stevenson journeyed overland from New York City to San Francisco. Not yet the successful author of *Treasure Island* and *Kidnapped,* he traveled on the rough, uncomfortable cars of an emigrant train. While his fiction celebrated outdoor adventure, the seemingly blank spaces of the Great Plains disoriented Stevenson. Just looking at such emptiness could, he insisted, produce "a sickness of the vision peculiar to these empty plains."

It had thundered on the Friday night, but the sun rose on Saturday without a cloud. We were at sea—there is no other adequate expression—on the plains of Nebraska. I made my observatory on the top of a fruit-wagon [a box car], and sat by the hour upon that perch to spy about me, and to spy in vain for something new. It was a world almost without a feature; an empty sky, an empty earth; front and back, the line of railway stretched from horizon and horizon, like a cue across a billiard-board; on either hand, the green plain ran till it touched the skirts of heaven. Along the track innumerable

Newbold H. Trotter's *Buffalo Crossing Railroad Track* portrays the new West of industry and railroads colliding with the most powerful symbol of the old west.

wild flowers, no bigger than a crown piece [an English coin about the size of an American silver dollar], bloomed in a continuous flower bed; grazing beasts were seen upon the prairie at all degrees of distance and diminution; and now and again we might perceive a few dots beside the railroad which grew more and more distinct as we drew nearer till they turned into wooden cabins, and then dwindled and dwindled in our wake until they melted into their surroundings, and we were once more alone upon the billiard-board. The train toiled over this infinity like a snail; and being the one thing moving, it was wonderful what huge proportions it began to assume in our regard. It seemed miles in length, and either end of it within but a step of the horizon. Even my own body or my own head seemed a great thing in that emptiness. I note the feeling the more readily as it is the contrary of what I have read of in the experience of others. Day and night, above the roar of the train, our cars were kept busy with the incessant chirp of grasshoppers—a noise like the winding up of countless clocks and watches, which began after a while to seem proper to that land.

To one hurrying through by steam there was a certain exhilaration in this spacious vacancy, this greatness of the air, this discovery of the whole arch of heaven, this straight, unbroken, prison-line of the horizon. Yet one could not but reflect upon the weariness of those who passed by there in old days, at the foot's pace of oxen, painfully urging their teams, and with no landmark but that unattainable evening sun for which they steered, and which daily fled them by an equal stride. They had nothing, it would seem, to overtake; nothing by which to reckon their advance; no sight for repose or for encouragement; but stage after stage, only the dead green waste under foot, and the mocking, fugitive horizon. But the eye, as I have been told, found differences even here; and at the worst the emigrant came, by perseverance, to the end of his toil. It is the settlers, after all, at whom we have a right to marvel. Our consciousness, by which we live, is itself but the creature of variety. Upon what food does it subsist in such a land? What livelihood can repay a human creature for a life spent in this huge sameness? He is cut off from books, from news, from company, from all that can relieve existence but the prosecution of his affairs. A sky full of stars is the most varied spectacle that he can hope. He may walk five miles and see nothing; ten, and it is as though he has not moved; twenty, and still he is in the midst of the great same level, and has approached no nearer to the one object within view, the flat horizon which keeps pace with his advance. We are full at home of the question of agreeable wallpapers, and wise people are of opinion that the temper may be quieted by sedative surroundings. But what is to be said of the Nebraskan settler? His is a wallpaper with a vengeance—one quarter of the universe laid bare in all its gauntness. His eye must embrace at every glance the whole seeming conclave of the visible world; it quails before so vast an outlook, it is tortured by distance; yet there is no rest or shelter, till the man runs into his cabin, and can repose his sight upon things near at hand. Hence, I am told, a sickness of the vision peculiar to these empty plains.

Yet perhaps with sunflowers and cicadae, summer and winter, cattle, wife, and family, the settler may create a full and various existence. One person at least I saw upon the plains who seemed in every way superior to her lot. This was a woman who boarded us at a way station, selling milk. She was largely formed; her features were more than comely; she had that great rarity—a fine complexion which became her; and her eyes were kind, dark, and steady. She sold milk with patriarchal grace. There was not a line in her countenance, not a note in her soft and sleepy voice, but spoke of an entire contentment with her life. It would be fatuous arrogance to pity such a woman. Yet the place where she lived was to me almost ghastly. Less than a dozen wooden houses, all of a shape and all nearly of a size, stood planted along the railway lines. Each stood apart on its own lot. Each opened direct off the billiard-board, as if it were a billiard-board indeed, and these only models that had been set down upon it ready made. Her own, into which I looked, was clean but very empty, and showed nothing homelike but the burning fire. This extreme newness, above all in so naked and flat a country, gives a strong impression of artificiality. With none of the litter and discoloration of human life; with the paths unworn, and the houses still sweating from the axe, such a settlement as this seems purely scenic. The mind is loth to accept it for a piece of reality; and it seems incredible that life can go on with so few properties, or the great child, man, find entertainment in so bare a playroom.

6. Walt Whitman Calls for a New Language for the West, 1879

Walt Whitman had already written about the American landscape and the West before traveling by rail to Colorado. Poems like "Pioneers, O Pioneers," "The Prairie-Grass Dividing," and "Passage to India" took up some of the largest and most complex questions in American history—questions of geography, national destiny, and the relationships of gender and race. In the fall of 1879, Whitman traveled across the Kansas plains to Denver. He recorded his impressions in a series of prose sketches. At once poet, tourist, and journalist,

Whitman came to see the Great Plains as the most clearly American of all landscapes.

Grand as the thought that doubtless the child is already born who will see a hundred millions of people, the most prosperous and advanced of the world, inhabiting these prairies, the great Plains, and the valley of the Mississippi, I could not help thinking it would be grander still to see all those inimitable American areas fused in the alembic of a perfect poem, or other esthetic work, entirely western, fresh and limitless—altogether our own, without a trace or taste of Europe's soil, reminiscence, technical letter or spirit. My days and nights, as I travel here—what an exhilaration!—not the air alone, and the sense of vastness, but every local sight and feature. Everywhere something characteristic—the cactuses, pinks, buffalo grass, wild sage—the receding perspective, and the far circle-line of the horizon all times of day, especially forenoon—the clear, pure, cool, rarefied nutriment for the lungs, previously quite unknown—the black patches and streaks left by surface-conflagrations—the deep-ploughed furrow of the "fire guard"— the slanting snow-racks built all along to shield the railroad from winter drifts—the prairie dogs and the herds of antelope—the curious "dry rivers" —occasionally a "dug-out" or corral—Fort Riley and Fort Wallace—those towns of the northern plains, (like ships on the sea,) Eagle Tail, Coyote, Cheyenne, Agate, Monotoyn, Kit Carson—with ever the ant hill and the buffalo wallow—ever the herds of cattle and the cowboys ("cow punchers") to me a strangely interesting class, bright-eyed as hawks, with their swarthy complexions and their broad-brimmed hats—apparently always on horseback, with loose arms slightly raised and swinging as they ride.

Speaking generally as to the capacity and sure future destiny of that plain and prairie area (larger than any European kingdom) it is the inexhaustible land of wheat, maize, wool, flax, coal, iron, beef and pork, butter and cheese, apples and grapes—land of ten million virgin farms—to the eye at present wild and unproductive—yet experts say that upon it when irrigated may easily be grown enough wheat to feed the world. Then as to scenery (giving my own thought and feeling,) while I know the standard claim is that Yosemite, Niagara falls, the upper Yellowstone and the like, afford the greatest natural shows, I am not so sure but the Prairies and Plains, while less stunning at first sight, last longer, fill the esthetic sense fuller, precede all the rest, and make North America's characteristic landscape.

Indeed through the whole of this journey, with all its shows and varieties, what most impressed me, and will longest remain with me, are these same prairies. Day after day, and night after night, to my eyes, to all my senses—

the esthetic one most of all—they silently and broadly unfolded. Even their simplest statistics are sublime.

7. Samuel Bowles Reveals the Shape of the New West, 1868

Like so many other newspaper journalists, Samuel Bowles (1826–1878) was attracted to the American West. His attraction was part national pride and part romance and adventure. The New England editor and printer made his first western trip by stagecoach in 1865, along with Vice President Schuyler Colfax and Illinois governor William Bross. In 1868 the party took a similar tour, this time by transcontinental railroad from Omaha.

Bowles's *Our New West* (1869), a virtual encyclopedia of the American West, offers observations on everything from mining and the Mormons to city life and federal Indian policy. In the selection reprinted here, Bowles describes the West's new industrial landscape.

So completely is the Pacific Railroad henceforth the key to all our New West; so thoroughly must all knowledge of the characteristics of the latter radiate out of the former as a central line, that its story should be told almost at the outset, even to the anticipation of earlier experiences. Marked, indeed, was the contrast between the stage ride of 1865 and the railroad ride of 1868 across the Plains. The then long-drawn, tedious endurance of six days and nights, running the gauntlet of hostile Indians, was now accomplished in a single twenty-four hours, safe in a swiftly-moving train, and in a car that was an elegant drawing-room by day and a luxurious bedroom at night.

The long lines of travel in our wide and fresh West have given birth to more luxurious accommodations for passengers than exist in Europe or the Atlantic States. With the organization of travel over the Pacific Railroad come cars that will carry their occupants through from New York to San Francisco, without stop or change, and with excellent bed and board within them. Only America could have demanded, conceived and organized for popular use such accommodations as the Pullman Palace and Sleeping Cars of the West. To some, as to ours, are added the special luxury of a house organ; and the passengers while away the tedious hours of long rides over unvarying prairies with music and song.

Omaha, in 1865, a feeble rival of Atchison, Leavenworth, and Nebraska City in outfitting emigrant and merchandise wagons for Colorado and Utah, and without a single mile of railroad within one hundred miles, has already become the greatest railroad center of the Missouri and Mississippi Valleys. It is the starting point of the Pacific Railroad, which stretches a completed line of eighteen hundred miles west to the Pacific Ocean; to the east are two or three completed lines of five hundred miles across Iowa and Illinois to Chicago, and others are in progress; to the south are open roads to St. Louis across the Missouri; and to the north is a finished road to Sioux City, and fast stretching to St. Paul. The three great states of the Mississippi Valley, Illinois, Iowa, and Missouri, the garden and granary of the nation, and the seat of its middle empire, are slashed in all directions by railroad lines, completed or rapidly constructing, meeting as a western focus at Omaha and Council Bluffs, sister towns on either bank of the Missouri, and converging on the east into either Chicago or St. Louis. Their consequent development, in population and wealth, is perhaps the most wonderful illustration of modern American growth. It is within this area that New England is pouring the best of her emigration, and reproducing herself, in energy and industry and intelligence, on a broader, more generous and more national basis.

Out now upon the continental Railroad. For five hundred miles, a straight, level line, across the broad Plains, along the valley of the Platte. It was but a play to build a railroad here. Yet there is a steady ascent of ten feet to the mile; and for the first two hundred miles the country has the exquisite roll and the fertile activity of the Iowa and Illinois prairies. Through this region the growth of Nebraska shares that of those two states; and she has the advantage of them, generally, in climate, in water, and in wood. But beyond this limit,—out upon the real Plains,—the first results of the Railroad are to kill what settlement and cultivation they had reached under the patronage of slow-moving emigration, stage travel, and prairie schooner freightage. The ranches which these supported are now deserted; the rails carry everybody and everything; the old roads are substantially abandoned; the old settlers, losing all their improvements and opportunities, gather in at the railway stations, or move backwards or forwards to greater local developments. They are the victims, in turn, of a higher civilization; they drove out the Indian, the wolf, and the buffalo; the locomotive whistles their occupation away, and invites back for the time the original occupants.

The day's ride grows monotonous. The road is as straight as an arrow. Every dozen or fifteen miles is a station,—two or three sheds, a water-spout and wood pile; every hundred miles or so a home or division depot, with shops, eating house, saloons uncounted, a store or two, a few cultivated acres, and the invariable half-a-dozen seedy, staring loafers, that are a sort of fungi indigenous to American railways. We yawn over the unchanging landscape and the unvarying model of the stations, and lounge and read by day, and go to bed early at night. But the clear, dry air charms; the half dozen soldiers hurriedly marshalled into line at each station, as the train comes up, suggest that the Indian question is not disposed of yet; we catch a glimpse of antelopes in the distance; and we watch the holes of the prairie dogs for their piquant little owners and their traditional companions of owls and snakes, —but never see the snakes.

SUGGESTIONS FOR FURTHER READING

Faragher, John Mack. *Women and Men on the Overland Trail*. New Haven: Yale University Press, 1979.

Fender, Stephen. *Plotting the Golden West: American Literature and the Rhetoric of the California Trail*. Cambridge, Massachusetts: Harvard University Press, 1981.

Hyde, Anne Farrar. *An American Vision: Far Western Landscape and National Culture, 1820–1920*. New York: New York University Press, 1990.

Stilgoe, John R. *Metropolitan Corridor: Railroads and the American Scene*. New Haven: Yale University Press, 1983.

Thacker, Robert. *The Great Prairie Fact and Literary Imagination*. Albuquerque: University of New Mexico Press, 1989.

Unruh, John D., Jr. *The Plains Across: The Overland Emigrants and the Trans-Mississippi West, 1840–1860*. Urbana: University of Illinois Press, 1979.

Ward, James A. *Railroads and the Character of America, 1820–1887*. Knoxville: University of Tennessee Press, 1986.

Learning the Country:
Some Thoughts
in Conclusion

In late December 1806, President Thomas Jefferson told members of Congress that the Lewis and Clark expedition had "learnt the character of the country." It was Jefferson's way of saying that exploration was more than wandering without purpose. Making journeys was part of a larger enterprise, a venture into inquiry, explanation, and possession. In referring to the character of the country, Jefferson employed the word *character* in a way mostly lost in modern usage. He meant that his captains had studied at least three realms of knowledge on their way to the Pacific.

The first realm was what Jefferson once called "the face of the country." Explorers and travelers learned the terrain, surveying all the varied features of the American landscape. Novelist Willa Cather (1873–1947) expressed the same idea when she wrote about a Nebraska farmer who "knew every ridge and draw and gully between him and the horizon." Early explorers studied these ridges and horizons, named them with new names, and claimed them as part of expanding empires. Jefferson also used *character* in a second sense. Eighteenth-century English literature was filled with character books, collections of word sketches depicting representative social and occupational types. Each type represented a unique locale or style of life and labor. As they examined and described varied biological communities, explorers were looking for characters. Such characters represented the distinctive attributes of a particular region. Finally, Jefferson meant *character* as an expression of promises, possibilities, and relationships between human societies and the environment. Each country, he and other geographers believed, had a special quality, or character, that fit its destiny. Describing the West as a garden or a desert was more than an expression of terrain and climate. It was a judgment about places suitable for settlement by American farmers and artisans. If the character of the country was right, republican virtues would grow and flourish. Character was all about the complex relationships between environment and culture.

In *Arctic Dreams,** Barry Lopez writes that "what one thinks of any region while traveling through it is the result of three things: what one knows, what one imagines, and how one is disposed." The reports, letters, diaries, and maps in *Revealing America* pose these questions and suggest some answers. The documents carry us along on all sorts of journeys, asking us what we know, how we imagine our own territory, and how we are disposed to the country around us. Exploration accounts are more than stray fragments from a distant past. Reading them, we are urged to ask the same questions about ourselves and the character of our world.

One day in early 1847, Hezekiah Packingham looked around his promised land—Oregon's Willamette Valley—and wrote the bitter complaint of a disappointed traveler. "My calculations are all defeated," Hezekiah reported to his brother in Illinois. This lament was more than the unhappy whine of a discouraged overlander. Hezekiah's calculations testify to the power of imagination in revealing America. Like so many explorers and travelers, Hezekiah thought that he knew what lay at trail's end even before making the journey. Generations of explorers had fashioned an image of Oregon that emphasized fertility, prosperity, and security. Hezekiah enthusiastically embraced this image, only to find it an illusion.

All the journeys traced in this book began with acts of imagination. Imagination joined with desire to invent whole countries of the mind. America was, in the words of art historian Hugh Honour, "the prejudged land." Fray Marcos de Niza imagined the golden wonders of Cíbola without seeing the Zuni pueblos. George and Tamsen Donner went "California dreaming" months ahead of their departure from Illinois. Desire took imagination and gave it the confidence of familiar form and reassuring substance. Imagination not only shaped the sought-after prize but also marked out the route to reach it. The force of imagination leveled mountains, cut passes, and straightened rivers. Imagination drew maps and then insisted on their accu-

---

Arctic Dreams: Imagination and Desire in a Northern Landscape, by Barry Lopez. New York, 1986.

racy no matter what experience taught. Conjecture hardened to wisdom as generation after generation hunted for the Northwest Passage. Not finding it in one place, believing minds simply moved it elsewhere or redefined it. Imagination built whole landscapes, entire geographies of promise and expectation. As historian Simon Schama explains, "Landscapes are culture before they are nature; constructs of the imagination projected onto wood and water and rock."

Outbound expeditions always began with interior voyages. Travelers and explorers journeyed close to home before striking out for distant places. The expeditions by land and water recounted in *Revealing America* offer more than a dash of color and adventure to perk up the standard outlines of American history. The stories of Coronado, La Salle, and Frémont are essential to an appreciation of the twists and turns of North America's intricate history. They show us the power of illusion to condition perception and direct behavior. Tracking each journey, we consider the complex motives behind each venture. Explorers did not go it alone, pursuing some elusive goal on a solitary pilgrimage. Instead, each explorer and traveler carried along the dreams and desires of entire societies and cultures. Some of these communities were nations bent on imperial domain. Explorers were warriors, marching and countermarching in a war for America that lasted more than three centuries. In the contest of cultures and empires, explorers scouted ahead of the main army of occupation. Other communities were founded on religious conviction. Missionary zeal sent a company of dedicated explorers and travelers to build cities of God. The war for America was fought not only for territory but for hearts and souls. Still other communities were directed by the capitalist rhetoric of markets and profits. Fur traders, land-company agents, and government surveyors marked up the landscape and assigned it value according to marketplace needs. But whatever the community and however it instructed its explorers, there was one motive common to all: the hungry desire to possess. Europeans and Americans defined some aspects of the indigenous world as wealth, the proper reward at the end of the journey. Whether fur, gold, land, or souls, these were the objects of wealth and the subjects of desire. Whatever else native peoples had, whatever learning, art, and wisdom they had gained over the ages, this was discounted as valueless in the calculus of global markets and the ledger book.

The passion for possession might have shaped one kind of future for North America if the continent had been empty of human inhabitants. But few, if any, explorers expected their journeys to reveal an empty America. Voyages of discovery and exploration inevitably meant encounters with native peoples. Such encounters were acts of invasion and explanation.

Explorers pushed their way into native worlds and then sought to explain that invasion in terms that would justify such violence. Through exploration accounts we can track the invasion and the changing rationales employed to justify it. These same accounts, read with an eye toward native peoples as actors on the historical stage, teach us the ways in which Indians explored the explorers.

Imagination and desire prepared explorers to expect that native peoples would match European preconceptions of non-Europeans. Some Native Americans, explorers thought, might be monsters who slaughtered and devoured their enemies. This powerful image convinced certain explorers that native peoples lived outside the boundaries of law and reason. Europeans and Americans were duty-bound to fight and destroy such savages, just as knights in the Crusades had waged holy war on Islam. If some explorers were prepared to meet monsters, others believed that America's native peoples were passive beings living as nature's own primitives. Long before English poet John Dryden coined the phrase "noble savage" in 1670, explorers had some Indians firmly located in the American Garden of Eden. Such natives might readily accept Christianity, eagerly join as partners in commercial or military ventures, and finally relinquish their homelands without resistance. And while some explorers populated America with hell's monsters or Eden's nobility, others planned grand quests aimed at finding Indians who lived in kingdoms of gold and silver. Cíbola, Quivira, Harahey, and a dozen other names conjured up visions of native peoples dwelling in exotic splendor. If Cíbola's guardians would not agree to share their wealth, simple force would arrange a more equitable distribution.

All these conceptions of native peoples revealed more about the explorers than the explored. Whether knowingly or not, explorers put their own deepest passions and fears into Indian mouths. Travelers were capable of writing accurate accounts of native peoples and often did just that. But when it came to judging and evaluating cultures other than their own, preconceptions usually weighed more than experience. In written records and on maps, explorers put native peoples in their "proper" places. Knowledge itself worked in the service of dispossession and imperial possession. Defining all too often meant confining. To define the proper native place was to chart steadily smaller places.

Three and a half centuries after Jacques Cartier, Hernando de Soto, and Francisco Vásquez de Coronado made their way into America, enterprising journalist Samuel Bowles took his passage on the new transcontinental railroad. Along with the luggage required for a long journey, Bowles carried aboard his railway coach the collective memories of generations of explorers and travelers. These memories, made up of images, illusions, and expectations, prepared Bowles to look at the Platte River Valley and see the garden

Acknowledgments

Text Credits

Chapter 2, page 56: Cleve Hallenbeck, ed. and trans., *The Journey of Fray Marcos de Niza* (Dallas: Southern Methodist University Press, 1949; new edition, 1987), pp. 20–21, 25–26, 33–34. Reprinted by permission of the publisher. **Chapter 2, page 57:** Pedro de Castañeda text from George P. Hammond and Agapito Rey, eds., *Narratives of the Colorado Expedition,* University of New Mexico Press, 1940, as found in David B. Quinn, ed., *New American World,* Arno Press, pp. 373, 377–78, 379, 387–88, 396–97, 404–5. Reprinted with permission from University of New Mexico Press. **Chapter 3, page 71:** George P. Hammond and Agapito Rey, eds. and trans., *The Rediscovery of New Mexico 1580–1594* (Albuquerque: University of New Mexico Press, 1966), 277–78, 282. Reprinted with permission from University of New Mexico Press. **Chapter 3, page 92:** Joyce Marshall, ed. and trans., *Word from New France: The Selected Letters of Marie de l'Incarnation* (Toronto: Oxford University Press, 1967), pp. 374–377. Reprinted by permission of Oxford University Press Canada. **Chapter 3, page 100:** Theodore C. Pease and Raymond C. Werner, eds., *The French Foundations 1680–1693* (Springfield, Illinois: Illinois State Historical Library, 1934), 1–4, 6–7. Reprinted by permission of Illinois State Historical Library. **Chapter 4, page 120:** Iris H. Wilson, ed. and trans., *An Account of Nootka Sound in 1792* by Jose Mariano Mozino (Seattle: University of Washington Press, 1970), pp. 46–50. Reprinted by permission of University of Washington Press. **Chapter 4, page 125:** Lois Mulkearn, ed., *George Mercer Papers Relating to the Ohio Company of Virginia* (Pittsburgh: University of Pittsburgh Press, 1954), 7–8. **Chapter 5, page 168:** From *Simon Fraser: Letters and Journals, 1806–1808,* edited by Dr. W. Kaye Lamb, published by Macmillan Canada, 1960, pp. 63–65. Permission granted by Dr. W. Kaye Lamb. **Chapter 6, page 190:** Reprinted by permission of the Publishers, The Arthur H. Clark Company, from *The Southwest Expedition of Jedediah Smith,* edited by George R. Brooks, Glendale, CA 1977, pp. 41–43. **Chapter 6, page 204:** Stella M. Drumm, ed., *Down the Santa Fe Trail and into Mexico: The Diary of Susan Shelby Magoffin, 1846–1847* (Lincoln: University of Nebraska Press, 1982), pp. 60–69. Reprinted by permission of Yale University Press. **Chapter 7, page 230:** From *The Journals, Drawings, and Other Papers of J. Goldsborough Bruff,* by Joseph Goldsborough Bruff. Copyright © 1949. Reprinted with permission of the publisher, Columbia University Press.

Illustration Credits

Chapter 1, page 8: Ptolemy Atlas, World Map. 1522 (3995.919). From the Collection of Gilcrease Museum, Tulsa. **Chapter 1, page 10:** Archiv Gerstenberg. **Chapter 2, page 58:** Library of Congress. **Chapter 2, page 63:** Western History Collection, University of Oklahoma. **Chapter 3, page 89:** By permission of the Houghton Library, Harvard University. **Chapter 3, page 94:**

Courtesy William L. Clements Library, University of Michigan. **Chapter 3, page 101:** Library of Congress. **Chapter 4, page 114:** Courtesy of the Oregon Historical Society. **Chapter 4, page 119:** National Museum of American Art, Washington, D. C./Art Resource, NY. **Chapter 4, page 127:** Courtesy of the John Carter Brown Library at Brown University. **Chapter 5, page 148:** National Museum of American Art, Washington, D. C./Art Resource, NY. **Chapter 5, page 159:** By permission of the Houghton Library, Harvard University. **Chapter 5, page 161:** National Portrait Gallery, Washington, D. C. **Chapter 6, page 187:** Codex Canadensis (4726.7 pg. 37). From the Collection of Gilcrease Museum, Tulsa. **Chapter 6, page 197:** Buffalo Bill Historical Center, Cody, Wyoming. Gift of the Coe Foundation. **Chapter 6, page 203:** J. Gregg, *Commerce of the Prairies*, 1844. "Arrival of the Caravan at Santa Fe" (2528 1451). From the Collection of Gilcrease Museum, Tulsa. **Chapter 7, page 221:** Library of Congress. **Chapter 7, page 226:** Library of Congress. **Chapter 8, page 247:** William Tylee Ranney, Old Scout's Tale (0126 2261). From the Collection of Gilcrease Museum, Tulsa. **Chapter 8, page 252:** This item is reproduced by permission of The Huntington Library, San Marino, California. **Chapter 8, page 262:** State Historical Society of Wisconsin (Whi 49845). **Chapter 8, page 264:** Transportation Collection, Division of History and Technology, The Smithsonian Institution.